The Price of Alliance

Studies in Canadian Military History

Series editor: Andrew Burtch, Canadian War Museum

The Canadian War Museum, Canada's national museum of military history, has a threefold mandate: to remember, to preserve, and to educate. Studies in Canadian Military History, published by UBC Press in association with the Museum, extends this mandate by presenting the best of contemporary scholarship to provide new insights into all aspects of Canadian military history, from earliest times to recent events. The work of a new generation of scholars is especially encouraged, and the books employ a variety of approaches – cultural, social, intellectual, economic, political, and comparative – to investigate gaps in the existing historiography. The books in the series feed immediately into future exhibitions, programs, and outreach efforts by the Canadian War Museum. A list of the titles in the series appears at the end of the book.

CANADIAN WAR MUSEUM
MUSÉE CANADIEN DE LA GUERRE

The Price of Alliance
The Politics and Procurement of Leopard Tanks for Canada's NATO Brigade

Frank Maas

UBCPress · Vancouver · Toronto

26 25 24 23 22 21 20 19 18 17   5 4 3 2 1

Printed in Canada on FSC-certified ancient-forest-free paper (100% post-consumer recycled) that is processed chlorine- and acid-free.

Library and Archives Canada Cataloguing in Publication

Maas, Frank, author
The price of alliance : the politics and procurement of Leopard tanks for Canada's NATO brigade / Frank Maas.
(Studies in Canadian military history)

Includes bibliographical references and index.
Issued in print and electronic formats.
ISBN 978-0-7748-3518-3 (hardcover). – ISBN 978-0-7748-3519-0 (pbk.). –
ISBN 978-0-7748-3520-6 (PDF). – ISBN 978-0-7748-3521-3 (EPUB). –
ISBN 978-0-7748-3522-0 (Kindle)

1. Canada. Canadian Armed Forces – Procurement – History – 20th century. 2. North Atlantic Treaty Organization – Canada – History – 20th century. 3. North Atlantic Treaty Organization – Europe – History – 20th century. 4. Leopard (Tank) – History – 20th century. 5. Canada – Military relations – Europe – History – 20th century. 6. Europe – Military relations – Canada – History – 20th century. 7. Canada – Military policy. 8. Europe – Military policy. I. Title. II. Series: Studies in Canadian military history

UC265.C3M37 2017   355.6′2120971   C2017-903775-7
C2017-903776-5

Canadä

UBC Press gratefully acknowledges the financial support for our publishing program of the Government of Canada (through the Canada Book Fund), the Canada Council for the Arts, and the British Columbia Arts Council.

Publication of this book has been financially supported by the Canadian War Museum.

Printed and bound in Canada by Friesens
Set in Minion and Helvetica by Apex CoVantage, LLC
Copy editor: Joyce Hildebrand
Proofreader: Carmen Tiampo
Indexer: Sergey Lobachev
Cover designer: Martyn Schmoll

UBC Press
The University of British Columbia
2029 West Mall
Vancouver, BC V6T 1Z2
www.ubcpress.ca

To my wife, Katrina, and our children, Annabelle, Frederick, Roger, Bridget, Charles, and the twins

Contents

Illustrations

Acknowledgments

This book was many years in the making and would not have been possible without the assistance of innumerable people along the way. Numerous scholars offered useful advice and helpful sources, and I am thankful for the insights and critiques provided by the anonymous reviewers. The help of archivists and librarians at various archives and colleges – notably, Canadian Forces College, Fort Frontenac Library, the Canadian War Museum's Military History Research Centre, the Directorate of History and Heritage, and Library and Archives Canada – was essential. I am sincerely thankful for all of my interviewees, who offered insights and enjoyable discussions and gave freely of their time. Bill Coupland provided invaluable assistance in tracking down other contacts, and Bob Caldwell gave me an excellent introduction to the army in the 1970s. The editorial staff at UBC Press, especially Emily Andrew and Randy Schmidt, guided the book through the publishing process with great patience and expertise. I am also grateful for the indispensable financial assistance of the Canadian War Museum, without which this project could not have been completed.

Kevin Spooner and Alistair Edgar suggested important improvements and revisions to key drafts of this book, and the advice and criticism of Joel Sokolsky of the Royal Military College of Canada was vital. Roger Sarty suggested the topic, and improved my work greatly as he shepherded me through the writing process. My parents, Andre and Linda, offered essential assistance and constant encouragement. Finally, I am grateful for the steadfast support of my wife, Katrina, who was always a patient sounding board for my ideas.

Abbreviations

ACE	Allied Command Europe
ADM	Assistant Deputy Minister
AMF	Allied Command Europe Mobile Force
ATOB	Army Tactics and Organization Board
CDS	Chief of the Defence Staff
CIBG	Canadian Infantry Brigade Group
CMBG	Canadian Mechanized Brigade Group
DFSV	direct fire support vehicle
DND	Department of National Defence
DSR	Defence Structure Review
DSS	Department of Supply and Services
EEC	European Economic Community
FDO	force development objective
IRBs	industrial and regional benefits
KM	Krauss-Maffei
MBFR	Mutual and Balanced Force Reductions
MBT	main battle tank
NATO	North Atlantic Treaty Organization
NORAD	North American Air Defence Command
OER	operational equipment requirement
RCDs	Royal Canadian Dragoons
RCEME	Royal Canadian Electrical and Mechanical Engineers
SACEUR	Supreme Allied Commander Europe
SCOD	Special Committee on Defence
STAFEUR	Special Task Force on Europe
VCDS	Vice Chief of the Defence Staff

The Price of Alliance

Introduction

In 1990, when I was a little boy, my parents started a six-person company to paint parts for armoured vehicles produced in London, Ontario. I played in the office during summer vacations and worked for the company from elementary school through university. This first-hand knowledge served me well when I was doing my master's degree and studying the production of the Light Armoured Vehicle in London, Ontario. For my next project, Roger Sarty, at Wilfrid Laurier University, suggested that I study Canada's purchase of the Leopard 1 tank in the 1970s, given my prior knowledge and experience. I was dubious, but as I began preliminary research, I realized that the Leopard was about much more than a forty-odd-tonne piece of metal. It was about the conclusion of a defence policy debate that lasted nearly twelve years, cutting across a number of important issues – Canada's defence posture and relationships with its allies, foreign policy objectives, civil-military relations, the defence budget, and of course, procurement.

The story begins in 1951, when Canada deployed a brigade of troops, with sixty Centurion tanks, to bolster Western Europe, both physically and psychologically, against the Soviet Union. In the 1950s, this unit, garrisoned a short distance from the Iron Curtain, made Canada an important player in the North Atlantic Treaty Organization (NATO), an alliance that was the centrepiece of Canadian foreign and defence policy. This honeymoon, however, would be short. Postwar European recovery, the cost of modern weaponry, a changed strategic context, and divisive debates in Canada and other alliance nations over tactical nuclear weapons caused many policy-makers to question the value of the brigade and to push for a reduction or repurposing. They made little headway, though, until Pierre Trudeau became prime minister in 1968. After a review of defence policy that went on for nearly eighteen months, he announced plans to reduce the brigade by half immediately and, in the longer term, to replace its aging Centurion tanks with lighter vehicles. The re-equipment with light vehicles was confirmed in the 1971 Defence White Paper, *Defence in the 70s,* and in 1973, Trudeau resisted pressure by the army to keep the tanks.

But two years later, Cabinet confirmed that Canada would indeed continue to operate tanks in Europe, and in 1976, the government signed a contract to buy 128 West German Leopard 1 tanks, which began arriving in 1978. This was accompanied by the purchase of light armoured vehicles for army units at home and by the promise of billions of dollars for new fighters, patrol aircraft, and ships. This about-turn was remarkable, given the prime minister's earlier reduction of defence spending and skepticism of NATO.

The explanation for this reversal can be found in the answers to several interrelated questions: What were the most important elements determining the character and composition of Canada's ground forces in Europe in the 1960s and 1970s? Why did Trudeau reverse his decision to field light vehicles in Central Europe? Why did Canada purchase the Leopard tank, and was it a successful procurement? The central question that ran through this era concerned the equipment of Canada's troops in Europe: Would they be supplied with tanks or with light direct fire support vehicles (DFSVs)?

Tanks were formidable machines weighing roughly forty to sixty tonnes and carrying the thickest armour and most lethal guns of any vehicle on the battlefield.[1] They were often accompanied by infantry and artillery in tracked armoured vehicles to produce powerful mechanized formations. Tanks, however, required a great deal of maintenance, supplies, and spare parts, and they were difficult to transport long distances. They were a requirement for most NATO ground forces in Central Europe, given the Soviet Union's enormous tank armies, but were less relevant for the defence of Canadian territory. The army could not deploy its tanks to any areas where an unlikely Soviet incursion into Canadian territory, like the Arctic, could occur, and they were considered ill-suited for use in domestic operations.

DFSVs, by contrast, had much thinner armour than tanks and were consequently only a fraction of the weight, about eight to sixteen tonnes, and much easier to transport. This small size limited the effectiveness of the main gun, which could only destroy soft-skinned or light armoured vehicles, but some had wire-guided anti-tank missiles that allowed them to destroy tanks at long range. DFSVs were fast and mobile and, because of their ease of transport, could accompany light infantry units to support them. Canada also had transport aircraft that could move them rapidly.

To analyze the research questions, particularly the tank versus DFSV debate, it was necessary to examine two intertwined issues: the ways in which the army structured and equipped itself and the broader defence policy debate over Canada's garrison in Europe. I relied on the literature on the Canadian army's combat-development process and defence procurement to study the first issue, including how the equipping of the army affected defence policy at a higher level.[2] To examine the defence policy debate, I relied on a sociological methodology from the history of technology, the social construction of technology approach, to explore the roles of five distinct groups involved in the defence policy process – NATO allies, the army, External Affairs, and supporters and skeptics of NATO in Cabinet – and their struggles to assert their views of the Canadian army and whether it would have tanks, DFSVs, or both.[3] Although the groups could be further subdivided, such an approach would multiply detail without correspondingly strengthening the analysis. The first four groups supported the maintenance in Europe of the mechanized brigade equipped with tanks: Canada's NATO allies; the Department of National Defence (DND), particularly the army; External Affairs; and supporters of NATO in Cabinet, referred to here as civilian traditionalists. Those in the final group, the civilian revisionists, were skeptical of both the alliance and the terms of Canada's participation in it and argued for either a reduced and restructured contribution or full withdrawal of forces from Europe.[4]

The first group, NATO allies, was large and diverse and included heads of government, ambassadors, foreign and defence ministers, and senior military commanders. These figures put pressure on Canadian officials, subtly or overtly, to keep tanks in Europe in order to maintain alliance solidarity. Some of the best-known efforts came from the West German chancellor from 1974 to 1982, Helmut Schmidt, but there were many other instances of pressure. The commander of NATO's military units, the Supreme Allied Commander Europe (SACEUR), is an important military and political figure responsible for identifying the forces required for missions and for requesting them from member nations; during the period examined here, SACEUR was at the forefront of NATO's response to possible changes in Canadian military contributions.[5]

The second group was DND, especially the army and the Royal Canadian Armoured Corps.[6] The army saw service with its brigade in Central Europe as a critical step in the professional development of its soldiers and generally supported maintaining tanks in Europe, with some notable exceptions. The army's role in defence policy debates was largely led by the top army officer. In the 1960s, General Jean Victor Allard pushed the army to adopt a lighter structure without tanks, but in the mid-1970s, General Jacques Dextraze made it a top priority to keep tanks.

The third group, External Affairs, largely worked in the background but was never far from high-level reassessments of Canada's forces in NATO. Membership in NATO directly involved Canadian diplomats along the central fault line of the Cold War, and they cooperated closely with major allies on the most important and sensitive issues. Ross Campbell, who held key posts in External Affairs and was Canada's ambassador to NATO from 1967 to 1972, was an ardent supporter of maintaining Canada's military contributions to the alliance. H.B. Robinson also held key posts in External Affairs during the period under study and was an observer and participant in many key meetings. The department held sway in the 1960s, but after Pierre Trudeau became prime minister, its influence diminished.

The fourth group comprised the civilian traditionalists – Cabinet ministers who supported NATO and, by extension, the maintaining of Canadian tanks in Europe. The key members of this group were Prime Minister Lester Pearson and his external affairs minister, Paul Martin, who together dominated foreign policy from 1963 to 1968. They were supported by Mitchell Sharp and Léo Cadieux, who were the external affairs and defence ministers, respectively, during Trudeau's review of policy in 1968. Pearson had serious doubts about NATO starting in the mid-1960s arising from the continued European dependence on American conventional and nuclear forces, but he and Martin appreciated the political significance of the mechanized brigade and prevented any dramatic changes to it. However, after Pearson resigned in 1968 and Martin went to the Senate, the traditionalists lost their two most important figures, and after the review in 1969, they no longer had a voice in defence policy.

The civilian traditionalists thus gave way to the fifth group, the civilian revisionists. This group started to develop in the mid-1960s and included Trudeau, Donald Macdonald, Eric Kierans, Jean Marchand, and Walter Gordon. Although these men had varying goals, all were united by their questioning of NATO and the Canadian contributions to it. The most important revisionist was Trudeau, assisted by his foreign policy adviser, Ivan Head, who fully shared Trudeau's critical view of existing policy. The revisionists pushed for either withdrawal of Canadian forces or their restructuring with lighter vehicles. They had little influence until Pearson's retirement, but after he left office, the revisionists came to dominate questions on Canada and NATO from 1970 to 1975.

There was no room for compromise between the first four groups and the revisionists. The tactical view, held primarily by the army but also by NATO allies, was that tanks were required to provide a credible Canadian contribution in Europe. This fed into the political perspective shared by allies, External Affairs, and the traditionalists that a credible Canadian force with tanks was necessary to affirm NATO's cohesion and solidarity. This was entirely at odds with the revisionists, who argued that Canadian defence policy should be based on domestic needs and that if Canada provided troops to NATO, it should be on its own terms.

In the end, NATO allies triumphed over the revisionists: they became the most important group determining the character and composition of Canada's ground forces in Europe. They did not need to assert their influence from 1963 to 1968 because External Affairs and the traditionalists ensured that the commitment of the mechanized brigade was maintained. Regardless, their presence was felt during those years. From 1969 to 1975, they exerted significant pressure on Canada to keep tanks in Central Europe but showed little interest in the rest of the army at home. Wanting the "cash" of forward deployed troops, they cared little for the "credit" of additional troops in Canada. During a major review of defence policy and the beginning of trade talks with the European Economic Community (EEC) in 1975, NATO allies, particularly Schmidt, applied major pressure on the Canadians to keep tanks near the Iron Curtain. After the army made the decision to do so, it chose the Leopard, the best tank on the market at the time, and by all accounts, it was a successful purchase.

This book contributes to four major bodies of work: the analysis of Trudeau's foreign and defence policies; Canada's relationship with its allies; Canadian defence procurement; and the history of the army, particularly the Royal Canadian Armoured Corps, during the Cold War. There is a significant body of work on nuclear weapons, and the material on Canada and the Arctic during the Cold War is increasing, but to date, exploration of Canada's forces in Europe has been limited.[7]

The central work on Trudeau's foreign and defence policies remains J.L. Granatstein and R. Bothwell's *Pirouette* (1990). They argue, correctly, that from 1968 to 1973, Trudeau did damage to the Armed Forces and to Canada's relationship with its allies. Trudeau, however, was right to be skeptical of the status quo and to challenge it, and although he certainly made mistakes, his record on defence policy after 1975 was much stronger. John English, in his 2009 biography of Trudeau, *Just Watch Me,* includes a short rejoinder to the anti-Trudeau authors, but no recent academic studies have challenged the historiographical consensus with an in-depth examination of defence policy.[8]

The second body of work to which this study contributes is that on Canada's relationship with NATO and key allies. In Roy Rempel's *Counterweights* (1996), the central work on Canadian-West German relations, Rempel concludes that multiple attempts by Canadians to forge a link with Europe's most dynamic economy from 1955 to 1995 faltered because of Canada's poor and frequently changing defence policy. The West Germans wanted a strong and vital NATO, and Canada squandered any leverage it had with cuts, especially in 1969.[9]

Although Rempel's thesis is valid, his analysis of the defence policy debate needs revision, and he overestimates the political value of Canadian forces in Europe.

Isabel Campbell takes a more nuanced approach in *Unlikely Diplomats* (2013). She examines the Canadian brigade in Europe during the 1950s and early 1960s and concludes that it quickly became more important as a political symbol than as a military asset. There was tension between the brigade's political and military imperatives, and she argues that although Canada's contributions to NATO bought it a place at the table, it had little real influence.[10] My work begins where Campbell's concluded, taking the analysis to 1975.

This book also builds on the small but growing body of work on Canadian defence procurement. Much of the literature, such as Aaron Plamondon's *The Politics of Procurement* (2010), has been negative, focusing on the inadequacies of the procurement system and the overpoliticization of various projects. Plamondon effectively examines why the navy's Sea King helicopters have been in service for nearly fifty years and why a successor has been delayed for nearly thirty. His negative interpretation is reinforced by many failed or delayed projects in the post–Cold War era and by the unveiling of a new secretariat to oversee procurement in 2014.[11] There have been some analyses of successes, such as Randall Wakelam's *Cold War Fighters* (2012), a study of Canada's fighter aircraft industries after the Second World War. My examination of the effective Leopard acquisition broadens the literature with another success story – specifically, with an example of the procurement of an armoured vehicle.

The final body of work to which this study contributes is the history of the Canadian army, especially the Royal Canadian Armoured Corps, during the Cold War. Sean Maloney is the most prominent author on this topic, having written several articles and books on it. Although his work is a strong examination of the tactical aspects of the Cold War, his analysis of defence policy at the highest levels requires some revision.[12] Andrew Godefroy has also published some key works on the army during the Cold War.[13] In addition, Peter Kasurak's *A National Force* (2013) provides a strong challenge to the "Golden Age" narrative that presents the Canadian army as having been ruined during the Cold War by reduced budgets and civilian incompetence, a challenge that he supports with an examination of the army's resistance to defence policy. Kasurak, however, largely ignores the foreign policy context of the brigade in Europe, which fundamentally affected defence planning. He also misses some key episodes and personalities in the crisis of civil-military relations in the 1960s and 1970s.

Chapters 1 and 2 of this book address the Lester B. Pearson era and the review of defence policy in 1963, which led to the Defence White Paper of 1964. The plan was to develop heavy and light wings of the army, but by 1966, it was clear that there was not enough money to implement it. By 1967, serious criticism of the alliance, even from Pearson, had grown, and the government reduced its NATO commitments. The next two chapters examine Trudeau's defence policy review in 1968 and 1969. Against opposition from External Affairs, NATO allies, and traditionalists in Cabinet, Trudeau and the revisionists cut the strength of the brigade in NATO and made plans to re-equip it with light vehicles in a few years' time.

This episode laid the seeds for a civil-military crisis, the subject of Chapters 5 and 6. The army pushed for tanks to equip the force in Europe, and NATO allies made some forays, but the revisionists held firm. Chapter 7 covers the pivotal year of 1975, when Trudeau made three visits to Europe and met with other NATO leaders, particularly Helmut Schmidt, multiple times. By the end of 1975, Trudeau had been convinced to keep tanks, and the army began the process of purchasing the Leopard, the subject of Chapter 8.

The central sources for this book are records of how policy-makers addressed the force in Europe in light of changing strategy in the 1960s and 1970s and reductions in defence spending. Interviews were used to explore gaps or inconsistencies in the archival record and to provide context. Although memory sometimes conflicted with the documents, I thought it worthwhile to work within these limitations because many of the surviving figures from the era are in their seventies, eighties, and, in some cases, nineties. Corporate memory of the era will have faded long before the full range of documents becomes available. The second group of sources comprises records of the army's attempts to implement changes in defence policy by restructuring and buying new vehicles. The development of force structure – how many soldiers and vehicles of what kind – produced a number of documents and studies that provide valuable insight into the army's attempts to implement policy.[14] The records generated during the army's procurement process for new armoured vehicles were also critical to my research. The third group of sources focuses on Canada's relations with NATO allies and was drawn from the official records of External Affairs and from personal papers, memoirs, or interviews. The records of the United States and Germany, especially during the Trudeau years, are also a central part of this third group of sources.[15]

The overarching theme of this book – that NATO allies exerted an enormous influence on Canadian defence planning – is not surprising and was readily apparent to observers at the time. A detailed examination of this defence policy debate, however, reveals some important insights into Canada's Cold War history, its relationship with NATO, and the development of Trudeau's defence policy. Trudeau came into office in 1968 skeptical of NATO and the relevance of Canada's military and left in 1984 as a stalwart supporter of the alliance and with a wholesale re-equipment of the Armed Forces underway. This examination of the Leopard 1 purchase also sheds light on some of the perils and opportunities for Canadian defence procurement.

1

The 1964 *White Paper on Defence*

Responding to a New Strategic Context

John Diefenbaker, Canada's prime minister from 1957 to 1963, made a mess of defence policy during his time in office. His handling of the Cuban missile crisis and the acquisition of tactical nuclear weapons for the Canadian military became political nightmares that contributed to the fall of his government. During the 1963 election campaign, the Liberals promised a review of defence policy, and Paul Hellyer, the new defence minister, began that review after the Liberals won a minority government in April. Hellyer, only thirty-nine years old, was ambitious and determined to make his mark on the defence portfolio, but he would have limited funds to do so. The Pearson government was intent on completing the welfare state that Mackenzie King had started, so the defence budget was frozen. Although the question of tactical nuclear weapons was the biggest issue facing the new Liberal government, the army would figure prominently in Hellyer's review.

The army's major commitment to NATO was one division composed of three brigades: the 4 Canadian Infantry Brigade Group (4 CIBG), comprising six thousand troops and an armoured regiment of sixty Centurions, was forward deployed in West Germany as part of NATO's ground forces, and two similar brigades, based in Canada, were earmarked for the alliance in case of war. In 1963, the army planned to reduce the commitment to two brigades, one in Europe and one in Canada, and this reduction occurred a few years later.[1] The divisional commitment to NATO dictated that Canada maintain three brigades with tanks and train them for high-intensity mechanized war against the Soviet Union and its allies. Not only was this costly in terms of equipment and maintenance, but it was also unrealistic, given that it would be exceedingly difficult, if not impossible, to actually transport the follow-on brigades to Europe in case of war. Canada did not have enough sea or air transport, and it was unlikely that allies could spare any during an emergency. During the Berlin Crisis in 1961, the government was simply unable to transport an additional brigade to Europe to strengthen NATO.[2] The final commitment was for a brigade to defend North America in conjunction with the United States.

The army was large by Canadian peacetime standards and was leavened with many veterans from the Second World War and Korea, but there were problems.

The air force and navy received the bulk of the funds for new equipment as defence budgets shrank in the late 1950s and early 1960s, and the army needed new equipment to keep pace with the Warsaw Pact and NATO doctrine. Canada's infantry and artillery still relied on trucks for transport and needed tracked armoured vehicles in order to protect troops more effectively on a battlefield with nuclear, biological, and chemical weapons, which NATO expected the Warsaw Pact to use from the outset of a conflict. In 1963, the most pressing need was for armoured personnel carriers, new reconnaissance vehicles, and self-propelled artillery, as well as anti-tank missiles.[3] The army's tank was the Centurion, which was still a good vehicle in 1963 but was beginning to show its age.

In the mid-1950s, the army bought 347 Mark V Centurions to equip its Regular Force armoured regiments. This popular and capable fighting vehicle was heavily armoured but very slow, and it had a limited range before it needed refuelling.[4] It also required intensive maintenance and frequently broke down, problems that worsened as the equipment aged. The Centurion was also difficult to move long distances because of its weight, roughly fifty-two tonnes; it required movement by sealift, rail, or special tank transporters. The Mark V Centurion had the British 20 pounder gun, an improvement on the famous 17 pounder mounted on Sherman Fireflys in the Second World War, which was a good gun in the early 1950s but was made inadequate by improvements in Soviet tanks and armour. In the 1950s, the British, to counter the new generation of Soviet tanks, produced the Mark XI Centurion, with the excellent 105 mm L7 gun and extra armour, and in the early 1960s, Canada improved seventy-five of its Centurions to this status for use in the 4 CIBG. Although these upgrades kept Canada's tanks up to alliance standards, the tanks at home were still Mark Vs, which were inferior and required different ammunition.[5] This would complicate the supply of Canadian forces if NATO ever cashed in the divisional commitment. Finally, allies were developing new tanks and planning to replace the Centurion, and once this occurred, the supply of spare parts would dry up. The Centurion would be a serviceable tank for a few more years, but it would need replacing or a major overhaul.[6]

As these tanks soldiered on into the 1960s, a new strategic context was emerging. In the 1950s, the US strategy was massive retaliation, which relied on a few ground troops equipped with tactical nuclear weapons and the threat of an instant and total nuclear response to any aggression. This policy had fallen out of favour because of the lack of flexibility in dealing with crises and because it did not deter war or communist subversion in other parts of the globe.[7] The US and NATO began moving away from the "tripwire" response in the late 1950s, with MC (Military Committee) 14/2 and a greater emphasis on conventional forces, and in 1960, President John F. Kennedy's secretary of defense, Robert

McNamara, began implementing flexible response.[8] In Europe, this strategy made the use of tactical and strategic nuclear weapons a last resort and required the development of strong conventional forces with a broad range of capabilities and versatile nuclear strike options. On a global scale, flexible response also emphasized the development of units that could fight across the entire spectrum of war, from low-intensity conflict to all-out nuclear war, and could deploy quickly to hot spots in transport aircraft and helicopters and put out brush fires around the world. There was enthusiasm for light, airmobile formations, and the Americans would also develop strategic concepts, units, and materiel to create formations that could respond rapidly to insurgency, subversion, or a breakdown of order, which seemed to be everywhere in the post-colonial world.[9]

With this changing strategic context in mind, Hellyer began his wide-ranging review of Canadian defence policy. One of the key reports, submitted in September 1963, was from the Ad Hoc Committee on Defence Policy, chaired by Dr. R.J. Sutherland of the Defence Research Board. He examined policy from the 1950s and early 1960s and offered alternatives for the future but no concrete recommendations. The report noted the central concern of the era – the defence budget – and stressed that the real decline in defence spending, the rise in operating costs, and the obsolescence of equipment would inevitably force a change in policy.[10] Canada's choices were constrained by geography, finances, and the relationship with the United States, but the country did have flexibility regarding its contributions to the defence of Western Europe. Sutherland noted:

> The object of Canada's participation in the defence of Europe is essentially political, to support Canada's membership in NATO and to maintain an independent position within an evolving North Atlantic Community. In principle, there are many ways in which this could be accomplished. In practice, the range of options is constrained, in the short run, by our existing investment in hardware and by diplomatic considerations vis-à-vis our allies, and in the long run, by logistic and other factors arising out of Canada's situation as a North American nation.[11]

He wrote that troops near the Iron Curtain were "proof of Canada's commitment" and that as long as they were there, "Canada's credentials with Europe can never be seriously challenged."[12] Withdrawal from Europe would reduce Canada's stature within NATO, but the status quo offered its own challenges – namely, the divisive issue of nuclear warheads and the expensive re-equipment of the forces. The Centurion, one of those pieces of equipment, would require replacing by 1967 or 1968, at the latest. Buying replacement tanks was costly but cheaper than the requirements of the navy or air force, and army units offered the best value for influence in relation to money spent. There was also the problem of transporting the balance of the division from Canada to Europe.[13]

The second option, withdrawal and disbandment of forces, would diminish Canada's stature in Europe and Washington, but it would by no means be disastrous. The real advantage was savings, which might amount to 30 percent of the defence budget. If Canada considered partial withdrawal, it should leave the brigade group in Europe because, Sutherland noted, "as a result of several centuries of European history, there is an attitude that armies represent the national will and purpose in a way which is denied to air forces and navies."[14] The third option was to base forces in Canada. This would bring less criticism from allies than total disbandment would, provided sufficient transport for them was available, but it would leave the problem of deploying them to Germany in case of emergency. The final option was to contribute to SACEUR's mobile reserves, which were intended to show the alliance's solidarity and were of military rather than political value. This option was appealing because these troops would be compatible with domestic requirements for the defence of Canada and would be light, which would solve the problem of the Centurion replacement. Canada, however, would lose the credibility of deployment on the Central Front, and the mobile reserve was of dubious military value.[15]

The idea of light mobile forces had already piqued Hellyer's interest and seemed to be where the strategic winds were blowing. It also had the support of one of Canada's top retired soldiers. Charles Foulkes, a veteran of the Second World War and chairman of the Chiefs of Staff Committee from 1951 to 1960, testified before the Special Committee on Defence (SCOD), convened to support the defence policy review. His position was that Canada should field a light force in Europe, and he continually emphasized the costs of keeping 4 CIBG in Europe and urged Canada and the United States to withdraw their forces slowly and let the burden of defence fall to the Western Europeans. He recommended that Canada's European brigade become a mobile reserve in Europe and then eventually be brought home.[16]

In August 1963, Hellyer instructed the Chiefs of Staff Committee to start studying the costs and structure of an airmobile division with its own air support, along with the air- and sealift needed to transport it. The emphasis was on portability, but Hellyer also wanted the division to have firepower and flexibility.[17] By November 1963, the committee's interim report was ready. The proposed new mobile division of three brigades would replace existing commitments for NATO and would be implemented in the late 1960s, after the obsolescence of current equipment – namely, the Centurion. The portability of forces would take precedence over armour or firepower.[18] There was considerable emphasis during the generation of the study that brigades should have

DFSVs to give them some teeth, especially against Soviet formations or countries supplied by the Soviets. The main contender for the role of the DFSV was the American Sheridan, weighing approximately sixteen tonnes and armed with a combination gun and missile launcher.[19] The study noted that the major problem was lift: Canada simply did not have the air or sea transport to deploy its mobile formations quickly, even with only light equipment.[20]

Hellyer recalled years later that he had had no interest in altering 4 CIBG and that one of his central concerns was equipping it with armoured vehicles.[21] The archival record, however, suggests that he at least considered repurposing it. In November 1963, Associate Minister of National Defence Lucien Cardin was in Europe and was due to meet with SACEUR, General Lyman Lemnitzer. Hellyer told Cardin "to make a special effort to ascertain views of the importance attached on both political and military grounds to maintaining the Canadian brigade in its present role and with its present equipment in the front line."[22] Cardin was concerned about the implications of this question and discussed it with Canada's NATO ambassador, George Ignatieff. External Affairs also learned that in a visit to NATO headquarters as part of the SCOD, a member of Canadian Parliament had asked SACEUR the same question. General Lemnitzer had responded with one word: "Disastrous!"[23]

SCOD submitted its report in December 1963. Much of the discussion focused on tactical nuclear weapons and the allies' differing strategies and reactions to flexible response. For the army, the committee recommended that Canada keep 4 CIBG in Europe and equip it with armoured personnel carriers and other high-mobility vehicles to mechanize the formation and put it on par with other NATO forces and that further study be conducted into the transport and mobility of the two brigades earmarked for NATO at home. The committee also recommended that the procurement of more transport aircraft for the Armed Forces be considered.[24]

Hellyer began drafting the White Paper in early 1964 and adopted many of SCOD's recommendations. Although 4 CIBG would stay in Europe with its tanks, External Affairs highlighted its importance. Commenting on the draft of the White Paper, the department stated: "The requirement for the second and third brigades to fulfill our divisional commitment to NATO admittedly exists, but there is no pressure from our NATO allies for us to do more than maintain the commitment in principle." External Affairs questioned the need to augment forces in Europe with new equipment or more personnel but was adamant that the brigade remain in place:

> The kind of army contribution that will count most with our allies and best contribute to the deterrence of war is a small, but highly trained and fully equipped

> Canadian force in the front line in Europe as we now have in the Fourth Canadian Infantry Brigade. Such a force is militarily more effective and politically more significant than any number of commitments to follow up with post-hostility reinforcements.[25]

Ross Campbell wrote to Frank Miller, the head of the Armed Forces and the chair of the Chiefs of Staff Committee, and repeated this assessment almost verbatim. NATO allies wanted the cash of a forward deployed brigade in Europe and cared little for the credit of more troops.[26] The brigade would remain in Europe, and with it, the problem of maintaining a mechanized force thousands of kilometres from home against the formidable Soviet army.

Hellyer revised the White Paper and published it in March 1964. By his admission, it was a short and sometimes ambiguous template that left many of the details to senior officers of the Armed Forces and civilian managers of the Defence Department.[27] The most notable result of the White Paper and the subsequent Hellyer years was the drama over the unification of the army, air force, and navy, but Hellyer's plans for the army were equally consequential. He wanted more deployable forces that could serve on peacekeeping operations, carry out counter-insurgencies, or wage all-out war. He noted in the White Paper that Canada's army would be as flexible as possible to contend with multiple threats: for example, peacekeeping operations required mobile and versatile units that could deploy quickly and then conduct a variety of operations on the ground.

The White Paper noted the discussion about converting the brigade in Europe into a light air-portable formation for use on NATO's flanks but stated that this proposal was rejected so as to maintain solidarity with the alliance. Four CIBG would remain in its current role, but the two brigades in Canada that were promised to NATO in case of war would be re-equipped and retrained as a mobile force for the full spectrum of conflict, from United Nations operations to service in the European theatre. The final brigade would be transformed into a special service force that would be air-portable and have some air-droppable equipment for rapid mobility. The re-equipping of "the Army as a mobile force" was the first priority for defence spending, although there was no direct reference to any types of vehicles.[28]

The 1964 White Paper was not a dramatic shift in overall defence policy; it affirmed that Canada's most important military priorities were the defence of its territory and participation in NATO, the North American Air Defence Command (NORAD), and the United Nations.[29] The paper was in line with Canadian internationalist foreign policy from the 1950s on but tried to produce a cheaper and more responsive military to meet these priorities. Hellyer took stock of the strategic climate and predicted that the future lay in more mobile forces.

At first, the army's plan called for only a slightly modified structure. The brigade in Germany would have some minor modifications, and the two at home would be similar but with an emphasis on making them transportable by air. There was no discussion of the types of tanks for these units.[30] The army's first priority was for tracked combat vehicles to give soldiers the mobility and protection they needed on the nuclear battlefield.[31] Hellyer put this at the top of his priority list and developed a five-year equipment-procurement plan for the entire Armed Forces, which he brought to Cabinet in November 1964. He noted that the critical needs for the army were for tracked armoured personnel carriers, reconnaissance vehicles, and self-propelled artillery to mechanize 4 CIBG and equip the units in Canada. The special service force also needed light equipment and long-range transport. These were the most important requirements, and Hellyer noted that the army would delay the replacement of the Centurion until 1968–69. By then, $96 million had been allotted to purchase 240 new tanks.[32] The army also budgeted $18.1 million to buy light reconnaissance tanks in the early 1970s.[33]

After some consultations with the Treasury Board, the five-year equipment plan was approved, and money started to flow into re-equipping the army. Over the next five years, it received more than 900 M113 armoured personnel carriers in various configurations, 174 Lynx reconnaissance vehicles based on the M113 chassis, and 76 M109 self-propelled 155 mm guns.[34] The army also bought new trucks, anti-tank missiles, radios, and mortars.[35] However, the purchases of armoured vehicles were backward rather than forward looking. Hellyer and the army began procurement before the army had completed intensive analysis of the restructuring required by the White Paper, so Hellyer equipped the army to the standards of 1963, not 1964.[36] There was little consideration of the demands of strategic mobility, which had been a key feature of the White Paper. Although the tracked vehicles were much lighter than tanks, they were still relatively heavy and difficult to transport by air, and they required significant maintenance. These vehicles were necessary for any forces fighting against the Warsaw Pact but unsuitable for rapidly deployable formations. The five-year equipment program and new budgetary techniques promised to impart greater rigour into defence procurement, but there was little overarching thought about reconciling NATO commitments with strategic mobility. As a result, the army bought much of the materiel for a mechanized division of three brigades but then tried to turn half of itself into a light mobile force with this unsuitable equipment.

This contradiction became clear in 1965. The army began planning for a mobile force of two brigades at home and a special service force, but the key structuring work came from the Army Tactics and Organization Board (ATOB), established in 1962.[37] This board ran combat development studies and coordinated changes in doctrine, force structure, training, and procurement. In 1965, the ATOB produced a report that served as the blueprint for the future organization of the army until 1967. The commitment of a division to NATO required that Canada maintain roughly half of its army as a mechanized force with tanks to fight the Warsaw Pact. Other commitments – the defence of Canada and the United States, the commitment of a battalion to a NATO rapid-response force, peacekeeping, and intervention in limited wars – required lighter and more deployable units. In essence, NATO commitments and the plans in the White Paper dictated that Canada develop two armies, one heavy and one light. The original plan in the White Paper to have two brigades that could serve in any role from peacekeeping to nuclear war was impossible. Units for service in NATO required heavily armed and armoured tanks and tracked combat vehicles, while mobile forces for peacekeeping or counter-insurgency required DFSVs and wheeled reconnaissance vehicles that could be deployed quickly. The key determinant of the heavy army was the need for armour and firepower, while for the light army, it was ease of transport.

An important feature in all these considerations was the shrinking size of the Canadian army. It was small compared to those of allies and needed to rely on an ally for logistics support so that the proportion of fighting troops to support troops could be reduced. The global reach and plentiful resources of the United States made closer relations with the US army preferable, especially because the United Kingdom's financial difficulties in the 1960s had caused severe problems in supply. The White Paper recommended that 4 CIBG be located in southern Germany with American troops and that the army standardize on North American–produced equipment, a priority since the end of the Second World War.[38]

The ATOB's recommended course of action to meet alliance commitments and the White Paper's emphasis on strategic mobility were to maintain a mechanized division composed of two beefed-up brigades and a light infantry division of two brigades. The heavy and light wings of the army would have the same pattern and organization, with the major difference between the two wings being combat vehicles: heavy formations would have tanks and tracked reconnaissance vehicles whereas light formations would have DFSVs and wheeled reconnaissance vehicles.[39]

This framework would guide attempts by the army to create two armies with limited manpower and money until the renegotiation of NATO commitments in 1967. One of the major problems was the clear inadequacy of Canada's strategic lift, by either sea or air, for transporting the reinforcements to Europe in a time of war or for deploying light units. The brigade in Canada earmarked for NATO would have to be shipped by sea, and it would take roughly two months to deploy it to Europe.[40] The air force had purchased twenty C-130s in the mid-1960s but still did not have enough strategic lift to transport a light formation rapidly. This was exacerbated because M113s were difficult to airlift because of their size and weight, and M109s would not fit into Canada's planes. The ATOB report noted that these purchases might have to be adjusted, given the problems they would present in rapid deployment, but this never happened.[41] The difficulties and expense of creating this bifurcated army quickly became apparent, but more reorganization and confusion was to come.

The first major change was the creation of the office of Chief of the Defence Staff (CDS) in 1964 to replace the position of chair of the chiefs of staff and to provide greater control over the services. It took time to sort out the reorganization, but in time, the CDS's deputy and principal adviser was the vice chief of the defence staff (VCDS), and below that role was the deputy chief of the defence staff, responsible for operations, overseeing the commands in Ottawa, and other day-to-day tasks.[42] In 1965, the service headquarters disappeared and were reorganized into five functional commands with administrative elements at Ottawa.[43] The army was broken into Force Mobile Command, with the high command at St. Hubert, Quebec, and Chief Land Doctrine and Operations, at Canadian Forces Headquarters in Ottawa. Force Mobile Command officially opened on 19 October 1965, absorbing the army's fighting units and intended to provide land and tactical air forces to fight across the entire spectrum of warfare.[44] The split resulted in years of confusion as the headquarters in St. Hubert and Ottawa tried to establish a division of responsibilities. The army as a legal entity would continue to exist until 1 February 1968, but it was effectively gone. Even the *Canadian Army Journal* ceased publication, and a new Canadian Forces magazine, *Sentinel*, replaced all three service journals. This reorganization seemed sleek, modern, and efficient – far superior to the hidebound and narrow service headquarters that preceded it. The change, however, weakened the army's combat development process, thereby stifling analysis of the land forces for the rest of the 1960s.[45]

A few weeks after Mobile Command opened, at the CDS staff meeting in November 1965, the VCDS, Lieutenant-General R.W. Moncel, presented on the difficulties of creating heavy and light armies. In the ensuing discussion, there was talk of the "desirability of organizing all the ground forces as light forces so that roles could be readily interchanged." The CDS, Frank Miller, suggested that it might be possible to renegotiate the role of the brigade in Europe and instructed the army to study alternative structures for 4 CIBG and any resulting advantages.[46]

A few weeks later, Miller travelled to Paris and met with General Lemnitzer. In a follow-up letter, Miller noted that DND was having difficulties re-equipping 4 CIBG in Europe, and even more trouble equipping and coordinating transport for the balance of the division earmarked for NATO. During a visit to NATO headquarters in Paris, Miller had asked for Lemnitzer's "appraisal of the effect of withdrawing the Canadian Brigade from Europe, and/or removing the remainder of the Canadian Division from its current status of being earmarked for NATO." Lemnitzer responded that the Canadian brigade was one of the most effective units in the critical Central Army Group; it was an essential contribution, he wrote, since it established "the credibility of NATO's overall deterrent." He also wished to maintain the promise of the full Canadian division in Europe.[47]

Miller responded a few days later, on 16 January. He said that he did not want withdrawal of the forces from Europe but recommended "that the nature of the Canadian forces be changed." Miller wrote that the only way to get the balance of the division over to Europe in a reasonable time was to stockpile equipment in Europe, and the reinforcement brigade in Canada would still require equipment to train effectively. He did not think the government would accept this. The CDS suggested that Canadian troops in Europe should be air-portable so that the balance of the division could arrive in a timely fashion. This change would be in accord with NATO's emphasis on mobile forces to defend the flanks, but Miller wanted to hear Lemnitzer's initial reaction to the idea before undertaking any comprehensive studies.[48]

Lemnitzer's response arrived a month later. He stated that the growing power and mechanization of Soviet armoured forces had caused him to press for the re-equipping of light units with heavier armoured vehicles. If the Canadian brigade was a light unit, it might indeed be more useful on the flanks, but it would weaken NATO's defences on the crucial Central Front. He acknowledged the financial difficulties of prestocking equipment in Europe and earmarking air transport, but given the need for these troops, he hoped it could be resolved.[49]

The reasons for Miller's interest in re-equipping as a light force are unclear. Ross Campbell and External Affairs had been careful to emphasize the importance of the "fully equipped" Canadian brigade to Miller, and it is certain that he knew there would be resistance from SACEUR or the army. Hellyer stated that he had no interest in repurposing 4 CIBG, although the archival record suggests that he looked into it quite seriously and that he might have asked Miller to pursue it on his behalf.[50] The pressure may also have come from below, from the first commander of Mobile Command, Jean Victor Allard, who was a proponent of light forces. Perhaps Miller was interested in standardizing the army and, as an air force officer, had no qualms about sacrificing any sacred army cows such as the tank. Whatever his reasons, Miller's forays came to little, and 4 CIBG stayed.

In February 1966, DND's highest administrative authority, the Defence Council, discussed the structure of Mobile Command. The council endorsed a plan that closely followed the ATOB's recommendations. The mechanized division for NATO would be composed of two brigades, one in Germany, one at Gagetown, and these formations would have tanks, M113s for infantry, Lynx reconnaissance vehicles, and M109 self-propelled howitzers. The other half of the army, the two air-transportable brigades based at Calgary and Petawawa, would have DFSVs and light, probably wheeled, reconnaissance vehicles. There would also be a tactical air force, a divisional headquarters, and support troops.[51]

CDS General Jean-Victor Allard gave a good characterization of the bifurcated army a year later. He described the heavy brigades as the "deterrent force" that contributed to NATO and kept the Russians out and the lighter brigades as the "intervention forces" that could quickly defuse conflicts before they had a chance to escalate and draw in the superpowers. He emphasized that this shift was not turning Canada's military into a peacekeeping force but was enhancing its capabilities. Allard also stated that there was no question of turning the NATO forces into light formations so that they would be more compatible with the mobile forces.[52]

The army completed its detailed structure based on this outline in August 1966, and Lieutenant-General W. Anderson, now commander of Mobile Command, came before the Defence Council to present it. The central procurement plan for the armed forces, the Integrated Defence Program, would have to be revised immediately if Mobile Command was to be organized and equipped by 1970. Anderson noted the declining personnel levels of his command and stated that "heavy mechanized troops which are most costly must be kept to the minimum necessary to meet NATO commitments and maximum emphasis must be given to operational requirements to meet commitments in the other areas of the spectrum." The CDS, now General Jean-Victor Allard, emphasized that this new structure "provided a good opportunity to review the equipment requirements of the army which was now enduring an appalling situation as the result of the policy in 1959 to emphasize manpower at the expense of equipment." Despite this, Hellyer deferred a decision, saying that the Integrated Defence Program needed to be formulated in concert with long-range plans and the costing of equipment, so Mobile Command was left only partially equipped even though the structure was approved a few months later in November.[53]

In 1966, it appeared that Canada would have the best of both worlds – a powerful mechanized force that could take on the formidable Soviet army and a light mobile force that was at the cutting edge of technology and strategic thought. If Hellyer seriously considered turning the entire army, including 4 CIBG, into a light mobile unit, External Affairs and SACEUR dissuaded him. NATO allies wanted the forward deployed brigade but cared little for additional units from Canada. The army had the blueprint for its heavy and light wings, and there was some excitement for the new structure but not enough money to fully equip Mobile Command. The year 1967 would see even more troubles.

2

The Traditionalists at Work

Renegotiating NATO Commitments in 1967

Are we not kidding ourselves when we say, "Oh what a boost to morale 6,000 Canadian troops give to West Germany and to Great Britain and the United States." Are we going along in a sort of dream world on this?

– Edgar Smith, Standing Committee on National Defence, 12 May 1966

Hellyer's plans for the army began to unravel as the parliamentary debate over unification of the three services peaked in late 1966 and early 1967. The first problem was finding a suitable vehicle to fill the requirement for a DFSV, which would be the principal striking element of the air-transportable brigades.[1] The army's operational equipment requirement (OER) for the DFSV, the document that outlined the key specifications of a prospective piece of equipment, noted that while the vehicle would have to be small and light to fit into the C-130 transport aircraft, it would also need a large enough gun to provide credible fire support to destroy other vehicles. The key justification of the need for the DFSV was outlined in that document:

> The increased use of armoured vehicles throughout the world makes it highly unlikely that Canadian Forces could ever expect to operate in an area in which the enemy would not have this type of vehicle. The present armament of scout vehicles, and support weapons in light armoured units is not adequate to deal with the large range of enemy armour[ed] vehicles. In addition, the scout vehicle does not possess a sufficiently powerful direct fire capability to deal with the great majority of other types of targets which may be encountered during any type of operation. At present the Canadian Forces have no equipment which can fulfill the requirement of a DFSV and still have the mobility required of this vehicle.[2]

The light brigades would lack crucial firepower without the DFSV. They were using an ad hoc mix of Centurions and reconnaissance vehicles in light armoured regiments, which was clearly a stopgap measure, since the Centurions were strategically immobile: no plane could carry them, and it would take weeks to deploy them by sea.[3]

The C-130 requirement was critical because the plane was in service with many NATO allies and Canada had them. The C-130 was also robust, easy to maintain, and able to take off from improvised airstrips, while larger transport aircraft were in short supply and required more maintenance and facilities. Upon arrival, the vehicle had to be ready to fight immediately, be easily maintained, and have a large operating range without significant maintenance or frequent refuelling.[4] It would provide support to infantry or take on other light armoured vehicles with its main gun. Planners wanted the DFSV to be able to destroy enemy tanks but would accept a complementary system, such as anti-tank guided missiles, if the main gun was too weak.[5]

The emphasis on strategic and tactical mobility and armament came at the expense of armour. The vehicle would have to be proof against light machine gun fire and 152 mm shell bursts and afford a degree of protection against heavier Soviet machine guns.[6] The armour would be thin, especially in comparison to tanks fielded by NATO and Warsaw Pact forces. There were few vehicles in service or development that could meet these stringent requirements: the two main contenders were the US Sheridan and the British Combat Vehicle Reconnaissance, then under development.[7]

The Sheridan promised to meet many of the demanding criteria of the OER. The US army started developing this vehicle in 1959 to function as a light tank for reconnaissance forces and to give airborne troops some armoured fire support. The vehicle could be carried in a C-130 Hercules and even dropped from the air. It was equipped with the Shillelagh 152 mm combination gun and missile launcher, which was also projected for use on the US army's new tank, and this would give the Sheridan the capability to engage heavier vehicles despite its small size and thin armour. This gun, however, suffered from numerous faults and never worked satisfactorily.[8] The Sheridan also suffered from some significant problems in armour protection; the Canadian army knew about these problems early on and shied away from the vehicle when its flaws were exposed in combat experience in Vietnam.[9] The British Combat Vehicle Reconnaissance, later named the Scorpion, was similar to the Sheridan, although it was a much less ambitious design. It was not ready in the 1960s, but Canada would come close to buying it in 1972.

The other problem was the replacement of the Centurion. Canada's Centurions in Europe, armed with the excellent 105 mm gun, were still capable, but the tanks at home had the obsolete 20 pounder gun, and the maintenance burden of the tank, always heavy, was becoming weightier with age. One of the major problems with the Centurion was that it had an aircraft engine, the Rolls-Royce Meteor, a development of the Merlin that was used in the Second World War era Spitfire and P-51 Mustang. The spark plugs were on the bottom of the engine to facilitate easy access for aircraft mechanics, but once they were in the tank, mechanics had to take the entire engine out just to replace them. This process could take from thirteen to thirty-six hours.[10] "To put it bluntly," concluded a 1966 report, "Centurion is fast becoming a liability, at least in Canada." There were serious shortages of replacement parts, and some of them were unreliable.[11] Colonel K.R. Ward, director of electrical and mechanical engineering, wrote, "To RCEME [Royal Canadian Electrical and Mechanical Engineers], the Centurion is a disaster which gulps a disproportionate share of maintenance manpower. From the turret basket up, it is a beautiful piece of equipment; the rest of it is a conglomeration of mismated, badly designed components, thrown together into the most ill conceived ease of maintenance complex imaginable."[12] As allies like the United Kingdom, Denmark, and the Netherlands retired the Centurion, spare parts would become increasingly scarce and costly, and Canada's access to rebuilds and improvements to keep the tank in service would become more expensive and difficult. The major deficiencies of the Centurion were its low speed and limited range, which were inadequate according to the standards for tanks for the 1971–80 period set by the American, British, Canadian, and Australian Armies' Program, an organization created to foster cooperation and standardization among these armies.[13]

The army's preferred candidate to replace the Centurion was the MBT-70 (main battle tank). The United States and West Germany started developing this tank in the early 1960s with the plan to produce a prototype in 1967 and put the vehicle into production in 1970. The Canadian army hoped that it could piggyback on this research and development and save money by buying from a large production run. The MBT-70 would also probably impose a lighter maintenance burden, since the largest armies in NATO were using it, so spare parts would be plentiful. This tank was also in accord with the recommendation to standardize on North American materiel.

In May 1964, Paul Hellyer sent a letter to his counterpart in the United States, Secretary of Defense Robert McNamara, expressing Canada's interest in participating in the MBT-70 program. McNamara was pleased that Canada was interested in the program, although the terms of participation were still unclear.[14] Little happened in response to Hellyer's initial letter, but the MBT-70 came up in July 1965 at a CDS staff meeting. Some army officers and Dr. R.J. Sutherland, head of operational research, presented on the status of the MBT-70, outlining its characteristics and the possibilities for Canadian participation. Canada was required to submit a request for partial participation in the program by 30 September 1965 and could evaluate prototypes in 1967 or 1968 before actually committing funds to the program. In the meeting, Sutherland stated that the tank replacement program was actually not a pressing matter; he thought the

Centurion could remain in service until at least 1975, given adequate maintenance and spare parts. The meeting concluded with the resolution that Canada would indicate its interest in the MBT-70 program but would decide on a replacement program only after examining how much longer the Centurion would last.[15]

Other papers confirm the army's interest in the MBT-70, interest that continued into 1967, even as problems with the development of the tank mounted and its production date was pushed into the mid-1970s.[16] The army studied its needs for tanks in the fall of 1966 and identified only two contenders that could meet the requirements for the 1971 to 1980 time frame and Canada's long-term need for tanks: the British Chieftain and the MBT-70. Although the Chieftain was good, it was not good enough to push Canada away from American sources. The MBT-70 promised to meet most of the standards; however, it would not be ready before the Centurion was obsolescent. A stopgap measure was needed, and although it was possible to upgrade Canada's Centurions, the army preferred the American M60. It recommended the purchase of 130 M60s to be fielded by the end of 1969; these new tanks would replace the Centurions in Europe. In the early 1970s, Canada could make a decision on the MBT-70; if purchased, they could be fielded in Europe around 1975, the M60s transferred to units back home, and the Centurion retired.[17]

The resulting discussion on this plan in the CDS staff meeting focused on the difficulties of actually equipping Mobile Command to its full scales. The deputy minister, Elgin Armstrong, suggested that Canada could re-examine the need for the second mechanized brigade and perhaps equip it to training scales only, to save money. Other officers commented that this was already the case, but Allard wanted to keep the cadre of a mechanized brigade at home in case it required deployment. Allard also stated that Mobile Command had been trying to produce forces to meet all possible commitments but budgetary limitations had produced only policing type forces. He stated that more guidance from Paul Hellyer would be required.

In the discussion on tanks, "the CDS [Allard] expressed the opinion that the time is drawing near when the concept of a main battle tank is becoming obsolete." He later added that "the development of an anti-tank weapon which is not dependent upon direct fire will probably mark the end of this type of weapon system." Given this consideration, Allard stated that it was impossible to determine the requirement to replace the Centurion with precision and that cheaper options, such as the German Leopard or French AMX-30, should be examined. Mobile Command's equipment needs would also have to be reconciled with budgetary limitations.[18]

In the end, the MBT-70 was plagued by technological problems, especially with the gun and missile launcher combination that it shared with the Sheridan.

It was difficult and time-consuming to switch between the gun and missile modes, and the ammunition for the gun was caseless. Early models frequently broke apart, spilling propellant in the turret. The ammunition also left residue in the barrel, which could cause a new round to detonate prematurely.[19] The West Germans withdrew from the program in 1969, and it was finally cancelled in 1971.[20]

Even if these vehicles had been ready, the military was running out of money. Inflation began rising in the mid-1960s, which reduced the Defence Department's purchasing power, forced personnel costs to rise to keep pace with the private sector, and increased operating and maintenance costs. Cabinet set the Defence Department's budget escalation at 2 percent per year, but personnel, operations, and maintenance costs rose at a rate of 3.5 percent.[21] The department was also affected by the reduction of federal spending in 1967, and six hundred soldiers were withdrawn from 4 CIBG that year.[22]

The military also could not establish its priorities for new equipment, despite a shrinking capital budget. To anticipate future equipment needs and to prevent isolated or ad hoc requests, the defence budget had a list of "future resources requirements" – items that the military wanted but that had no money allotted to them. This list was first developed in September 1966, and requests from services totalled nearly $1 billion of equipment. There was nowhere near enough money in the capital budget for all these programs, so the criteria became more stringent, and each item on the future resources requirement list had to be justified by an OER. The list dropped to $154 million in April 1967, but it was then too limited to properly anticipate new needs. A new list created in June 1967 returned to the start and resulted in 187 requests for roughly $3.5 billion. The future resources requirement list was as good as useless, given the difficulties of accurately costing new materiel and assessing necessary items. The army got its requirements for new tanks and DFSVs put on the future resources requirement list but never into the budget, where money was actually allocated for them.[23]

While the army examined new vehicles, NATO was scrambling to respond to France's withdrawal from the military structure of the alliance in early 1966. On 16 March 1966, Prime Minister Pearson, External Affairs Minister and NATO supporter Paul Martin, and Hellyer met to discuss the issue with, among others, the CDS, Jean Victor Allard. H.B. Robinson recorded that Hellyer thought there were some financial and organizational advantages to be gained from reducing strength in Western Europe, mostly by the elimination of the Air Division headquarters at Metz, France. Hellyer noted that the actions of the next eighteen months would determine NATO military arrangements for the next ten or twenty years. Robinson recorded Hellyer's recommendation to "take a very hard look at the scale of effort which Canada wished to assume between now and the 1980s," noting that Hellyer "was not sure of the strength of the political case for keeping our forces in Europe at their present level." Martin firmly opposed a reduction, but the prime minister wanted to see the arguments for and against it clearly laid out. Pearson noted

> that he had thought for the past two or three years that some re-apportionment of defence responsibility would be appropriate as between Europe and North America. The Europeans had looked as if they were in a better position to take a bigger share of the burden of defending Europe, and he thought there would have been much to be said for a certain amount of re-deployment, permitting the United States and Canada to reduce (not of course, altogether) their European obligations but maintaining interlocking arrangements across the Atlantic.

Hellyer proposed that DND and External Affairs should examine the arguments for maintaining the current forces in Europe and other alternatives, but he "thought it unlikely that the Department of External Affairs could produce arguments persuasive enough to offset the case for some relief in our balance of payments difficulties." Robinson noted that "Mr. Martin again demurred."[24]

Two weeks later, Cabinet discussed the implications of the French withdrawal. Hellyer explained that the French did not accept a key premise of flexible response, that conventional ground forces could stop the Warsaw Pact. The only real deterrent to Soviet aggression in Europe was a strategic nuclear response, and several ministers concurred with the French position. Pearson disagreed, stating that this "philosophy" only increased the chance of a nuclear war starting in Europe. For this reason, Pearson stated that the burden of defence should increasingly fall to the Europeans to prevent the American arsenal from being used too hastily, although Canada would continue to make the "appropriate contribution to the collective defence program."[25]

Pearson was quite serious about the need for the Europeans to shoulder a greater share of the defence burden. He hastily typed out some ideas on France's withdrawal to Paul Martin, developing his thoughts from the earlier meeting.

> The basic DeGaulle thesis that NATO had outlived its usefulness is right – up to this point; that there should have been a radical re-examination of the whole NATO structure in the light of the changes that had occurred since the Treaty had been signed 16 years ago. Everybody seemed to agree that changes had to be made to give the European side of the coalition greater influence and power in its direction and control. Everybody talked about the need for a new NATO, but nobody did anything about it.

He later added:

> My own view for some time has been that Europe should take primary responsibility for the organization and control of the NATO European, and the North American members should take the same responsibility for the defence of this continent. There should be trans-Atlantic defence co-ordination by some form of joint command structure – looser than at present – while the U.S.A. and Canada should keep some, but smaller, forces in Europe. [26]

Pearson was concerned about the apparent permanency of the Canadian military commitment. Martin opposed a reduction and argued strongly that Canada should maintain its current contributions so as not to upset allies in a tumultuous time and to maintain links with them but should gradually transfer its forces back home.[27] H.B. Robinson commented that after discussions with Pearson, Martin would "return dreadfully upset. ... Pearson would say that relations with Europe had to be reappraised, and Martin would react with horror. 'I wish he wouldn't talk that way.'"[28]

On 14 July 1966, Cabinet again discussed Canadian forces in Europe, and the resolution was made to maintain Canadian troops in Europe over the short term, with the long-term goal being to get European countries to contribute more and gradually draw down North American military forces in Europe.[29] A few weeks later, Pearson met the American president, Lyndon Johnson, in the small town of Chamcook, New Brunswick, near Maine, and the two discussed De Gaulle and NATO. According to the US Department of State's archival record of that conversation, Pearson stated his now familiar idea that the Europeans should bear more of the burden of defence, but Johnson was skeptical: "What worried him [Johnson] most is that we might do less and they [the Europeans] won't do more." Pearson said that he was not suggesting a full-scale withdrawal; indeed, "Canada had had an opportunity to withdraw when France asked them to leave," he noted, but had resisted. Rather than proposing "that the US should pull out wholesale," his idea was "that the British, for example, could involve themselves more in the defense of Europe and ought to give up trying to play the role of nineteenth century imperialists."[30]

The 1966 resolution to slowly move the burden of defence to the Europeans set the stage for the renegotiation of Canada's NATO commitments the next year. This effort focused on the persistent thorn in the army's side – the transport of the second mechanized brigade from Canada to Europe. Hellyer directed the military to study this problem, and in June 1967, VCDS Lieutenant-General Frederick Sharp submitted a paper titled "Optional Contributions for NATO" to Jean Victor Allard. He noted that Canada still did not have the lift to transport the brigade quickly and that stockpiling equipment in Europe was too expensive. The cuts to the army in the 1960s meant that both 4 CIBG in Europe and its reinforcement brigade at home were under-strength, and in case of war or an emergency, the formation at home might be left at only half-strength. Maintaining the status quo of the follow-on mechanized brigade was clearly untenable.

For the period of 1967 to 1972, when the Centurion tank and the Honest John tactical nuclear rocket launcher would still be in service, Sharp's paper recommended a more realistic alternative to the follow-on mechanized brigade – an air-transportable brigade with tactical air support to reinforce NATO's flanks. Canada already contributed some forces to NATO's mobile reserves, and the alliance was working on making it more robust. Sharp suggested that the Canadian Airborne Regiment and an air-transportable brigade would be good candidates for this role. With some modest improvements in strategic lift, Canada could transport these forces to NATO's northern flank but not to the southern flank. The paper recommended that airlift capabilities be studied and that Canada open negotiations to replace the follow-on mechanized brigade with an airmobile one.

For the period after 1972, the paper drew on recent studies that investigated NATO's future needs – more close support aircraft and more troops as highly mobile regional reserves in continental Europe and the United States. If Canada could acquire such a role, it could standardize on light forces and replace the Centurion with a lighter and cheaper vehicle. The paper pronounced that "air mobility is the next major cycle in land force development" and that "land force air mobility ... is held to be a superior concept for conducting mobile warfare." It recommended that Canada investigate a role as a regional reserve and examine the development of a standardized land force that could fight in any conflict.[31]

One of the critics of Sharp's paper, Brigadier-General N.H. Ross, stated that it failed to follow Hellyer's direction, which was that "one option to be considered, and by inference considered seriously, is provision of the mechanized Brigade from Canada." He was critical of the recommendation to gradually shift into an airmobile role and wrote that the variability of Mobile Command's tasks "implies a heterogeneous but balanced force structure" and that standardization of the army "ought not to be pursued as an end in itself." There was some merit to reinforcing the northern flank, he wrote, but air transport would be too costly. Finally, he was opposed to the replacement of the Centurion with a lighter tank, noting that the Sheridan was $547,000 per vehicle while a Chieftain tank was $330,000.[32]

Although Ross was opposed and sent his comments to Sharp, Allard was in general agreement with the paper, and a modified version of its plan for the period of 1967 to 1972 formed the basis for planning in the summer of 1967.[33] No changes would be made to 4 CIBG, but the second mechanized brigade would be replaced by a light one for service in Norway or Denmark, a brigade that would come to be called the Canadian Air-Sea Transportable Brigade Group.[34] This would save a sizable sum of money and would be palatable to allies, who cared most about Canada's brigade deployed near the Iron Curtain.

In the Cabinet discussion on the reduction, Walter Gordon, president of the Privy Council, stated that Canada should remain in the alliance but reduce contributions, "probably to a greater extent than that proposed by the Minister of National Defence in the document under consideration." He was isolated and effectively countered by Martin, Pearson, and Mitchell Sharp. Pearson voiced strong support for NATO by affirming Martin's points and "emphasized that the present Canadian contribution constituted the 'minimum price for club membership'" and that he "did not consider that Canada could reduce her commitments beyond those proposed and retain respectable membership in the Organization." Although there had been far-reaching discussions of Canada's role in NATO, the winds of change were still blowing, and Martin concluded by saying he would instruct Norman Robertson to write a review of Canada's defence policy.[35]

These reductions caused some serious questioning of the need to replace the Centurion with an equivalent. Allard had already stated that he thought the tank would not last much longer.[36] He had mentioned the West German Leopard, which until now had played no role in army planning, and had expressed interest in a small purchase to equip the brigade in Germany, with the Germans responsible for the bulk of maintenance and logistic support.[37] The recent history of maintaining the Centurion probably weighed heavily on Allard. In the fall of 1967, teams from DND and the Department of Defence Production visited Munich to discuss the purchase of approximately 150 tanks, including maintenance arrangements, and to explore opportunities for Canadian industry with the German manufacturer, Krauss-Maffei (KM). In December 1967, Allard brought officials from KM to Ottawa to discuss his plans and the company's estimate of costs for the purchase of new tanks and maintenance. But there was no substantial financing planning for the purchase of a new tank, and these initiatives came to naught.[38] A few months later, the army began considering a retrofit of the Centurion to squeeze a few more years out of it. The Netherlands had been working on an overhaul of the Centurion, including replacing the tank's unreliable Meteor gasoline engine with a more powerful and reliable diesel engine.[39]

The renegotiation of commitments caused no shortage of turmoil, but even more was in the offing. In the late summer of 1967, the army and External Affairs started to investigate moving the brigade to southern Germany in the American sector, near Canadian air units at Baden-Soellingen. Locating all Canadian forces in Europe in one area would ostensibly save money by cutting down on administrative and headquarters personnel, and Canada could tap into the American logistics system. Although it is possible that Hellyer initiated this examination, Allard spearheaded it. Hellyer moved out of the picture on 19 September, taking over the Department of Transport, and was replaced by the associate minister for DND, Léo Cadieux. In September 1967, five working groups began studying the operational, logistical, accommodation, administrative, and foreign policy aspects of a possible move.[40]

External Affairs sounded out its ambassadors on the plan in October 1967. The ambassadors to the United States, United Kingdom, and West Germany – A.E. Ritchie, C. Ritchie, and R. Bower, respectively – were cautious, highlighting that the British would not like the plan, that there were few advantages to be gained from an even closer relationship with the US, and that European allies would be hesitant.[41] Ross Campbell had discussed the plan with General Allard in Ankara and had noted the problems, but he did see some advantages in consolidating the forces to save money and to highlight the Canadian contribution that had been partially subsumed in the British army. The British had taken to calling their six brigades and Canada's 4 CIBG the "British Army of the Rhine." Although this was a semantic issue, it still rankled some Canadian sensibilities. Campbell also noted that the British were on the verge of cutting their forces in Europe to relieve the burden on their balance of payments and that it might be time to move now to avoid a repetition of the hasty withdrawal of air units from France in 1966. He suggested that if Canada's commitments were restructured, "we might think in terms of a switch to a self-contained mobile role in ACE [Allied Command Europe] involving colocation of the brigade and airdiv [air division] in southern Germany."[42] External Affairs, however, was against the plan. The fear was that a move would upset the British, subsume the Canadian contribution into American forces, or make the Germans think that this was a prelude to a Canadian reduction.[43] This did not, however, dissuade Cadieux from examining it further. In February 1968, he instructed the military to study other possible roles for the brigade, the possibility of a reduction of troops, and withdrawal or major overhaul of the brigade or air division. He directed the military to pay particular attention to making 4 CIBG a mobile regional reserve, which would determine whether or not the Centurion tank would be replaced with a DFSV or a tank.[44]

Allard informed Cadieux in a memo that his staff was studying the options, but the possibility of total withdrawal of forces, which would make long-term planning redundant, should be determined. He also suggested that SACEUR should be consulted about repurposing the brigade.[45] He attached a draft of a letter to Lemnitzer in which he informed SACEUR that he wanted to send his deputy chief of staff, Major General N.G. Wilson-Smith, to discuss the colocation of 4 CIBG and the air division, as well as the possibility of a new role for the brigade. Given Canada's obligations and resources, he highlighted that the Canadian military should have the "greatest degree of mobility, flexibility of employment, and quick reaction." He saw a similar emphasis on European defence with NATO's recent "Special Study" on the use of light mobile forces against the Warsaw Pact in Central Europe and thought it was a good opportunity to dovetail these efforts.[46] He also informed H.B. Robinson and Canada's ambassador to NATO, Ross Campbell, of his plan.[47] Campbell was supportive, although he suspected that SACEUR would raise objections. He stated that the "proposal not only makes Canadian sense, but NATO sense, if the current accent on mobility of land forces and augmentation of conventional air strength is converted into revised force requirements by SACEUR."[48]

The briefing for Major General Wilson-Smith left no doubt of Allard's intentions: he wanted to move the brigade south and make it into a light regional reserve. In its present location, 4 CIBG was not compatible with land forces at home; the Centurion would need to be replaced, and possible British reductions would ensnare Canada in the north and make it difficult to change the brigade's role or structure. Allard wanted Wilson-Smith to sound out SACEUR on the possibility of a phased alteration in which the mechanized brigade would be a corps reserve, then a mobile brigade at regional reserve level, and then a highly mobile brigade for SACEUR's reserve.[49] Although the Canadians emphasized that this was a more effective use of defence dollars, Wilson-Smith characterized Lemnitzer's reaction in the March meeting as "basically unenthusiastic." The headquarters associated any change with reductions, saw the plan as a decrease in much needed front-line strength, and feared weakening the Northern Army Group further.[50]

The renegotiation of commitments in 1967 prompted another round of revisions of the army's structure. In January 1968, at a Defence Council meeting, Lieutenant-General W. Anderson pointedly expressed his frustration, since the plans to equip Mobile Command had stalled. The structure had been recast several times to contend with financial and personnel limitations, the need to create a tactical air group, and the reduction in NATO ground commitments. The new plan was to maintain the formation in Europe at full strength as a mechanized brigade but convert the brigades at home into four reduced-strength "combat groups," based at Calgary, Petawawa, Valcartier (the operating language of this formation would be French), and Gagetown. The formation at Gagetown would be mechanized with heavy tanks and self-propelled artillery to provide a training pool for 4 CIBG, but "the main implication of these revised commitments was to reduce the need for mechanized forces and to place greater emphasis on the need for air transportable forces." The other three formations based in Canada would be light air-portable units with equipment that could fit in a C-130, except for the Centurions in light armoured regiments, which would be replaced by a lighter vehicle in time. Anderson emphasized that a decision on this force structure was required quickly, and even more importantly, Mobile Command needed stable funding and personnel levels to actually make it work. The combat effectiveness and morale of the army had declined precipitously because financial and personnel limitations had forced units to reduce their strength, crucial equipment like the Centurion was rusting out, and there was no DFSV in sight. The European brigade was the only real combat formation left. Anderson commented on the equipment program: "This Command has never had an approved programme because it has never had an approved structure. The two go hand in hand." Cadieux sympathized with Lieutenant-General Anderson, approved the structure, and noted that the equipment procurement program would be given top priority.[51]

Although the restructuring took place, the re-equipment program did not come to pass. A few months later, in April 1968, Pierre Trudeau seized the Liberal mantle and initiated his own review of defence policy, which went back to "first principles." The key element that runs through the Pearson years is the declining defence budget. Canada could have paid for a large and modern armed forces: its spending as a proportion of gross domestic product was one of the lowest in the alliance, and the country was by no means poor. The Pearson government, however, correctly surmised that the Canadian people wanted more butter and fewer guns, so it put the military on a lean budget. There was little political impetus for increased defence spending when the Liberals introduced costly but popular social programs as antiwar sentiment grew during the conflict in Vietnam and détente with the Eastern bloc seemed a possibility. Inflation mounted in the mid-1960s, causing personnel and operations costs to rise dramatically while lowering the army's purchasing power. Despite attempts to save money by making the Armed Forces leaner through integration and unification, spending on new equipment never reached the 25 percent of the defence budget that Hellyer promised. In the 1962–63 fiscal year, capital spending stood at 21.6 percent of the defence budget, and by 1967–68, it had decreased to 18.9 of the budget, and to 16.7 percent the following year.[52]

The army was also weakened by rapid changes in structure. The reorganization of the command structure wreaked havoc with combat development, and although it tried to restart this process, successive reorganizations and cuts stifled proactive thinking about the army in the late 1960s and early 1970s. To some extent, such thinking was impossible given the rapid changes in defence policy and budget and the personnel cuts that ensued over the next few years.[53] The brigade in Europe remained a viable and well-trained formation, but at home, the army wasted away. It suffered cuts of roughly ten thousand soldiers to stay under the budget ceiling during the 1960s, and it took nearly four years and numerous rounds of restructuring to approve Mobile Command's organization.[54] Within months, a shift in the political leadership rendered this approval moot.

A progressive shift to light forces was also occurring, largely at the instigation of Allard, in the belief that such forces were the future of ground combat and that they would be cheaper than mechanized forces. In 1963, the army had been primarily equipped with tanks, and most of it, except for the brigade for the defence of North America, was tasked to fight against the Warsaw Pact's heavily armoured armies in Central Europe. By 1965, half of the army was to be light; by 1967, that proportion had increased to roughly three quarters, and the army was left with the rump of a heavy force in Canada.

Despite the turmoil at home, 4 CIBG remained in Europe. SACEUR General Lyman Lemnitzer did his part to stymie General Jean Victor Allard's attempts to repurpose the brigade, but the real work came from the civilian traditionalists. Although the prime minister became increasingly critical of NATO, Martin and Pearson, the most prominent traditionalists, effectively shut down any discussion of radical changes to Canada's commitments in Europe. They realized that six squadrons and a ground brigade was the minimum buy-in at the NATO table, and they could not reduce further, despite hopes that the situation would change in time.

Their defence, however, was ultimately flawed. Some of the new members of Cabinet, especially Trudeau, were revisionists and were frustrated at being blocked out of any serious discussion of foreign policy. They probably had no idea of the depth of Pearson's doubts about NATO, and if they had been brought into the process, it might have dampened their ardour to review policy. Instead, as the Liberals gathered to elect a new leader in April 1968, the revisionists were intent on overturning the status quo.

3
Trudeau Takes the Reins
The Triumph of the Revisionists

At this time, Mr. Kierans said External Affairs tells us as a Cabinet what our allies think. The Department should be relating to our allies what we as a nation were attempting to accomplish.

– Cabinet Conclusions, 30 March 1969

We had to get them [National Defence and External Affairs] out of the frame of mind that we had to be in everything.

– Marc Lalonde, interview by R. Bothwell and J.L. Granatstein, 30 November 1987

NATO had in reality determined all of our defence policy. We had no defence policy, so to speak, except that of NATO. And our defence policy had determined all of our foreign policy. And we had no foreign policy of any importance except that which flowed from NATO.

– Pierre Trudeau speaking to the Alberta Liberal Association, 12 April 1969

Pierre Elliott Trudeau won the Liberal convention in April 1968 and electrified the country during the federal election in June. He was telegenic and seemed much younger than his forty-eight years, and "Trudeaumania" seemed to signify the coming of age of a new generation as the elderly Pearson and Diefenbaker faded from the scene. Although Trudeau's first interest was maintaining Canadian unity, foreign and defence policy was a close second.[1] Soon after becoming prime minister, he frightened allies and External Affairs with his public statements about the need for a review of Canadian defence policy. On 7 April, the day after being elected leader of the Liberal Party, he stated, "We are not as important as we used to be in Europe," adding that "Canada should concentrate on what it does best – defence of Canadian air-space." This comment prompted Léo Cadieux to read a prepared statement to allies stating that he was convinced there would be no major changes to Canada's military presence in the near future.[2] External Affairs sent a memo to Trudeau advising him of a wide-ranging departmental review of NATO in process, overseen by Norman Robertson, and of the certainty that allies would be quite sensitive to any changes in Canada's commitments.[3] When the Robertson report, produced at the behest of Paul Martin, was submitted, Trudeau rejected it because it recommended the status quo. After his election win in June, he instructed DND and External Affairs to submit a new review of policy.[4] This review would focus on the land forces in Europe, which External Affairs Minister Mitchell Sharp referred to in May 1968 as the review's "thorniest problem."[5]

Trudeau's views on Canada and NATO are significant because he was the major figure leading the charge against the status quo; without him, there would have been no reduction. No other critic had the same power or determination to overcome the traditionalists or the bureaucracies. Thomas Axworthy, in the Prime Minister's Office from 1975 to 1979 and from 1980 to 1984, commented that Trudeau had read much of the strategic thought on nuclear weapons in the 1950s and 1960s, and although he accepted the logic of deterrence, he was horrified by nuclear weapons and the possibility that events might overtake leaders as they had in the summer of 1914. Trudeau was unsettled by NATO's continued reliance on tactical nuclear weapons despite European recovery, and in addition to wanting to rid the Canadian Armed Forces of nuclear weapons, he wanted to reduce the risk of global nuclear war.[6]

There is little evidence to support the view that Trudeau wanted to withdraw Canada from the alliance entirely and adopt neutrality like Sweden or Switzerland. Some, like Allard, thought that Trudeau wanted Canada to be neutral, and the prime minister certainly investigated that possibility.[7] He also made inquiries about James Eayrs's theory that if one of the smaller NATO members withdrew, one of the weaker Warsaw Pact members could withdraw, leading to gradual de-escalation.[8] This, however, is not necessarily evidence of intention. Indeed, Allan Gotlieb noted that there was the perception among some External Affairs officers that Trudeau wanted a full review, from root and branch, of Canadian foreign policy and that he questioned everything and sought out the full range of opinion on these questions.[9]

Trudeau probably did want full withdrawal of Canadian troops from Europe, if not in 1968, then in the very near future. His statements from a press conference in May 1968 are revealing:

> What I have said is that so far as the military involvement in NATO is concerned, this does need a very strong and perhaps drastic reassessment. This is based on one of the realities which I have described, that Europe of 1968 is no longer the Europe of 1948 and 1949. It does not need at this time the Canadian military "might" to defend itself. Our role in the defence of the free world would be much better discharged, I believe, if we were more concerned with continental defence because if there was going to be a world conflict it will take place over our air space, in our air space, and therefore talking about isolationism does not

> mean in my mind isolationism. It means on the contrary being more realistic, playing the role as Canadians in an area in which we perhaps have more to say than we do in Europe today. ... But once again, politically, I do not ask for the withdrawal. Perhaps eventually politically NATO will be done away with but I do not propose that we do it one-sidedly. Perhaps we can de-escalate with the Warsaw Pact countries.[10]

Trudeau was indeed being realistic; he knew that a few thousand Canadians with five dozen tanks on the Iron Curtain was a small contribution to the strategic balance. Like Pearson, he thought that a rebuilt Europe should shoulder the burden of defence.

Trudeau diverged from Pearson in that he discarded the internationalism of the 1950s and aggressively espoused concrete national interests as the key determinant of foreign and defence policy. Allan Gotlieb and Max Yalden, both in External Affairs at the time, wrote a paper in early 1968 critiquing Canada's foreign policy for its continued reliance on internationalism and multilateralism and arguing for a policy based on enlightened national self-interest. They passed their paper to Trudeau, Marc Lalonde, and Michael Pitfield. Clearly, the emphasis on national interests appealed to Trudeau, and it became a central feature of his thinking on foreign and defence policy.[11] For Trudeau and the revisionists, the brigade in Europe was clear evidence of the adherence of External Affairs and the military to the outdated internationalism of the 1950s that no longer served Canada's interests.

They had a point. Although External Affairs was adamant that Canada had influence in Europe, there were no particularly close economic or cultural relationships between the continent and Canada. To the contrary, the protectionist EEC built trade walls that effectively blocked many Canadian exports, particularly agricultural products. In early 1968, H.B. Robinson suggested that the defence minister send Trudeau a paper titled "Rationale for Canadian Defence Forces," in which a report from Canada's ambassadors to NATO countries led to a strong defence of the status quo in Europe. The paper argued that allies would be very critical of a withdrawal of Canadian troops, nor would they accept a promise of air-transportable troops.[12] R.L. Raymont, executive staff officer to the CDS, was skeptical about Trudeau being convinced by this and thought that more concrete evidence of the alliance's value should be presented: "Mr. Trudeau will probably want to know what specific examples of particular influence and advantage Canada has received during the last 5 years, both political and economic because of Canadian troops based in Europe."[13] External Affairs could point to precious little, and A.E. Ritchie later stated that Canada's "affection for Europe was unrequited."[14] Canada also paid the costs of stationing its troops and their families in Europe, receiving no money or trade preferences to offset the drain on the balance of payments. This was in contrast to the United States and United Kingdom, both of which threatened Germany with significant troop reductions in the 1960s if the Germans did not offset their costs.[15]

Finally, Trudeau had grave doubts about flexible response, NATO's official strategy, and they were warranted. Although the rhetoric of flexible response was appealing and promised to reduce the chances of an all-out nuclear war, there was significant debate between Europe and the United States over how much was enough to deter the Soviet Union. In the early 1960s, many Europeans argued that enhanced conventional strength only invited aggression by weakening the implied resolve to use nuclear weapons and that if the Europeans built up conventional strength while the US retained its monopoly on nuclear weapons, European allies would be "second-class citizens" in NATO. At the extreme end, France argued that flexible response was simply a means for the United States to begin its disengagement from Europe. Although there was a rough consensus by 1967 that NATO needed conventional forces to resist a non-nuclear attack, the required troops and capabilities were unclear.[16] NATO countries also had little appetite to increase defence spending to bolster the defences on the Iron Curtain. The Europeans were skeptical of flexible response, and Kennedy, McNamara, and Lyndon Johnson never seriously considered increasing strength in Europe. To the contrary, they threatened the Europeans for financial considerations, and they withdrew two divisions in 1967, the same year the alliance adopted flexible response.[17] Although the Americans promised to return these troops by air in case of emergency, it was a major reduction in NATO's strength, which complicated the other problem—nuclear parity.

In the 1950s and early 1960s, the Soviet Union had superior conventional forces in Europe, but until the late 1960s, its strategic nuclear arsenal lagged behind that of the Americans. The leaders in the Kremlin were aware that any move against Western Europe could be greeted by an American first strike and the obliteration of the Soviet Union, while the United States could survive with less damage. As the Soviets achieved strategic parity in the late 1960s, NATO's nuclear umbrella became mutual assured destruction. This change caused Richard Nixon to state memorably in a National Security Council meeting that the flexible response strategy was "baloney." The meeting notes record the gist of his (and other participants') comments: "They have possibility of conventional option, greater numbers. We remember our massive retaliation, gave us freedom to act. This has changed. In Europe, we may have to face up to a drastic increase in our conventional capability." A few moments later, Henry Kissinger remarked on how the situation had changed: "Europeans don't realize American nuclear umbrella depended on first strike. No longer true. Need review of strategic doctrine." The US secretary of defense, Melvin Laird, pointed out, "We don't have flexible response because of drawdowns," to which Nixon responded: "Nuclear umbrella no longer there. Our bargaining position has shifted. We must face facts."[18]

As Nixon and Kissinger had noted, NATO's strategy rested on dubious premises in the late 1960s. Strategic parity had made NATO's nuclear "sword" less effective and highlighted the need for a stronger "shield" – that is, more conventional forces. But it was clear that no NATO country was going to pay for this and that flexible response as a military strategy was largely a veneer. Pierre Trudeau and Ivan Head recalled this later: "Official NATO policy in the late sixties argued for conventional containment, but in reality its military formations still dictated employment much more akin to the earlier trip-wire strategy than to the more sophisticated flexible-response strategy then officially in place."[19] Trudeau thought that the status quo was untenable and only increased the chances for the occurrence of a nuclear war. He would be unyielding in forcing the bureaucracies to review policy, but the funding crunch from the mid-1960s had already forced that to begin.

On 30 April 1968, Cadieux submitted a memorandum to Cabinet outlining the fiscal difficulties and asking for an extra $250 million per year to bring the budget up to $1.975 billion and increase capital spending to 20 percent. He and Allard continued to pursue revising the role of Canadian troops in Europe, and Cadieux wrote that in the period from 1968 to 1974, "it would be planned to convert the forces in Europe from a Mechanized Brigade Group and a separate Air Division to a Mobile Brigade Group supported by integral tactical air forces similar to the forces maintained in Canada." Although a withdrawal of Canadian forces from Europe could save the desired funds, the memo also argued strongly against this move, which would cause Canada to lose credibility with its allies and would undermine NATO.[20]

A few days later, the Cabinet Committee on Priorities and Planning considered, and rejected, Cadieux's proposal to increase funding and change the role of the forces in Europe. Trudeau did not want a decision to lock the government into a role for multiple years while the defence review was ongoing, and the committee recommended "that no action should be taken at this time which would precipitate, as an unavoidable consequence, the withdrawal of Canadian forces from Europe." The committee instructed DND to make a comprehensive review of policy and alternative force structures.[21] Cabinet rejected any increase in funding but directed a study of the military's future roles and costing. Cadieux said that the guidance provided by a review of Canadian foreign policy would allow him to develop more specific proposals for Canada's military, but he thought it was likely that he could repurpose it to be more deployable around the world.[22]

Cabinet rejected the report by External Affairs on foreign policy, tabled in July 1968, because it recommended the status quo, although it did contain some discussion of other options for Canada, such as neutrality. The government would maintain the status quo until the end of 1969 while a more detailed review continued, to be completed by November 1968.[23] The Soviet invasion of Czechoslovakia in August 1968 affected the review process, and most NATO members responded to the invasion with largely symbolic plans to increase strength to show the alliance's resolve. The United States sent a note with specific requests for Canada's Armed Forces, asking that Canada return to the full divisional commitment of the two brigades and restore the six hundred troops that had been withdrawn in 1967. Cadieux rightly pointed out that Canada had no sealift to transport the reinforcements; in any case, Trudeau resisted making any commitments, saying that this contribution was strategically useless and that it would prejudice the outcome of the review.[24]

The review was not completed by November 1968, and as it started to drag on, it began to affect the morale of the Armed Forces and to unsettle allies.[25] Despite Cadieux's attempt to reassure allies, they suspected, correctly, that a change was in the offing and feared a major reduction, if not an entire withdrawal. At the autumn NATO meeting in November, Sharp met with his German counterpart, Willy Brandt, who asked that Canada not reduce its commitments in Europe. Sharp responded that Canada was reviewing foreign and defence policy thoroughly and had great interest in Europe, especially since the recent invasion of Czechoslovakia. He assured Brandt that the government would carefully examine its NATO plans, that no one had suggested withdrawal, and that a review of the nature and size of Canada's commitment was underway.[26]

A few months later, in early 1969, the review finally came to Cabinet. Trudeau was anxious to complete it before a series of NATO meetings in Washington in April and Brussels in May. The bureaucracies of External Affairs and DND produced two reports. The first was written by the Special Task Force on Europe (STAFEUR), composed of some of Canada's most experienced diplomats in Europe, such as Paul Tremblay, ambassador to Belgium, Luxembourg, and the European Community from 1966 to 1970; Robert Ford, ambassador to the Soviet Union from 1964 to 1980; and John Halstead, head of the European Division in External Affairs from 1966 to 1971. As evidenced by the Gotlieb and Yalden paper, External Affairs' view of Canada's relationship with Europe was not monolithic, and there was division during the drafting of the STAFEUR report. Halstead recalled later that Canadian security interests in Europe was the most controversial topic in the report and that H.B. Robinson chaired an informal group in External Affairs that considered whether Canada should keep troops in Europe.[27] However, Michael Shenstone, head of the NATO and North American Defence Division at External Affairs in 1968, recalled that the critiques of policy caused the department to "circle the wagons" in defence of Canada's commitments.[28] The STAFEUR paper focused on the political aspects of Canada's relationship with Europe and addressed the military contribution in broad terms, examining nearly every facet of Canada's relations with Europe and offering alternatives to the status quo. It emphasized the importance to Canadian security of a free and independent Europe, but the crux of the paper was the assertion that membership in NATO meant having influence and active relations with some the largest military and economic powers in Europe. Western Europe could be a counterweight to American influence and domination, but it came at a price. Canada needed to commit to the alliance military forces that were taken seriously by allies and that were based in Europe.[29] As Pearson had noted in 1967, this meant a mechanized brigade and six squadrons of aircraft.

The companion to STAFEUR's report was the *Defence Policy Review,* which examined all the military possibilities for Canada, including nonalignment, withdrawal from NATO, and the maintenance of a bare-bones Armed Forces solely for internal security. It cautioned against withdrawal of troops from Europe, stating that Central Europe was the most important possible battleground of the Cold War; if Canada were to withdraw its forces from this theatre, it would squander the influence it had with allies. Just as Paul Martin and External Affairs had argued in 1963, the defence policy review emphasized that military units deployed near the Iron Curtain bought the most influence.[30] The Soviet Union, although it entertained no serious thought of trying to seize Western Europe or grab a slice of territory, was still menacing, and European allies wanted to keep Canadians on the front line. The paper was vague about what kind of influence these troops bought and whether influence meant having a say in alliance strategy or sway with allies.

The Cabinet Committee on External Affairs and National Defence, having considered these two reports throughout February and March 1969, reached no consensus on whether Canada should keep forces deployed in Europe as part of NATO. The committee noted that Cabinet would need to consider the shortfall between Canada's commitments and the budget, the possibility that alternative military roles would be better suited to Canadian interests, and the use of forces based at home for surveillance of Canadian territory.[31] In *The Canadian Way,* Head and Trudeau recount that they were frustrated at External Affairs supporting the status quo despite a changed strategic context: "Innocently, but effectively, officials had held onto the ball while the clock ran down. There now remained only a few weeks before the final decision had to be made."[32]

From this point on, Trudeau was extremely skeptical of the External Affairs assessment of the brigade in Europe and turned to alternate sources of advice. H.B. Robinson commented later that Michael Pitfield, in the Privy Council Office, thought DND and External Affairs were "in cahoots" and were trying to frustrate the review.[33] Trudeau instructed his foreign policy adviser, Ivan Head, to draft a report that would challenge the orthodoxy of the bureaucracies.

Head was a lawyer and had been an External Affairs officer for a short time in the early 1960s. He was skeptical of the importance placed on the Cold War and military containment of the Soviet Union and thought that inequality between the developed North and the developing South was of greater concern than the ideological conflict between East and West. Head relied on a group of advisers called the Non-Group, so named to hide its true purpose.

Head's report, "Canadian Defence Policy: A Study," was at odds with the two reports of the bureaucracies and was, ironically, grounded in a military assessment of the brigade while downplaying its political significance.[34] Head argued that Canada's defence priorities were not located in Europe; rather, they were defending the American nuclear deterrent, reducing the chances of nuclear war, and fostering economic development and peace. Western Europe had more than enough soldiers and money to replace Canada's contributions; the brigade on the Central Front was fundamentally symbolic and represented resolve more than any real military need. A large commitment was unnecessary, but even more troubling was the fact that Canada's Armed Forces were ill-suited to discharge fundamental tasks for the government, such as aid to the civil power. The military had become specialized in alliance roles, especially the NATO brigade, which was of little use outside Central Europe. The paper advocated not for withdrawal from NATO but for a drastic reappraisal of Canada's military contribution to Europe based on the fundamental assumptions that it did not make a significant difference to European security and that it was at odds with Canadian needs. Head argued that the brigade should be replaced with a light combat group, only one-third of which would be stationed in Europe.[35] This reduced force of roughly fifteen hundred to two thousand would give NATO allies some Canadian hostages in the unlikely case of conflict with the Soviet Union, but the light combat group would be compatible with domestic requirements.[36]

Head's study closely reflected Trudeau's thinking on defence policy when he came into office. Trudeau's draft of "Canadian Defence Policy: A Study," nearly identical to the Cabinet submission, is full of notations and underlined passages that recurred in his speeches and statements both before and after the writing of the paper. Trudeau noted the passages emphasizing that Canada's most important contribution to the Cold War was protecting the second-strike capability of the United States. This was the real deterrent, not sixty Canadian tanks on the north German plain. He underlined the passages noting that Europe had recovered economically and no longer needed Canada's military contribution. Trudeau also noted Head's statement that "the role of the Canadian Armed Forces is not, initially, to impress our enemies, but rather our friends. This is a political, not a military, role."[37] A few weeks later, Trudeau stated, "Our defence policy was more to impress our friends than our enemies."[38] Finally, Trudeau noted the point that Canada's military was poorly structured to perform tasks at home, underlining the section on replacing the mechanized brigade with lighter, smaller forces.[39]

The strategic criticism in Head's report was accompanied by skepticism of NATO's importance for Canada. In *The Canadian Way*, Trudeau and Head recount that Canadian contributions to NATO infrastructure totalled $175 million, while NATO defence purchases in Canada were $1 million. Keeping Canada's forces in Europe cost $120 million per year. Head and Trudeau scorned Canada's influence in Europe: "This 'influence' could be jeopardized, argued the STAFEUR authors, were Canada to withdraw from, or substantially diminish, its NATO role. Not surprisingly, this argument failed to impress many ministers."[40] Indeed, the Department of Finance's assessment of the defence policy review in March 1969 was that "while the NATO countries of Europe attach importance to Canada's continuing military presence, this has not led them to give any special consideration to Canadian trade interests."[41]

Ross Campbell, ambassador to NATO, frequently jumped the chain of command – sometimes to the prime minister himself, sometimes publicly – in appeals to deflect the review.[42] Someone with intimate knowledge of the defence policy review had alerted the Americans to Trudeau's skepticism of NATO, and on 25 March 1969, Henry Kissinger wrote to Richard Nixon that "members of his [Pierre Trudeau's] entourage have expressed concern that he is still flirting with reducing Canada's role in NATO; they believe some low key remarks by you in private might be beneficial." Kissinger suggested that the president underscore the continued vitality and relevance of NATO, although no mention was made of any specific military commitments.[43] There is no record of the ensuing conversation between Trudeau and Nixon, but Nixon was familiar with the arguments for reducing American troop levels and later stated that he had impressed upon Trudeau the idea that the "Europeans could not expect Americans to do more if Europe did less."[44]

The reports by STAFEUR, DND and External Affairs, and Head were submitted to Cabinet a few days after the meeting of the two leaders. Head's report, however, was withdrawn at the protest of Cadieux.[45] At the beginning of the Cabinet meeting on 29 March 1969, Trudeau emphasized that Head's report, although it had come from his office, did not necessarily reflect his viewpoint.[46] The debate in Cabinet was largely split between pro- and anti-NATO wings. The prominent civilian traditionalists were Léo Cadieux, Charles Drury, John Turner, Mitchell Sharp, Paul Hellyer, and Paul Martin as leader of the government in the Senate, although he did not speak much. These men offered the same defences of Canada's commitments to NATO as had been made for the preceding five years: the value of military contributions because of the nation's stake in European security, the importance of alliance solidarity, and the maintenance of influence and good relations with allies.[47] Although the revisionists did not have as consistent an outlook, they questioned Canada's influence, and all were generally in favour of a reduction of forces – and in some cases, total withdrawal from Europe. Trudeau frequently interjected and argued that Canada's small military contributions did little to maintain security in Europe and that the most important defence priority for Canada was to help defend the American second-strike capability and preserve the balance of terror.[48] The Cabinet meeting minutes record some of Trudeau's comments as follows (underlining in the original):

> The Prime Minister suggested that an observer would find it strange that Canadian troops were off contributing to the defence of Europe to impress politically our friends while leaving exposed our vast coastline, our territorial seas, and air space. The Prime Minister believed that the policy was inverted. We should be protecting our internal security, defending our three seas, and then considering other possible international commitments. It was not logical or rational to protect that which was not ours. If we did not contribute specific forces to Europe, it did not mean that we did not share the same interests in defence, nor did it mean that we would not participate with Europeans in time of trouble. Forces in situ, however, should first be in Canada to protect Canadian interests.[49]

Donald Macdonald vociferously called for withdrawal of all forces from NATO throughout the review, and John Munro stated that "it was almost pretentious on our part to assume that we had great influence, or that we had much of a role to play in NATO."[50] It is likely that some of the traditionalist arguments were less convincing for other members of Cabinet because of European recovery; in Sharp's memoirs, he recalls the review with a measured tone and notes that with European revival, he could justify reconsidering the size of the commitment.[51] It is also likely that many Cabinet ministers defined "influence" differently than External Affairs did. For Cabinet, influence was measured by trade or concrete demonstrations of sway with allies, but for diplomats, it was more subtle and intangible.

The Cabinet debate resulted in a consensus by 1 April. Canada would remain in NATO but would implement a phased reduction of its forces in Europe and move to a defence policy based on domestic needs.[52] The Privy Council Office and External Affairs disagreed as to whether this meant total withdrawal from Europe.[53] Gordon Smith – who was working for the Canadian ambassador to NATO, Ross Campbell – later recounted that he and Campbell were shocked to read the initial press release, which implied full withdrawal.[54] Cadieux recalled that on 1 April, he threatened to resign if all troops were withdrawn from Europe. He met with Trudeau, and they agreed to use the term "planned and phased reduction," which would leave no doubt that Canadian troops would remain in Europe. Cadieux also insisted on consultation with allies.[55] Sharp, mindful of the consequences this reduction would have for the alliance, emphasized that it should not be arbitrary but should be made in light of prospective Mutual and Balanced Force Reductions, an attempt by NATO and the Warsaw Pact, which ultimately failed, to reduce each other's military forces in Europe at the same rate to avoid destabilizing the balance of power. Trudeau's response is recorded in the minutes of a Cabinet meeting:

> After 20 years of NATO participation we were now able to witness a rebuilt Europe which had the capacity to control and meet European security problems. The GNP of European countries including Britain had reached a combined national income equal to some 500 billion U.S. dollars. This change in the ability of European countries to provide defence forces for their own security must be recognized when we considered the necessity for restructuring our defence forces to take into account our own priorities. The Prime Minister continued that now was the time for the Canadian government to act and decide. The government should now make its position clear so that a new defence structure could be built and developed. For some years, the Prime Minister said, we had been told that Cabinet should not reduce its force commitment in Europe because of the acquisition of new equipment or new roles. Now we were told that we should not reduce our force contribution in Europe for other reasons such as the morale of Canadian forces. With these kinds of pre-conditions when could the government effectively change its foreign and defence policies?[56]

On 3 April, the press release announcing the results of the review came out. It affirmed Canada's continuing support for NATO and NORAD but stated that there would be "a planned and phased reduction of the size of the Canadian Forces in Europe." The four defence priorities for Canada were listed as follows:

> (a) the surveillance of our own territory and coast lines, i.e., the protection of sovereignty; (b) the defence of North America in co-operation with the United

> States forces; (c) the fulfilment of such NATO commitments as may be agreed upon; and (d) the performance of such international peace-keeping roles as we may, from time to time, assume.

The "structure, equipment and training" of Canada's military had to be compatible with Canadian requirements, and Trudeau announced that "our eventual forces will be highly mobile and they will be the best-equipped and best-trained forces of their kind in the world."[57] Brandt visited Cadieux and Sharp a few days after the review, and the German foreign ministry's report of that meeting was that the pro-NATO group in the Canadian government expected support from the German government to oppose troop reductions or withdrawal.[58] After meeting with allies in Washington, Cadieux reported that the Americans were more sympathetic to the plans for reduction, provided that Canada maintain some presence in Europe and consult with SACEUR.[59]

Although the reduction was based on a strategic reappraisal of Canada's role in the Cold War given Europe's recovery and Canada's needs, Trudeau and the revisionists were also making a political point. In Alberta on 12 April 1969, Trudeau commented on the review: "In the situation we had reached, NATO had in reality determined all of our defence policy. We had no defence policy, so to speak, except that of NATO. And our defence policy had determined our foreign policy. And we had no foreign policy of any importance except that which flowed from NATO."[60] In a lunch with J.L. Granatstein in 1988, Trudeau expressed regret about the speech, saying it had been unfair to Pearson. He said that he had been tired from skiing and "that the audience wanted to hear about oil, and he didn't want to talk about oil."[61] Regardless, Trudeau's formulation was probably an accurate reflection of his thinking in the late 1960s; later, in 1995, he and Head characterized defence policy in 1968 as a "parody of NATO."[62] Although the press conference on 3 April and the speech on 12 April came roughly a year after the first intimations of a review, the defence policy review was far from over. The revisionists had won this round over the traditionalists and External Affairs, but the clash with NATO allies was still to come.

4
The Summer of 1969
Consultations with Allies

You cannot turn foreign policy on and off like a tap, and the results of the review did not substantially change our policies or commitments.

– Paul Martin, *A Very Public Life II*, 1985

Although SACEUR had thrown numerous roadblocks in the way of Allard's plan to repurpose the brigade in Europe and move it south, Trudeau's defence policy review would finally give Allard the momentum to implement these plans. Allard corresponded with Lemnitzer on the move throughout 1968 and early 1969, and on 29 March 1969, the day the critical Cabinet discussions on the review began, Allard received a message from SACEUR. Lemnitzer was wary of any changes to the status quo, and although he appreciated Allard's interest in light mobile forces, he emphasized the need for mechanized troops on the front line. If absolutely necessary, Canada could move to a reserve role in Northern Army Group, provided it maintained the same equipment.[1] After the 3 April press release, a group was tasked to produce a new force structure for the military and for Canadian troops in Europe. The group comprised Deputy Minister of Defence Elgin Armstrong; CDS Jean Victor Allard; Henri de Puyjalon, from the Treasury Board; Hume Wright, from the Privy Council Office; and H.B. Robinson, from External Affairs. The revised structure would be presented in late May at a meeting of NATO's Defence Planning Committee, the most important committee on the military structure of the alliance. The plan, presented to Cabinet on 30 April, was to reduce the military's personnel from 98,000 to 81,000 in order to remain under a frozen budget ceiling of $1.815 billion, reduce the contribution to NATO from 10,100 troops to 3,500, and restructure the military in accordance with the priorities announced on 3 April – the defence of Canadian sovereignty and security, the defence of North America, the fulfilment of NATO commitments, and UN peacekeeping roles. The plan specified that Canada would remain in NATO and deploy forces in Europe, but it emphasized that these forces would be compatible with units at home.[2]

This meant going light, since the bulk of Canada's army was now ostensibly a light mobile force, although light armoured regiments kept using Centurions for lack of a DFSV.[3] The army would abandon mechanized warfare and retire the Centurions in Canada and the Shermans used for militia training; it would withdraw more than two-thirds of the recently delivered self-propelled M109 howitzers.[4] The submission to Cabinet warned that reacquiring a capability for high-intensity mechanized warfare would involve great expense.[5] Canada would withdraw more than half of the 6,000 strong brigade in Europe, which, in 1968, was renamed 4 CMBG (Canadian Mechanized Brigade Group), and convert it into a light mobile force for use on NATO's northern flank (either Denmark or Norway) as part of Allied Command Europe Mobile Force (AMF). This was a small, rapidly deployable reserve composed of contributions from several NATO allies and intended to reinforce threatened areas and show the alliance's resolve in crises.[6] This idea may have come from Ross Campbell in October 1967; he was certainly talking with Allard during the review. The rump of 4 CMBG would move south to Lahr and be re-equipped by the end of 1972.[7] This move made little military sense – the unit was moving hundreds of kilometres *away* from the area it was supposed to defend – but it made political sense. Lahr was about an hour away from Canadian air units based at Baden-Soellingen, and the move would consolidate all Canadian forces in Europe in the same location, an idea that had been floated since the late 1950s. Cabinet discussed the changes on 15 and 20 May and approved the restructuring, although a small door was left open for revision in case of vociferous protests by allies.[8]

Léo Cadieux must have been anxious as he flew over the Atlantic on his way to Brussels, knowing he would receive a rough ride from his colleagues. The reductions did not make a sizable dent in NATO's overall strength, and the reduction of sixty-six hundred troops was not going to alter the balance of power. The cut would, however, further weaken the alliance after a decade of tumult that had started with the problem of sharing nuclear weapons and continued with the American and British effort to extract more money from the Germans to offset the costs of stationing forces in Europe. France withdrew from the military structure of the alliance in 1966, and the United States sent more and more troops to a war that the Europeans wanted no part of. Not only were all member nations under pressure from their own citizens to reduce defence budgets in favour of social spending, but the war in Vietnam had provoked strong currents of antiwar sentiment. Henry Kissinger, in *The White House Years,* recalls the debates over "burden-sharing" and the European fears of American reductions, coupled with American resentment at Europe's unwillingness to do more.[9] Canada had not undermined NATO since its inception and had been the "good ally," sacrificing its own national interests for the good of the alliance.[10] This was all to change when Cadieux announced the results of his government's review at Ross Campbell's residence in Brussels on 25 May 1969.

Cadieux began by emphasizing that Canada was neither withdrawing from the alliance nor cutting defence spending. Although some troops would come home, the remainder would become a highly mobile force in line with recent NATO thinking and requirements. His colleagues would have none of it. The Belgian defence minister stated that the results of the decision were "catastrophic" and "could have the gravest consequences for the free people of Western Europe." How could he get more funding for his budget if opponents could point to the recent Canadian example? The defence minister for the Netherlands stated that the news of the reduction would be a "considerable shock." Ross Campbell recounted that the two ministers from the Low Countries both had tears running down their faces.[11] The Germans were worried, and the Americans had not anticipated such a drastic reduction and hoped it could be postponed. When the US secretary of defense, Melvin Laird, asked if there was room for negotiation, Cadieux replied that there was little. Laird hoped that the reductions could be postponed, given that "there had been certain difficulties in USA Congress concerning the maintenance of current level of USA forces in Europe. ... Canadian example if followed would be of material assistance to those interested in USA force reductions in Europe." Denis Healey, the British defence minister, frankly stated "that the proposals were totally unacceptable" and in clear contravention of the rules for reductions. He "suggested that Mr. Cadieux report the views of his colleagues back to Canadian Cabinet, knowing that such actions could not be taken with the acquiescence of other members of the alliance, nor could it be expected that such proposals would receive support or sympathy." At this point, Allard chimed in, emphasizing that the new force would be more efficient and cheaper than the current mechanized brigade, but his rejoinder had little effect. NATO's secretary general, Manlio Brosio, summed up the fears of Canada's allies. If Canada presented its reductions as a fait accompli, "we rule out and invalidate consultation. Such an action could initiate a chain reaction with great inherent danger and reduce, in the minds of our members and the general public, the credibility of NATO's obligations and undertakings." He concluded by recommending that Canada consult with its allies on the new structure to preserve NATO's viability and the principle of consultation between allies.[12]

As Brosio noted, Canada's cut would make it more difficult for allies to maintain defence spending and NATO commitments, let alone increase them, during the era of détente. In Washington in early 1969, alliance members had pledged that there "should be no reduction in NATO's overall defence capability except in the context of agreed reductions with the forces of the Warsaw Pact." As Healey noted in an official Defence Planning Committee meeting, the Canadian proposal was clearly going to undermine this principle, and other countries would probably have to pick up the slack.[13] Sharp had told Trudeau about this, but the prime minister was intent on making policy without foreign influences. One of the central concerns was the effect the reduction would have on the United States. Although the American leadership, State Department, and Pentagon had no interest in reducing troops, the Europeans were always fearful of a return to American isolationism. Later in 1969, Henry Kissinger passed a memorandum on the strategic situation, written by an acquaintance to Nixon. In a paragraph on the Canadian reduction, he wrote:

> Unaware of Trudeau's marked sense of independence, many Europeans actually believe that Canada could not very well take such a measure without the, at least tacit, approval of Washington. This, then, leads to the further conclusion that the entire North American continent is beginning to turn inward and [is] intent on ultimately withdrawing all its forces still stationed on foreign soil.[14]

Both sides also worried about the efforts of Senators Mike Mansfield and William Fulbright to bring about US troop withdrawals and about the Canadian example strengthening the senators' cause.[15]

The American position on the reduction was generally less hostile than the European response. Kissinger, in a memo to Nixon before the meeting, recommended that the American position should be to mitigate the effects of the reduction and to keep as many Canadian troops in Europe as possible. The memo suggested a conciliatory approach: "We are willing to discuss a change in the role of Canadian forces in Europe if this would increase the chances of retaining more Canadian forces." Kissinger thought that reversing the decision was unlikely but that it could be moulded to "the over-all interests of the Alliance by affecting its scale and timing."[16] Later, while discussions in Brussels were ongoing, Helmut Sonnenfeldt, from the National Security Council Staff, tried to moderate the American reaction, fearing that a strong protest would magnify the consequences of the decision and close any room for negotiation. The US secretary of defense, Melvin Laird, was very disappointed with the announcement but did not critique the Canadians strongly.[17] He was more pessimistic than his colleagues about the prospects of the Canadian reduction and reported to the Germans that he thought almost all Canadian forces in Europe would be gone within three years and that the Germans and the Americans should create a united front and remind the Canadians that the decision was harmful and weakened NATO.[18]

Brosio had called for consultations, and on 29 May 1969, a group of Canadian officers made a detailed report on the new force structure to Supreme Headquarters Allied Powers Europe. Deputy Chief Plans Rear Admiral Robert

Timbrell opened by stating that the military had reviewed its budget, structure, and priorities and had concluded that it could devote thirty-five hundred soldiers to the defence of Europe. By 1971, Canada's contribution in Europe would be reduced to two squadrons of CF-104s, based at Baden-Soellingen, and a ground formation of fifteen hundred, based nearby at Lahr. This latter unit would be very light: the heaviest vehicle was the Lynx, nine tonnes with a heavy machine gun, and the heaviest anti-tank weapon was the handheld Carl Gustav. It would be entirely air transportable, relying on helicopters for observation and transport.[19] Some officers questioned why the force did not have tanks. Timbrell responded that the principle of compatibility for Canada's army had dictated the decision to go light: "There is no need for a heavy tank in North America, therefore we will be moving out of the heavy tank role." SACEUR's deputy was dismayed by this decision.[20] A week later, the discussion continued. Again, Timbrell emphasized that Canada was getting out of the tank business: everything related to tanks – whether heavy, medium, or light – would be deactivated.[21] The German envoy to NATO, Günter Gnodtke, reported that Brosio thought that all that would be left of the unit would be a reinforced battalion with inadequate anti-tank weapons and that the justification for eliminating tanks was "grotesque."[22]

Although Timbrell was adamant that the Canadian force in Europe would have no tanks of any kind, at home, the army was planning for the European force to have DFSVs and even attack helicopters. There are no papers in the archives to explain the divergence; the most likely scenario is that Allard was personally directing the revised structure in Europe, while the rest of the army was working on its own studies. The senior officers at the Defence Council in June must have been exasperated, if not despairing, as they discussed another major restructuring of the army, with declining funds and personnel levels, for the third time since 1964. Three combat groups in Canada would each have a reconnaissance regiment equipped with DFSVs and wheeled reconnaissance vehicles, while one unit would be equipped primarily with helicopters for close support and for transport. The formation in Europe would have Cobra attack helicopters, recently introduced in the United States, and a reconnaissance regiment with light helicopters, DFSVs, and a tracked vehicle. All Centurions would be retired, along with fifty of the recently acquired M109 self-propelled howitzers. Although this structure was much lighter and more deployable than it had been in 1963, it was also expensive, and the current budget would not come close to allowing for re-equipment of the entire army with the full complement of attack helicopters and DFSVs.[23] The structure presented at the Defence Council had much sharper teeth than Timbrell's force with Lynx vehicles and Carl Gustav anti-tank weapons, but it was still a radical change from the postwar

Canadian army. Since the buildup of NATO's strength in the early 1950s, preparing for high-intensity mechanized warfare in Europe had been the army's central mission. It had started to cast its eyes towards the rest of the world in the 1960s, but now it was turning inward. In June 1969, an army officer stated: "In a very real sense the restructuring of the land force component in Canada is a revolutionary event. The raison d'être of the land component in Canada is no longer to prepare for a war which would be fought abroad – it is instead to prepare for emergencies which could occur at home."[24] Light armour had apparently eclipsed heavy armour, and the life of the tank in Canadian service had a firm expiry date of 1973.

By June, Allard was beginning to retreat from the AMF option that he had concocted in April and that was approved by Cabinet in May. At the CDS Advisory Council meeting on 11 June 1969, there was discussion about the possibility of SACEUR wanting a restructured 4 CMBG on the Central Front, and that he would not want it tasked to Norway. Allard did not give up on a highly mobile Canadian army equipped with light vehicles and helicopters, but he wanted it to be able to fight in Central Europe.[25]

NATO stalled in responding to Canada's force proposals, and SACEUR stated that he needed to consult with his political masters before he could respond.[26] Brosio was particularly worried by the Canadian government's defence priorities. In a discussion with German Chancellor Gerhard Kiesinger, Brosio stated that Canada was reducing the strength of its military from 98,000 to 81,000 but maintaining its defences in North America while reducing strength in Europe from 10,100 to 3,400. Brosio said this was unacceptable, but Kiesinger remarked that it would not be easy to impress Trudeau.[27] When the Defence Planning Committee met to discuss the reductions on 27 June 1969, the members expressed their reservations about the plan to Ross Campbell. Brosio noted that the basic problem was balancing national versus alliance requirements, especially given the agreement that NATO would not reduce its strength unless there was a corresponding reduction by the Warsaw Pact. Each national representative noted his concern that the Canadian plan would weaken the solidarity of the alliance; in addition, the Dutch, Belgian, and Italian representatives pointed out that the plan was too nationalistic and undermined the principle of collective defence.[28] Two weeks later, Brosio remarked, correctly, that the Canadian actions were "extremely nationalistic" *(äußerst nationalistisch)* and could have repercussions, especially with weaker allies. As a compromise, Brosio was considering proposing that Canada reduce its forces in Europe in line with the overall reduction in the strength of the Canadian military.[29]

Brosio sent a letter to Trudeau in late June asking that the Canadian government review its decision, and Goodpaster sent a similar letter on 19 July.[30] In late July, an exasperated Cabinet instructed Cadieux to expedite negotiations with SACEUR.[31] Goodpaster sent along his counterproposal and, in another telegram, requested that either he or his chief of staff meet personally with Cadieux to discuss the restructuring. He wrote:

> On 1 August, I visited your force in Germany to inform myself at first hand of the current Canadian role and contribution to ACE. I was impressed with the professional calibre and the efficiency with which your country's resources have been converted into a qualitatively unsurpassed military contribution. ... The prospect of a change involving reduction in this Canadian capability is of deep concern to me and my force commanders.[32]

The NATO counterproposal recommended that the unit be a reserve for the Central Army Group, capable of limited actions, or for rapid reinforcement of AMF. The paper noted that Canada's proposed structure of 3,500 troops was too small and lacked heavy equipment, notably tanks. Goodpaster wanted 8,300 Canadian soldiers in Europe but was prepared to accept 6,500 with plans to augment the force to 8,300 in case of war or tension. This would include 4,099 ground troops with an armoured cavalry squadron of roughly seventeen light tanks, probably the Sheridan, which would give it some staying power against Soviet tank columns.[33] The American ambassador to Canada, Harold Linder, commented that although the proposal would be unacceptable, it was a useful bargaining tool and would strengthen the hand of the Canadian military who argued for a more robust contribution. Linder cautioned against a harsh tone, which would only make the Canadians more rigid and eliminate any wiggle room in the timing or actual size of the eventual contribution.[34]

Canada's initial response to the proposal was directed by VCDS Major-General Mike Dare. He was chair of the Force Structure Working Group, which was tasked with implementing the defence policy review and the new structure of Canadian forces in Europe. Well aware of Cabinet's limit of thirty-five hundred in Europe, Dare proposed a land component of nineteen hundred, but with an armoured regiment of a reconnaissance squadron and two tank squadrons of roughly twenty tanks each. His proposal did not mention whether they would be heavy or light, although a good guess would be that the Centurions would remain in service until a lighter alternative was available. There would be a mechanized infantry battalion, an artillery regiment with twelve guns, and associated headquarters and support troops. This brought the total strength of Canada's NATO troops to roughly four thousand, and Dare suggested that Allard ask the minister for five hundred more.[35] Allard was satisfied with the structure but evidently thought it needed more infantry; he wanted to add another battalion of roughly nine hundred troops, a number that was probably the result of informal consultations with Trudeau.[36] To Dare, Allard emphasized that the formation should be as air portable as possible but that current equipment should be maximized to save money. Army planners would develop an entirely airmobile structure and test it with wargames, equipping it when money became available, probably after the budget freeze ended in late 1972. Canadian forces in Europe, including air and support units, would be approximately five thousand strong.[37]

Cadieux took this revised plan to Cabinet the next day, 13 August. He stretched the truth, saying that SACEUR had proposed a Canadian force of eighty-three hundred, which Cadieux had rejected, and then sixty-five hundred. Cadieux wanted to propose a ground contribution that was half the present size of the brigade, approximately three thousand, and that would remain mechanized with tanks and self-propelled artillery until lighter equipment was available in two to three years' time. The new structure for Canada's forces in Europe was possible at a reduced strength of eighty-one to eighty-two thousand military personnel and a budget ceiling of $1.815 billion. There was some concern that this plan appeared to be just a reduction, not a use of better equipment with fewer people. Trudeau questioned, with prescience, "whether it would be possible to say that the new force structure was different. He wanted to be sure that there was no surprise in store for the government at the end of the three year period." He summarized the plan, saying that the force would be reduced by half, from its present strength of ten thousand to five thousand, with a further reduction to forty-three or forty-four hundred when the new equipment arrived.[38]

Cabinet wanted to announce the results by 15 September 1969 and finally end the review. Cadieux thought that inviting SACEUR would bring too much attention, so he invited Goodpaster's chief of staff, General Horace Wade, to Ottawa on 11 August to resolve the restructuring of Canada's contribution. Wade arrived four days later, and emphasized the loss to NATO and the consequences of further reductions, stressing that Canada was needed in the Central Region. Allard countered by stating that the new force would be smaller and more efficient and could still be tasked to the Central Front. The CDS outlined the interim structure of five thousand troops, with a land force component of twenty-eight hundred that would be replaced in the early 1970s by an airmobile formation with DFSVs. Not only would this unit be compatible with Canadian units at home, but it would also be more effective and useful in Europe. When Wade noted that he would need some time to review the proposal, Allard stated that a decision was needed quickly and that the government was not willing to negotiate further. The meeting ended at that point.[39] External Affairs communicated to Campbell in Brussels that the meeting had gone well and that Wade was probably happy with the revised structure.[40] In a message a week later, Campbell informed External Affairs that he would take the appropriate steps to inform allies before the public announcement on 15 September and that he would also resist any more pressure to extract more troops from Canada.[41]

By Labour Day 1969, the consultations were complete. When SACEUR, General Goodpaster, passed on his approval of the five thousand–strong Canadian force, Cadieux responded that he was happy that SACEUR thought this force would be meaningful. Not only would it have mobility and staying power, noted Cadieux, but it was an increase of fifteen hundred over the original proposal. He pointed out that the specific mission of the unit would "be dependent on the ultimate organization of the force" and that "the roles ... would appear reasonable for employment of this force in the central region and can be the subject of further discussion as the structure of the post 1972 force develops."[42] The defence minister had asked the service chiefs if the revised force structure met NATO commitments; their response was yes, but just barely.[43] At NATO headquarters, Campbell wanted to stress that Canada had consulted its allies despite their reluctance about the reduction; he wanted to finish the review with the "maximum of concurrence and minimum of recriminations."[44] He emphasized in a later message that Canada's "careful adherence to consultative requirements and readiness to make some adjustments in our original proposals has gone a long way towards ensuring the continuing goodwill of our allies." His conclusion was conditionally optimistic:

> If the public and private handling of this final phase of the force adjustments can be managed broadly as indicated above and if the reaction of the remaining eight is as constructive and comprehending as that of the key five, I am satisfied that we will have accomplished a fifty percent reduction of our force commitments with ninety percent of our standing and influence in the organization intact.[45]

On 19 September, with Léo Cadieux's announcement of the new structure to the House of Commons, the review of European defence policy was finally over.[46] The revisionists had won, largely because of Trudeau's force of personality and determination to overcome bureaucratic inertia from External Affairs, the resistance of the traditionalists, and opposition from allies. In a report on Canadian foreign policy in September, Hans Ruete, in the German foreign office, accurately commented that Trudeau espoused the independence of Canada and its own interests and "tenaciously and persistently pursued his line" and acted against the advice of his bureaucracies.[47] Trudeau focused on a primarily strategic assessment of Canadian defence policy and argued, with justification, that a rebuilt Europe no longer needed a contribution of ten thousand troops. This was at loggerheads with the politically based assessment of External Affairs, also justifiable, that Canada needed to provide forces deemed acceptable by NATO in order to have the benefits of membership in the alliance. But Trudeau would not compromise. He continually pushed past numerous protests, meetings, and memoranda until Canada's troops in Europe were, if not withdrawn, at least reduced and restructured in accordance with Canadian needs. The restructuring also made a political point. It was an assertion of sovereignty, a statement that Canadian defence policy would not be dictated by allied expectations. The traditionalists dissipated after this decision, and defence policy was now in the hands of the revisionists.

The final player in this drama, the army, was largely represented by Jean Victor Allard, who, as the record clearly shows, was the major figure in the plan to eliminate the Canadian tank. Some have asserted that Trudeau forced a reluctant army to eliminate its tanks. There is the story, for example, that while visiting a Centurion firing demonstration, Trudeau remarked that the army should enjoy this because it would be their last chance to fire off the big guns.[48] This episode may very well be true, but it was probably a flippant comment and not necessarily evidence of Trudeau's attempts to undermine the army. He might have inherently disliked tanks, or wanted to eliminate them because of unsavoury pictures of Soviet tanks crushing reform movements in Hungary in 1956, or Czechoslovakia in 1968, but there is no documented evidence for such antipathy. To the contrary, Dare recalled that during the October Crisis of 1970, Trudeau wanted tanks on bridges in Quebec and Montreal; the army needed to dissuade him from such a step.[49]

It is possible that Trudeau instructed Allard to eliminate tanks, but regardless of his personal perspective on them, it was Allard who spearheaded the shift to light forces, which had already begun in 1963, and this shift made some sense. By early 1968, the bulk of the army was ostensibly light, with the only mechanized formations being the brigade in Germany and a training pool in Gagetown, both of which had tanks that were aging maintenance nightmares. There was also significant debate in this era over the future role of armour, and not for the first time or the last, many argued that improvements in weaponry and technology had made the thick slabs of armour on tanks like the Centurion anachronistic.[50]

For the rest of the army, the change was difficult. The mechanized brigade had been the one constant during the preceding six years of change and uncertainty. It was garrisoned near the Iron Curtain, where American and Soviet forces faced each other with their most important allies across a divided

Germany that was at the root of the Cold War. Canada had played an important part in this standoff, its mechanized brigade on the front line the gem in the army's crown and the buy-in for Canada's diplomats at the North Atlantic Council. Now this had been cut in half, and the brigade, now a battle group, would become a light airmobile force by late 1972 or early 1973.

5
The Revisionists Assert Control
Defence in the 70s

The revisionists had won, but they had little faith in the Department of National Defence (DND). In September 1970, one of Trudeau's aides made the following points in a memo to Prime Minister Trudeau:

- It is anticipated that shortly there will be strong representations by DND for increased amounts to carry out present force commitments.
- No effective and compelling presentation has been made to Cabinet which warrants and substantiates an increased budget.
- No five year forecast or acceptable program review has been presented.
- If budgetary allocations for military programs are not substantiated and justified on the basis of their military effectiveness, the government will again be forced to fix an arbitrary budget for DND for future years.
- In those circumstances it would be legitimate to arbitrarily reduce the defence budget.

He also wrote that DND's plan for restructuring the forces in order to meet the revised priorities of April 1969 was deficient.[1] Marc Lalonde was in Trudeau's office as principal secretary from 1968 to 1972, after which he became a member of Parliament and had a number of Cabinet posts throughout the 1970s and early 1980s. He recounted that the perception in Cabinet was that the military had no strategic plan and that each service was always pursuing its own growth.[2] When Donald Macdonald asked for and received the DND portfolio, Trudeau told him to raise the morale of the troops, develop policy, and accept the NATO cuts and the budget freeze as final.[3]

In 1970, the army officially retired the Centurions in Canada and continued to work on the 1973 force structure for 4 CMBG. By March 1970, it had some preliminary reports ready, having run a series of war games called Bronze Nimbus. These tested out 4 CMBG's capabilities as a light tactical reserve on the Central Front; there was no discussion of the AMF option at all. In Bronze Nimbus IV and V, 4 CMBG's main anti-tank capability was six Cobra attack helicopters, anti-tank missiles, and nine DFSVs with a powerful main gun. The opponent was a reinforced Soviet motorized rifle regiment, and although 4 CMBG inflicted heavy losses, the Soviets were prepared to break through once the war game ended. The authors concluded that more study was required.[4] The army presented this force to SACEUR, who stated that it needed more mobility and staying power, and in May 1970, more war games were carried out. After this, Dare instructed that the structure should be truly airmobile, relying almost entirely on helicopters for movement, and it would still be a reserve for NATO's Central Army Group. The army's director of combat development, Colonel F.T. Harris, noted that allies were investigating airmobile units and that any major decisions should wait until certain trials of helicopters in central Europe in 1972 were completed. He thought it was worthwhile to wait and adopt an airmobile role in the late 1970s.[5] By September 1970, the army had developed a partially airmobile structure, but its combat effectiveness was doubtful.[6]

Dare presented this to the CDS Advisory Committee on 9 September 1970 and argued that 1971 was too early to make a definitive plan for the force in Europe to present to SACEUR. The United States, United Kingdom, and West Germany were researching airmobile units but saw them as an "ancillary." Dare stated that the army should continue in the mechanized role in Europe until the late 1970s and procure a new tank in the interim. In response to Dare, the CDS, now Frederick Sharp, directed that more research should be conducted on the rationale for a new tank and possible force structures.[7] A few days later, NATO planners asked about Canada's contribution to the alliance past 1973 and about whether it would keep tanks in service. They had either been misinformed or, more likely, had decided to ignore the decision to go on the flanks and withdraw the tank. The army responded that it had little information to pass on because it was still testing the structure with war games.[8]

The frozen budget stifled capital spending, and by November 1970, the army thought that there was not enough money to adopt the new structure by late 1972 or early 1973; it would be necessary to postpone the restructuring to 1975 or 1976. Deputy Chief Plans Major-General H. Tellier discussed the matter with Ross Campbell and presented him with four options for the interim force past 1974: (1) increase the land contribution but withdraw the air component, (2) increase the air component but withdraw ground troops, (3) maintain the status quo, or (4) undertake all commitments from Canada. The army was in favour of extending the status quo to 1974 or 1975 with rebuilt Centurions or leased M60s, which would buy more time to study the requirements for an airmobile force. Although this was at odds with the compatibility of ground units, Tellier noted that SACEUR was happy with the current Canadian contribution to NATO. Campbell contended that maintaining the status quo was the most attractive option and that any other changes would disquiet allies.[9]

The following month, the army presented the problems and costs of making an effective air-deployable force to Macdonald at the Defence Council. It recommended an extension of the status quo beyond 1 September 1974 and continued study of air mobility. The deputy minister, Elgin Armstrong, said that an airmobile force would probably be more expensive than purchasing new tanks to replace the Centurion and continuing with the present arrangement. Also, Canada could probably afford only one effective formation like this and could not equip units at home to the same standard. Dare stated that SACEUR preferred the current Canadian role, but a decision was needed quickly because the Centurion would probably be worn out by 1 September 1974 and it would take years to either buy and field a new tank or develop a deployable force. More time would be needed to analyze comparative costs, said Macdonald, who directed the army to open discussions with the Americans on the possible acquisition of a tank and to compare the costs of remaining in the armoured role versus creating an airmobile force.[10] He would pay particular attention to the contribution in Europe during the drafting of the White Paper.

At first glance, the paper seemed a simple elaboration of the policy announcements of April and September 1969, but it concealed a controversy. Macdonald brought in Gordon Smith, fresh from a PhD at the Massachusetts Institute of Technology, to write the paper, but Macdonald took direct charge of the section on the forces in Europe.[11] He wanted to know why Canada's troops were committed to the Central Army Group and asked Frederick Sharp and Armstrong about the Cabinet conclusion of 20 May 1969 that put Canada's force on the flanks: "How did we get into the situation where we are committed to CENTAG [Central Army Group] rather than to the AMF?"[12] Sharp responded with a lengthy memo on 1 February 1971 detailing the series of events; at some point, he wrote, the tasking to AMF was lost, although the plan to become airmobile was not. Macdonald wrote to Trudeau in March 1971, stating that he had investigated the status of Canadian forces in Europe. He attached a detailed memo from January 1971 that set forth the series of Cabinet resolutions and discussions on the issue and wrote that Canada was faced with the unpleasant choice of either continuing in a heavy role on the Central Front, contrary to Cabinet instruction, or facing accusations that it was not meeting its commitments. He wanted to discuss the matter with Trudeau.[13] The prime minister, in his response, agreed that it was a grave matter and said that they needed to investigate DND's failure to task Canadian land forces to AMF and implement the 20 May 1969 decision. Trudeau wanted a full report from the deputy defence minister and the CDS, who needed to address Canada's apparent commitment to a heavy role in Central Europe and the incompatibility of that force with units based at home.[14]

The problem flowed from NATO's apparently total ignorance of the plan to task 4 CMBG to AMF. SACEUR's counterproposal of 3 August 1969 had effectively kept Canada on the Central Front as a tactical reserve, although it noted that 4 CMBG could reinforce AMF. This was contrary to the Cabinet instruction of May 1969, and it meant that Canada would have to maintain a robust force to make a realistic contribution to the deterrent. Light airmobile formations, suitable for use on the flanks because of the need to deploy quickly, would be brushed aside by waves of Soviet tanks rolling across the Iron Curtain.

Trudeau instructed his staff to look into the matter. The deputy secretary to the federal Cabinet, M.A. Crowe, wrote that DND had never let Cabinet know that the AMF tasking was impractical or unfeasible, adding, "This leads to the conclusion that there has been either a deliberate or an unplanned failure by responsible Defence authorities to implement a Cabinet decision or to return to Cabinet for further direction when that decision could not be implemented." The consequences for the responsible administration of defence policy were grave if such basic decisions went unheeded.[15] For the revisionists, this was incompetence, at best, and outright disobedience, at worst.

Gordon Robertson, clerk of the Privy Council, prepared a more detailed paper outlining the various policy decisions and DND's options for equipping Canadian land forces in Europe, all of which were based on the assumption that Canada would remain on the Central Front. The brigade would need either tanks, contrary to defence policy, or prohibitively expensive anti-tank helicopters. DND's first option was to replace the mechanized combat group with an airmobile force, with helicopters for transport and firepower, and this was costly – $450 million. The second alternative was to create a mechanized infantry group, which was cheaper but still $100 million. The third option was to continue in the present arrangement and either lease Leopard tanks or extend the life of the Centurions to 1980. DND preferred this last option, estimated to cost only $1.5 million.

Robertson noted that no mention at all had been made of putting Canada's forces on the flanks, contrary to the Cabinet decisions in May 1969. Each of the three options was incompatible with army units in Canada, and although keeping the Centurion was cheap, he stated that "to stick with tanks ... is to decide that a fairly substantial part of Canadian land forces will train and operate in a dead end direction since the concept of compatibility with light mobile forces in Canada would have been sacrificed." In order to eliminate any ambiguity over the equipment needs of the Canadian troops in Europe, which ranged from attack helicopters to modified Centurions, Robertson recommended a review of where they would serve.[16] Trudeau responded to Robertson's memo: "Spoke to Macdonald. Shared his concern about perhaps five high level people having subverted the will of Cabinet. Told him that he and the Government would lose all credibility if he did not pursue this with the utmost firmness. He will do so and report to me."[17]

Macdonald followed up, discussing the issue with Deputy Minister of Defence Armstrong, the CDS, Sharp, some officers involved in the planning, and Cadieux. He summarized the story for Trudeau: Allard was particularly enthusiastic about airmobile formations but knew they could not survive on the Central Front. They needed to go on the flanks, and a light force could reinforce Norway as part of AMF. During intensive planning with NATO, this decision went unmentioned, for unknown reasons, and by that summer, Allard seemed to have lost his enthusiasm for the AMF role. Not only would it require expensive new helicopters and aircraft, but it would not make use of existing equipment. In short, it was impossible to do with a frozen budget. The thinking in DND evolved to maintaining an interim force for two or three years until money became available to re-equip the formation. Discussions with NATO in August and September focused on the size of the interim force, timing, and the move to Lahr, but not on the final structure of the contribution to AMF.

In a memo to Trudeau, Macdonald wrote that he had phoned Cadieux, who did not recall whether the AMF proposal had come up again in Cabinet or in discussions with the prime minister after May 1969. Cadieux stated that during intensive consultation over the summer, NATO military staffs had been evasive, so the post-1972 structure of the ground contribution remained an open question. The AMF decision was never implemented because no concrete military planning was done for the period after 1972. Macdonald wrote to Trudeau that although Cabinet had ratified Canada's continued presence on the Central Front with an interim force, a serious question remained: Could Canada ever leave the Iron Curtain without intense criticism from allies? Reinforcing Norway from bases in southwest Germany would require expensive and substantial amounts of air transport, and Macdonald concluded that this "was an unsound idea, one developed on the spur of the moment by the then CDS."[18]

Trudeau responded that "whatever excuses they [senior military and civilian officers of DND] may have, failure to conform to Cabinet decisions cannot be accepted." The role of Canadian land forces in Europe would be addressed during discussion of the 1971 White Paper, *Defence in the 70s*, but Trudeau found it "hard to understand how it is now feasible to employ this [light mobile] force in the Central Region when two years ago it was not considered sound to do so."[19]

Despite this reservation, Macdonald resolved to keep Canada's troops in Central Europe and equip them with light vehicles. In his memo to Cabinet introducing *Defence in the 70s*, Macdonald concealed the debate over the structure of Canada's troops in Europe. It had been impossible to task Canada's interim brigade to AMF, he wrote, and further study had revealed that a re-equipped force would not work either. He discarded the AMF role and enshrined the interim status quo. Canada's ground force would still be a tactical reserve in its current structure and would remain at a strength of five thousand rather than decreasing to forty-four hundred, as previously planned. Any more reductions would engender too much criticism from allies. Macdonald would not budge on the principle of compatibility of Canadian army units at home and in Europe, stating that they would be mobile, flexible, and general purpose. The Centurion would be replaced with a light tracked DFSV, the same vehicle the army had been looking for since 1964, and then every vehicle in the Canadian army, save the M109 155 mm self-propelled howitzer, would be transportable in the air force's fleet of C-130s. The Cabinet Committee on External Affairs and National Defence approved the resolutions.[20]

In preparing for the Cabinet discussion of the White Paper, Trudeau's staff suggested some questions to ask Macdonald; once again, the role of European land forces figured prominently. Trudeau knew from the defence policy review in 1969 that a light unit would not last long on the Central Front, and his staff counselled him to question its intended role and its ability to stand up to the Warsaw Pact.[21] Trudeau did not disappoint, but the Cabinet meeting did not appreciably alter Macdonald's conclusions or the final shape of the White Paper. The consensus was that participation in NATO was valuable because it gave Canada a toehold in Europe: it bought Canada a place at the Mutual and Balanced Force Reductions talks and helped Canada negotiate trade links with Europe. Trudeau then summed up the controversy over the AMF decision and questioned whether senior personnel in DND had done their job. Little could be done now, but "this experience led him to look at new suggestions with a particularly critical eye." Trudeau asked whether the light role was credible on the Central Front, given that two years earlier, it was not. Macdonald replied that the restructuring was in line with the principle of compatibility of army units; the continued presence of Canadian troops near the Iron Curtain, he said, had been dictated by the location of Canada's air units in Southwest Germany. He affirmed that NATO and Canadian staffs had judged that 4 CMBG as a light formation was viable on the Central Front and that it would undertake reconnaissance for larger US formations. The only major change for the brigade would be the replacement of the Centurion by a DFSV; it would keep its current personnel levels. Cabinet agreed to Macdonald's plans.[22] The decision to withdraw the tank from Canadian service in 1969 had flowed from an attempt to reorder Canada's defence priorities, but the explicit replacement of the Centurion with a light vehicle was the assertion of civilian control over the military.

Defence in the 70s, released in August 1971, began by describing the climate of the early 1970s: détente, a general antimilitary feeling spurred by the divisive war in Vietnam, and the pressure from citizens for more money for social and economic programs. It affirmed the defence priorities from April 1969 – Canadian sovereignty, the defence of North America, the fulfilment of NATO commitments, and UN peacekeeping missions – and stated that the reduction in 1969 arose from economic circumstances and a need to focus on Canadian requirements. The paper left no ambiguity about the plans for 4 CMBG:

> The Government has decided that the land force should be reconfigured to give it the high degree of mobility needed for tactical reconnaissance missions in a Central Region reserve role. The Centurion medium tank will be retired, since this vehicle is not compatible with Canada-based forces and does not possess adequate mobility. In its place a light, tracked, direct-fire-support vehicle will be acquired as one of the main items of equipment. This vehicle, which is air portable, will be introduced later into combat groups in Canada. The result will be enhanced compatibility of Canadian and European based forces, and a lighter, more mobile land force capable of a wide range of missions.[23]

The revisionists had asserted their authority but still had little regard for the military's ability to plan and budget, so Macdonald initiated the Management Review Group, which began the amalgamation of the military Canadian Forces Headquarters and the civilian Deputy Minister's Office, producing the National Defence Headquarters.[24] The military chain of command and the functional and administrative military commands produced in the 1960s remained relatively intact, but the civilian deputy minister now shared authority with the CDS in a confusing arrangement.[25] The civilian and military staffs overseeing procurement, finance, and other matters, hitherto separated, were now combined into four new departments overseen by Assistant Deputy Minister (ADM) offices, each with a civilian at the head and a military officer as deputy. ADM – Policy was the most senior office responsible for developing policy options and ensuring that planning was in accord with objectives and resources, ADM – Materiel oversaw procurement and supply, and the final two ADM offices were Personnel and Finance.[26]

NATO allies made some forays after the publication of the White Paper in an attempt to reverse policy, especially in light of the Soviet Union's conventional buildup in Europe in the 1970s and its increased defence spending under Brezhnev.[27] SACEUR, still Goodpaster, pressed the government to reverse the decision and invoked one of NATO's key reports in this era, "Alliance Defence Problems for the 1970s." It included a section on the status of armour and emphasized the Warsaw Pact's numerical superiority – 33,607 compared to 10,585 NATO tanks – and its plan for a relentless drive to the Channel if war ensued between East and West. At a modest rate of advance, the Warsaw Pact would be able to break through NATO's forward defences and overrun the Federal Republic of Germany, the industrial heart of Europe, within days. NATO would try to redress its numerical inferiority with tactics and infantry anti-tank weapons, but above all, it needed new tanks. Many NATO vehicles were old or obsolete, and the Warsaw Pact was threatening to take qualitative superiority. As the NATO report noted, "The modern tank with its advanced fire control system, 24-hour fire support capability, all-season mobility, range of action, and relative invulnerability in a nuclear environment will continue to dominate the modern battlefield and be the critical heart of a modern army."[28]

Goodpaster drew upon this report when he responded in March 1972 to Canada's plans to turn 4 CMBG into a light tactical reconnaissance formation equipped with the British Scorpion DFSV. He discussed the matter with the Canadian liaison officer at NATO, beginning with a description of the Warsaw Pact's already formidable numerical superiority, which was only going to improve. The Soviets were deploying two thousand new T-62s in Europe, adding to their already substantial stock of fifty thousand tanks, and were nearing qualitative superiority. The best structure for 4 CMBG's current mission as a reserve would be a mechanized force with tanks, and Goodpaster suggested that the status of Canada's contribution should be reviewed. The Canadian officer reminded Goodpaster of the plans to retire the Centurion and turn 4 CMBG into a light reconnaissance force that was entirely air transportable, except for the M109 howitzer. Goodpaster responded by saying that this was not what he needed – he needed mechanized troops with tanks – but his pressure did nothing. The Canadian responded by saying that the army was examining airmobile forces, but it was too early to give a clear answer on what they would look like. Regardless, the Centurion would be gone after 1973.[29] Goodpaster also sent comments to Ottawa and asked for a "fresh review" of policy. Frederick Sharp responded that "the question of armour capability ... is a long standing and irreversible decision of the Canadian government associated with the firm decision that Canadian land forces based in Europe should be compatible with those based in Canada." Sharp then reminded Goodpaster of the many times Canada had made this intention known: it was not up for discussion.[30]

The German and US senior political leadership also questioned the decision to retire the tank. Helmut Schmidt, the West German defence minister from 1969 to 1972, spoke with Donald Macdonald about tanks and made no headway.[31] He also tried, unsuccessfully, to speak with Trudeau, but despite being rebuffed, Schmidt had a "soft spot in his heart for Canada" and had a brother-in-law who lived in Canada.[32] In 1971, he suggested to Macdonald that West German troops should train in Canada. In part, this was because there was limited space available for large-scale training in Germany, but Schmidt had political motives, as is evident from a memo A.E. Ritchie wrote to Mitchell Sharp on the plan:

> He [Schmidt] wished to help the Canadian public understand Germany's role in Europe and NATO and to help the German public in turn understand Canada's approach to foreign policy and defence issues. He was concerned that NATO might become bi-polarized by its stress on European-USA relationships and its primary concern for European security. He alluded to the tendency of the

> Eurogroup of NATO to ignore Canadian considerations and said that he was extremely interested in doing something positive to develop greater mutual understanding between Germany and Canada.[33]

Schmidt also directed the West German ministry of defence to consider purchasing more products from Canadian companies to offset Canada's costs of stationing troops in Europe.[34]

James Schlesinger, US secretary of defense from 1973 to 1975, wanted to bolster NATO's conventional capabilities and increase defence spending across the alliance. In a December 1973 meeting with Henry Kissinger, he stated, "We need to have a long word with Canada. They are doing nothing in NATO, nothing in NORAD." He wanted them to put the full brigade back in NATO. Kissinger said, "They'll never do it," but suggested that Schlesinger "take a run at the brigade."[35] The next day, Schlesinger, his assistants, and the chair of the Joint Chiefs of Staff, Admiral Thomas Moorer, met with Richardson, the CDS, General Jacques Dextraze, and some other officials from External Affairs. The discussion focused on the air defence of North America, but at the end of the meeting, Schlesinger slyly floated the idea of an enhanced Canadian contribution. He "wondered if NATO might not be more vigorous by demonstrating to the Soviets a capability to maintain and reinforce its forces in Europe. Perhaps we might work together to determine what Canada could do in this regard." Richardson responded that he did not know if the contribution could be enlarged, but he would listen to any ideas. Schlesinger said he thought that reinforcement of NATO's northern flank would be useful.[36]

Although there was no ambiguity about the plan to replace the Centurion, the army would struggle over the next few years to develop a standardized structure, and internal resistance to the withdrawal of tanks grew. After the White Paper's publication, the army developed a timeline to implement the new structure and retire the Centurion by September 1974. There would be an interim force from 1974 to 1980, while the army developed plans for a fully airmobile unit to be fielded in 1980.[37]

The army was not alone in the need to re-examine its structure. The entire military was developing force development objectives (FDOs), papers that detailed each major operational role of the military and outlined costs, priorities, and alternatives. The FDOs would provide a stable framework by guiding the development of force structure, doctrine, training, and procurement for at least the next decade, thus preventing ad hoc or reactive decisions. These papers had been in development for some time, but the publication of the White Paper gave added urgency to finish them.[38]

In the spring of 1973, the military produced a draft FDO for the land force for the period of 1974 to 1985. It relied on *Defence in the 70s;* the American, British, Canadian, and Australian armies' frameworks for 1981 to 1990; and the NATO report "Alliance Defence Problems in the 1970s." The FDO argued that Canada needed a variety of brigade groups to meet disparate tasks, such as an armoured brigade for use in Central Europe, but simply could not afford it. It would have to choose one type of brigade group and then use it as a pattern for the rest of the army. For a template, the planners chose 4 CMBG as a light tactical reconnaissance formation, equipped with Scorpion DFSVs instead of Centurions. Although this unit could not stand up to Soviet tank columns, the FDO drafters argued that there was a place in NATO planning for airmobile forces to counter Soviet airborne or helicopter assaults and to be a mobile reserve.[39] The rest of the brigades in Canada, probably three but hopefully four, would then be structured as tactical reconnaissance formations once the Scorpion entered service in 1974.[40] After this, the army would study the possibility of adopting the structure of US airmobile brigades, which were expensive but put the most troops on the ground. The goal was to get the government to approve the re-equipment of the army as a total package so as to field a newly equipped and coherently structured army by 1985.[41]

Senior commanders' critiques focused on the proposed structure of 4 CMBG in 1974 and the decision to replace the Centurion with a DFSV. The commander of Canadian Forces Europe, Major-General W.C. Leonard, thought that replacing the Centurion with the Scorpion was a terrible idea and that using an airmobile force in Central Europe was just as bad. He counselled re-examining the Scorpion purchase, perhaps renting a tank to replace the Centurion, and reviewing defence priorities before any drastic decisions were made. The commander of Force Mobile Command, Lieutenant-General Gilles Turcot, supported Major-General Leonard's critiques, stating that the brigade needed tanks.[42] One brigadier-general wrote that relying on the US pattern for units was a mistake and that re-equipping the army in one package had merit but could also be dangerously inflexible. Changing 4 CMBG to a light role had limited value, he argued; the planners had too easily discounted the armoured brigade. Finally, he was dead set against the decision to structure the brigades at home as tactical reconnaissance formations like 4 CMBG, which would be largely useless for operations in Canada.[43] The replacement of the Centurion with a DFSV and 4 CMBG's role as a light reconnaissance formation was official government policy, however, and was explicitly stated in the White Paper. One FDO drafter wrote that this decision "was a thorn in our side in writing the FDO."[44]

The FDO amounted to little, and the next exercise, the land force policy review, arose in August 1973.[45] This originated in the office of the freshly minted office of ADM – Policy and was the responsibility of Major-General Roland Reid, of Chief Land Operations, who was assisted by Colonel Phil Neatby (Director Land Plans / Director Armour), charged with developing plans for the army, and Brigadier-General Dan Loomis. Other participants in the review were representatives from

External Affairs, Finance, the air force, and the navy. The paper was supposed to provide a policy framework for the army for the next fifteen years, in alignment with *Defence in the 70s*, and was a wide-ranging and expansive analysis of global trends, threats, and anticipated technological development. It was similar to the FDO in its assessment of Canada's security needs in the context of the four defence priorities from April 1969, but it shied away from making explicit recommendations on the future shape of the army. Jim Fox, who succeeded Phil Neatby as Director Land Plans / Director Armour, commented that in original drafts of the land force policy review report, writers were prohibited from using the word *tank* in reference to the Canadian Armed Forces.[46]

The report offered a number of choices for the Canadian army, with varying capabilities and costs. For example, the section on NATO land operations gave four possible capabilities for the force in Europe – from being able to engage a Warsaw Pact airborne regiment, to a tank regiment, to a tank division, to a tank division at two places. Maintaining a force designed to engage a Warsaw Pact airborne regiment would be relatively cheap: the enemy unit would be small and would not have heavy vehicles. One designed to engage a formidable Soviet tank division would be much more expensive. Policy-makers could choose the capabilities they wanted for each defence priority and structure the army according to defence policy needs and the dictates of the budget.[47] The army wanted to finish the land force policy review by May 1974.[48] The document arrived at Dextraze's office in July 1974, and by this time, the choices for the Canadian troops in Europe were either to replace or retire the Centurion or to create a highly specialized anti-air and anti-tank unit that would support allied countries. Dextraze wanted the report to go to Cabinet, but instead, the land force policy review was subsumed into another review in late 1974.[49]

While these examinations continued in Ottawa, there was a growing consensus in the rest of the army that it needed to structure itself with a more rigorous process in order to improve the jumble of force structure, training, equipment, and doctrine that had resulted from years of ad hoc and reactive decisions caused by policy changes and budget cuts. The army chose to rebuild by preparing for the worst-case scenario – a conventional war in Central Europe against the Warsaw Pact and its allies. This decision was rooted in the army's interpretation of a passage from *Defence in the 70s* that noted the government's intention "to maintain within feasible limits a general purpose combat capability of the highest professional standard within the Armed Forces." In a letter commenting on the land force policy review, Lieutenant-Colonel G. Simpson, commander of the third battalion of the Royal Canadian Regiment, wrote:

> The meaning of this statement in the White Paper was discussed at great length at the Combat Arms Conference in Kingston 6-9 Nov 73. There was a general

> consensus that the statement had a pretty definite meaning when translated into military terms. To those attending the meeting it meant: "the capability to wage war effectively in a nuclear environment at divisional level against the Russian forces using professional soldiers equipped with modern but not necessarily the latest sophisticated equipment."[50]

Lieutenant-General S.C. Waters, commander of Mobile Command at the time, asserted that "the White Paper of August 1971 must continue to be the basic start point for the development of any review of land policy as it continues to be the currently approved expression of Canadian Government Defence Policy." He referenced a passage in the White Paper, which was also included in the 1973 speech from the throne: "the Government re-affirmed its intention to maintain a high degree of military capability as the primary and most essential role of the Armed Forces" (underlined in the original). Waters concluded that the army needed to maintain a high level of combat capability: "In other words, it is dead wrong in my judgment to try to design para-military forces at the outset, and then attempt to have them grow into balanced combat forces with effective military capabilities. Stated another way, you can give professional servicemen boy-scout tasks, but you cannot give boy-scouts the tasks of the professional military service-men."[51]

The decision to prepare for a Soviet onslaught in Central Europe was one of the central planks of the army's next attempt to structure itself – the Combat Development Committee, which first met in 1974. The committee included every army officer in senior appointments, whether at Mobile Command, Ottawa, or 4 CMBG. Over the next seven years, it developed the intellectual framework for the Canadian army for the period 1986 to 1996, termed Corps 86. Army planners based their thinking on the mobilization of a Canadian corps for service in Central Europe against the Soviet Union and its allies in a large-scale, conventional war. It then analyzed the training, doctrine, force structure, and equipment required to field this corps.[52] This premise was similar to the American army's attempts to rebuild itself after Vietnam that focused on preparing for war in Europe. The studies and planning for Corps 86 had little effect on procurement in the mid-1970s, but they represented an important shift in the army's thinking, as well as dissatisfaction with both the letter and the spirit of *Defence in the 70s*. The dissatisfaction would morph into open revolt when the army was close to purchasing a DFSV to replace the Centurion.

FIGURE 1 Canadian Centurions roll past for the last time with the barrels dipped in salute on 21 June 1977.

Source: Library and Archives Canada/Department of National Defence fonds, e011157048

FIGURE 2 Canadian rental Leopard 1A2s on exercise in 1977. Note the cast instead of welded turret.

Source: Library and Archives Canada/Department of National Defence fonds, e011157034.

FIGURE 3 Project Manager Dave Hampson and Commander of Canadian Forces Europe Charlie Belzile with a commemorative key to one of the first Leopards.
Source: George Metcalf Archival Collection, Canadian War Museum, CWM 19790111-003

FIGURE 4 Dave Hampson *(foreground)* and D. Henderson of the Royal Canadian Dragoons *(background)* crew a freshly delivered C1 in early 1979.
Source: George Metcalf Archival Collection, Canadian War Museum, CWM 19790111-001

FIGURE 5 *From left to right:* D. Henderson, Terrey Seeley, and Clive Milner of the Royal Canadian Dragoons and Jim Fox celebrating the delivery of a Leopard C1.

Source: George Metcalf Archival Collection, Canadian War Museum, CWM 19790111-006

FIGURE 6 A Canadian Leopard C1 in a defensive position in a village during Exercise Certain Sentinel in early 1979.

Source: Library and Archives Canada/Department of National Defence fonds, e011166239

FIGURE 7 A Canadian Leopard C1 moves through a western Bavarian town in the winter of 1979.

Source: Library and Archives Canada/Department of National Defence fonds, e011166217

FIGURE 8 Children gather around a Leopard C1 as it stops during the annual Fall Exercise (Fallex) in September 1984.

Source: Library and Archives Canada/Department of National Defence fonds, e011166275

FIGURE 9 A Leopard drives down a Bavarian road during Fallex in 1984.

Source: Library and Archives Canada/Department of National Defence fonds, e011166285

FIGURE 10 A Leopard tank with mine rollers advances in 1987. A Lynx reconnaissance vehicle is in the background.

Source: Library and Archives Canada/Department of National Defence fonds, e011157139

6

The Scorpion and the Centurion

The Nadir of the Civil Military Crisis

THE MAIN CONTENDER for replacing the Centurion was the Combat Vehicle Reconnaissance (Tracked), or Scorpion, which was the only DFSV or tank that actually made it into the official budget from 1963 to 1974.[1] Ironically, the army wanted none of it, since the Scorpion, although a capable reconnaissance vehicle, paled in comparison to a tank. It was part of a family of vehicles that was developed in the early 1960s to form the basis of light, easily deployable forces that would rush to hot spots in the fading British Empire, a less expensive alternative to maintaining large garrisons. The vehicle was designed primarily to be small and light enough to fit into a C-130. In September 1967, the British Ministry of Defence granted a contract to Alvis to produce thirty prototypes, and on 23 January 1969, the first one rolled off the lines in Coventry.[2]

The British first passed information on the vehicle to the Canadians in December 1968, and its first mention as the prime candidate for the DFSV was in October 1969.[3] A briefing to CDS Sharp in 1970 on the needs of the DFSV noted that the two contenders remained the American Sheridan, in service since the late 1960s, and the British Scorpion, supposed to go into production in 1972. The army now preferred the Scorpion, estimated at $200,000 per vehicle, as opposed to $750,000 for a Sheridan. At about nine tonnes, the Scorpion was small, with the main gun being a low velocity 76 mm gun that could only take on soft-skinned or lightly armoured vehicles. The aluminum armour was proof against Soviet heavy machine guns from the front and light machine guns on the side and rear. The army budgeted $15 million to purchase seventy-five Scorpions – forty-five for units in Canada, twelve for Europe, eleven for support stocks, and seven for training.[4] The government needed to initiate contract talks with the manufacturer by September 1970 in order to start receiving vehicles by 1973 and to repurpose 4 CMBG within the proper time frame.[5]

The army's major directorate for assessing armoured vehicles – Director Equipment Requirements Land, headed by Colonel Ian MacDonald Grant at Canadian Forces Headquarters – knew that the British army would decide, in December 1970, whether to accept the Scorpion. Acceptance was a crucial stage in the British Ministry of Defence's procurement and sales process. If the new vehicle was successful, the British could aggressively market it to other countries, but if the army rejected it, then it would have to go back for redesign, and export opportunities could suffer.

In the summer of 1970, the British ministry brought in Captain R.H. Caldwell from the Strathcona's armoured regiment with the intention of establishing a small Canadian Trials Detachment at the Royal Armoured Corps Centre at Bovington, Dorset, England. The detachment consisted of Caldwell, a three-man crew drawn from the other regiments, and a vehicle mechanic. They were allowed to participate in the final technical and tactical trials for the Scorpion at the Armoured Trials and Development Unit at Bovington. Captain Caldwell led a troop of four Scorpions in tactical comparison trials with a squadron of The Life Guards, a British reconnaissance regiment. Caldwell was on the ground to witness the nonacceptance of the vehicle due to the small and cramped turret, the risk of the hardened aluminum cracking, insufficient stowage, and the difficulty of looking around a corner without exposing the bulk of the vehicle. Yet the Canadian trials process continued, and in December, the detachment accompanied two Scorpions and two Foxes, delivered in a Canadian Forces Hercules transport aircraft, to Camp Wainwright, Alberta, for cold weather trials. While other crews participated in these trials, the trials detachment returned to Bovington for final work in early 1971.[6] Doug Green was assigned to help the British with the trials at the base and to further examine the Scorpion as a replacement for the Centurion. Following the trial, one Scorpion and one Fox were shipped to Ottawa for investigation by technical and operational staff.[7] Alvis finally delivered the first production models of the Scorpion to the British army in January 1972.[8] One other option to buying a new vehicle was to mount the Scorpion's turret on the Canadian Lynx reconnaissance vehicle, but the Canadian army did not like this option because it was slower, noisier, and bigger than the Scorpion, and there were higher engineering and production costs, as well as a later delivery date.[9]

By 1970, after the restructuring of 4 CMBG had been delayed by a year, the initial requirement for seventy-five vehicles had risen to 131, and in February 1972, the Defence Management Committee, DND's highest committee, considered the Scorpion purchase. Seventy Scorpions would remain in Canada – thirty-six as part of reconnaissance squadrons divided across three regiments, nineteen for training, and fifteen for support stocks – while sixty-one would go to Europe. Four CMBG would have forty-eight operational Scorpions divided into three squadrons, as well as a reserve of thirteen vehicles. The army could acquire four vehicles by February 1973 and sixty by July 1974, and it would be able to restructure 4 CMBG within a reasonable time frame.[10] The submission went to the Treasury Board on 6 March 1972 and was approved ten days later.[11]

Delays in production complicated the purchase a few months later. In the summer of 1972, Alvis was affected by strikes and go-slow tactics, resulting in poor production performance. Negotiators from the Department of Supply and Services (DSS) could not get firm prices from the British Ministry of Defence, and the slowdown meant that the delivery schedule might be delayed by up to six months and force purchases of spare parts for the Centurion.[12] A few weeks later, a report painted an even grimmer picture of the delivery schedule. DSS negotiators reported on 28 July 1972 "that they have no confidence whatsoever in the delivery promises made either by ALVIS or MOD [British Ministry of Defence] and that the programme may well end up being over a year late to complete." They also felt they were being taken advantage of by a foreign company that knew it was the sole source, so the army began studying a one-year life extension of the Centurion to make up for the expected delay.[13] By late September 1972, L.G. Crutchlow, the head of ADM – Materiel, requested that DSS postpone negotiations until the recently appointed CDS, General Jacques Dextraze, returned from discussions in Europe with NATO officials, Goodpaster among them, over the role of Canadian forces in Europe.[14]

Despite these difficulties, the army was fully prepared to buy the Scorpion. Gerry Koeller, tasked with setting up training on the vehicle, recounted that he had secured places for Canadians at British schools, displacing British soldiers. Training was to begin on 4 September 1972 (Labour Day), but late on Friday, 1 September, Koeller was informed that the training would be cancelled and he should stop movement of soldiers to Britain. The troops, already en route, turned back at Koeller's orders, and Koeller sent a message to the Canadian liaison officer in London to inform the British staff of the cancellation. By that time, it was 10:00 p.m. in Britain, the liaison officer was at a party, and the duty officer did not pass the message along. No messages came from Canada on Monday, 4 September, because it was a holiday. It was not a holiday in Britain, however, so the British were furious when they started their training with a number of empty seats. Koeller stated that it was "a terrible way of doing business."[15]

General Jacques Dextraze, who had been appointed the CDS in the summer, was the main figure behind the abrupt cancellation of training.[16] A veteran of the Second World War and Korea, he was a gruff and stubborn man with a clear goal for the army. He was adamant that Canada should keep tanks, and he knew that if Canada bought Scorpions, the army would not have tanks for years, if not decades. During the trip to Europe in September, Goodpaster, to no one's surprise, stated that he wanted a mechanized force with tanks.[17] After Trudeau replaced Donald Macdonald with James Richardson as defence minister in November, Dextraze began serious attempts to cancel the Scorpion deal and keep the Centurion. Richardson came from a wealthy Winnipeg family and headed the family grain business until he entered politics, but unlike Macdonald, he exerted little control over his department, particularly over

Dextraze. The general wrote a letter to Richardson explaining that the Centurion could be kept in service until 1976 for a cost of $10 to $12 million.[18] On 20 December, Dextraze drafted a memo to Cabinet arguing that the Scorpion purchase should be cancelled and the Centurion rebuilt to extend its life for a few years so that the army could study the needs of the forces in Europe. He explained that negotiations for the Scorpion were suspended because the United Kingdom was not forthcoming on price, delivery dates, and industrial offsets. Furthermore, he wrote, recent studies had shown the Scorpion's viability on the Central Front to be "highly questionable," and SACEUR had questioned the purchase, which might undermine NATO during the Mutual and Balanced Force Reductions negotiations.[19]

Richardson submitted the memo to Cabinet, and Donald Macdonald, now minister of energy, mines, and resources, stated that Cabinet was well aware of the details and had decided to go light. There was no need to re-examine the matter now, he contended, and the minutes record that "he feared that in 1976, the recommendation placed before Cabinet would be for using heavy tanks." Trudeau recounted that Cabinet had decided to go light when the NATO force were to go on the flanks and then had decided to keep the force on the Central Front after it was argued that a light unit could be valuable there. He stated that he "could, at most, accept a decision not to switch to a lighter vehicle now. But since the viability of the role of the force was being questioned, the Cabinet should be informed fully of the new factors which had changed the situation." Richardson quickly retreated, stating that although he had been satisfied with the decision to retire the tank, SACEUR had questioned Canada's equipment, and negotiations with the manufacturer of the Scorpion had been unsatisfactory. Several ministers wondered why the matter had been reopened and proposed that if Richardson wanted to reconsider the policy decision, he should submit a new paper explaining why a mobile force in Central Europe was no longer viable. The 1971 policy of a light force would stand, and Richardson would decide the fate of the Scorpion.[20]

Although his first attempt to cancel the Scorpion deal had failed, Dextraze did not give up. Less than a week later, he and Richardson drafted another memorandum arguing that the government should reconsider replacing the Centurion with a DFSV. They noted the report "Alliance Defence Problems in the 1970s," which highlighted the disparity in tank strength between the Warsaw Pact and NATO, and they emphasized that SACEUR thought the formation needed tanks to be effective in Central Europe. Their paper also challenged the principle of compatibility of Canada's army units, one of the major results of 1969. They argued that Canada's army at home needed to be light so it could be transported easily, but the forces in Europe required tanks, since there was no other way to offset the Warsaw Pact's numerical superiority. The paper outlined three alternatives – effecting a total withdrawal, with obvious consequences for Canada's relations with its allies; continuing with the present plan to go light, which would be largely ineffective; or keeping the Centurion in service for two more years to facilitate detailed study of the land forces' needs in Europe. These resolutions were identical to those from the January submission and left no doubt of the army's preference.[21] The memo did not state it directly, couching its language to avoid overtly challenging *Defence in the 70s*, but it was clear that Richardson and Dextraze wanted to overturn policy and keep tanks in 4 CMBG.

L. Denis Hudon, one of Trudeau's secretaries, reviewed the paper and concluded that the military argument was sound. In a memo to Trudeau analyzing Richardson's paper, Hudon wrote that light mobile forces were ill-suited for the Central Front, but this was obviously at odds with policy. He stated that the paper argued strongly for a tank and that pushing the matter to 1976, as the document suggested, would only delay the inevitable decision on whether to keep tanks. For Hudon, the question was "which shall prevail – a force configuration based on theatre requirements and military principle, i.e. a tank-equipped land element, or one based on existing political direction, i.e., a lightly-equipped force with no tank." Trudeau, or one of his staff, underlined this passage in Hudon's memo. If Trudeau were to override his military advisers to make a point, this had to be absolutely clear.[22]

Head, who also weighed in on the matter, saw it as a clear-cut question of who dictated defence policy – the civilians or the military and allies. Recounting the priorities announced in April 1969, he declared, "To decide now that we should turn our resources, our priorities, indeed our principles, upside down in order to meet the wishes of SACEUR is unacceptable." He concluded by stating that unless Richardson and Dextraze's recommendations were acceptable on some grounds, such as a cost-benefit analysis, it should be stated clearly that Canada would retire its heavy armour and that 1976 "represents a terminal date for the heavy armoured role."[23]

Head drafted a response for Trudeau and, on 12 April, sent it to Richardson. In the letter, Trudeau stated that he did not take Richardson's memo as a challenge to the April 1969 policy or to *Defence in the 70s*, but he was concerned that keeping the Centurion would delay reconfiguration of the forces in Europe, which had already been postponed once. Trudeau asked that Richardson redraft his memo – particularly the second-last paragraph, which opened the door for a change in policy – and revise those sections that might argue for a continued mechanized role in Europe when Canadian policy called for lighter, more mobile units.[24]

Richardson assented, changing the offending paragraphs and removing the section asking for a reconsideration of the 1971 policy on land forces. He replaced the latter with a section explaining that the major object of the Cabinet submission was to keep the Centurion until 1976 and cancel the Scorpion. The subsequent statement read: "In recommending that two year delay, however, it does not propose reconsideration of the decision to retire the medium tank from the equipment inventory of the Canadian Forces including the land forces in Europe." Apart from those changes, the paper was identical to the first draft memo, produced in February 1973; although Richardson deleted explicit references to a revision of policy, the paper still clearly argued that light forces were unsuitable.[25]

The memo came to Cabinet at the end of May 1973. Trudeau dominated the discussion, intent on making his point absolutely clear. He pointed out that the paper was not in accordance with *Defence in the 70s,* and stated: "The government had decided on a configuration for its land forces in Europe. It did not intend to change that decision. If the configuration was not acceptable to Canada's NATO partners or if the Canadian Forces could not play a worthwhile role within that configuration, withdrawal of the forces from Europe would become necessary." He was willing to cancel the Scorpion and keep the Centurion in service until 1976, "as long as the Cabinet Record of Decision re-affirmed in explicit terms the 1971 policy decision and leave no doubt that this decision was not open for re-consideration." Richardson stated that it was neither his nor the CDS's intention to question the policy. The minutes record categorically that "the force would contain no heavy or medium tanks, but would be a light mobile force, and its equipment would be compatible with that of Canada-based forces."[26] Although Trudeau spoke strongly and drew a line in the sand on defence policy, Dextraze's gambit was successful. Cancelling the Scorpion meant that the two most promising candidates for the DFSV had been rejected and 4 CMGB would not be able to go light for years. Withdrawal was also not a serious option, because if NATO allies were embittered by the reduction in 1969, they would be infuriated by total withdrawal.

The army, probably at Dextraze's instruction, had already begun examining an overhaul of twenty-four Centurions to squeeze two more years of life out of them and keep the bare minimum of a tank capability in Europe. The Centurion's armour and firepower were still first class, but the vehicles were more and more difficult to keep in service. Memorably, one Centurion broke down on the way to the start line for an exercise and remained out of service for the entire duration.[27] In early 1973, the military sent out its request for proposal to the two main candidates for the rebuild program – Vickers-Armstrongs Limited in cooperation with the British 23 Base Workshop in Wetter, Germany, and the Dutch Tank Werkplats in Amersfoort, Netherlands.[28]

It was possible to retrofit the Centurions to greatly improve their performance, but this would cost $250,000 per vehicle, roughly three times the cost of a simple rebuild for each vehicle.[29] The retrofit would have replaced the Centurion's gasoline-burning Meteor engine with a more compact General Motors engine that was easier to maintain, was in service with other tanks, and burned cheap and plentiful diesel, which Canada could procure from other allied armies. The final drive and gearbox would also be replaced, and the gun control equipment would be improved. The Israelis had recently refurbished their Centurions along these lines, resolving many maintenance problems and improving the tank's speed and range.[30] The second option was a simple rebuild and refurbishment of existing components, which was much cheaper and involved rebuilding the engine and power train, inspecting and repairing the turret as necessary, and folding in some minor improvements. Rebuilt assemblies were not always reliable, so the overhaul would only marginally improve the Centurion's maintenance burden.[31] The army estimated the cost of the rebuild at only $80,000 per vehicle and the total cost of the rebuild program – excluding ammunition, operations, and maintenance costs – at $2,746,400.[32]

The army started working on the contract on 28 May, three days before Richardson brought his ill-fated memo before Cabinet.[33] The Program Control Board, the senior committee in DND that reviewed defence spending and procurement projects, approved the program in November 1973, and the Treasury Board approved the contract a few weeks later. The army chose the Dutch workshop at Amersfoort.[34] Rebuilt Centurions started rolling off the line in early September 1974, and the full complement of twenty-four had been delivered by January 1975. Mac Campbell was the life cycle material manager for the Centurion at this time, and he noted years later that the Dutch workshop was efficient and the tanks performed well, although there were some problems because the tanks were so old and major assemblies had been rebuilt many times.[35] The rebuild kept the Centurions running for a few more years, and, as an article in a Canadian armoured regiment's journal noted, the rebuild "kept the Canadian Forces in the tank business and, hopefully, it will lead to something better in the future."[36]

The army was intent on keeping the tank in Canadian service and perhaps even getting a new one, but it had considered attack helicopters since mid-1969. These were frequently suggested as a complement to DFSVs and a replacement for the Centurion's anti-tank capability. Attack helicopters with guided missiles were exciting and offered potent firepower in a small and flexible package, but they were also fragile, expensive, and difficult to maintain.

In 1972, the Americans, West Germans, and Canadians cooperated in a trial of attack helicopters in southern Germany, near Ansbach. American Cobra helicopters armed with wire-guided missiles faced off against German Leopards and Vulcan anti-aircraft defence vehicles. The attack helicopters worked in pairs and used "hide and seek" tactics to knock out opposing tanks. Helicopters would wait behind hills or even buildings and then peek out and fire their missiles at tanks sometimes two or three kilometres away. The tanks had trouble spotting the helicopters and were often eliminated before they knew what hit them. The loss ratio in the trial was eighteen tanks for each helicopter; however, helicopters were only effective in territory held by friendly forces because they were susceptible to small arms fire.[37]

Despite this initial success, the Canadian army never had any real interest in purchasing attack helicopters because they were far too expensive to buy and maintain and keeping tanks was the major priority.[38] One article in *The Springbok* suggested that Canada would need a combination of four observation and six attack helicopters for the brigade in Europe to produce an effective unit. This still could not replace the anti-tank capability of a regiment of tanks and would only be a gilded complement.[39] In a report from 1976 on the employment of the helicopter in the Canadian Armed Forces, Brigadier-General Gordon Kitchen concluded by saying that attack helicopters were only suitable as part of large formations, such as divisions or corps, because of their expense and the maintenance burden. The Canadian brigade was too small to merit this costly force.[40] Canada did buy Chinook, Kiowa, and Twin Huey helicopters in the early 1970s.[41] But it never came close to fielding attack helicopters.[42]

The frozen budget from 1969 to 1972 ensured that inflation would continue to force personnel cuts and increase operations and maintenance costs, as it had since the mid-1960s. Cutting another twenty thousand or so personnel between 1969 and 1972 had not reduced the budget dramatically, since personnel costs had risen to keep pace with inflation.[43] Consequently, the capital budget had declined in real terms for years: in 1972, it was at a nadir of 9 percent of the defence budget. In comparison, the capital budget for the 1956–57 fiscal year was 37.5 percent of the budget, and in 1963–64, it was 19.6 percent.[44] Although there is no hard and fast rule for determining how much should be spent on new equipment, the recommendation for modern armed forces is generally 20 to 30 percent of the budget.[45] The military did not help itself, in that the Treasury Board was frustrated by the lack of an approved program for DND purchases in terms of operational requirements and numbers and saw each submission for a new program with skepticism.[46] By 1972, the military needed billions of dollars of new equipment to replace its ships and planes from the late 1950s and early 1960s. The army was in solid shape in the early 1970s, with a relatively new fleet of armoured personnel carriers and self-propelled artillery and a few new helicopters, although its tanks and trucks were old. In a memo to the Program Control Board, Rear Admiral J.A. Charles said that if sufficient resources were not made available, the capability of Canada's Armed Forces would "rapidly decrease to that of a para-military force for use in the aid of civil power."[47]

To improve the capital budget and start getting new equipment, DND started working on a new financing system. Sylvain Cloutier recalled that it was his priority to increase the capital budget to re-equip the military when he was appointed deputy minister of national defence in 1971.[48] He had his special assistant, J.C. Arnell, draft a letter that explained the effects of inflation to Bud Drury, Treasury Board president. Arnell noted that nearly $2.5 billion worth of new equipment was needed if the Armed Forces were to effectively meet the policy aims of the government, and he recommended a real increase in spending to increase the capital budget to 20 percent of the defence budget by 1978–79 to re-equip the military.[49] Cabinet discussed and approved this in principle in the summer of 1972, and by early 1973, DND and the Treasury Board had prepared a submission to Cabinet outlining "formula financing." The central element of this plan was to double the capital budget over a five-year period, which would be achieved by a 7 percent annual increase in the defence budget for five years, starting at $2.143 billion, and by cutting or consolidating bases and activities.[50]

At the same time, Jean-Jacques Blais, a parliamentarian who took an interest in defence issues and was the minister of supply and services in the early 1980s during some major defence acquisitions, made a trip to Europe in early 1973 with some other colleagues from Parliament, including Monique Bégin and Francis Fox. They visited NATO headquarters and Canadian troops at Lahr and were told at a briefing in Brussels that Canada's image in NATO was not positive. They returned to Canada and mounted a campaign in caucus with the help of Leonard Hopkins, parliamentary secretary to the defence minister from late 1972 to 1975, to convince the government to increase defence spending. Blais recounted that Trudeau was impressed and moved by these efforts.[51] This assertion is supported by some of Trudeau's later speeches, especially in 1975, when he spoke of the need to have full public support for NATO's policies and stated that Canada's "overwhelming support" for collective defence allowed the government to increase the budget.[52] Cabinet approved the increase in the defence budget on 31 May 1973. This was the same day that it addressed Richardson's hapless memo on the Centurion and the Scorpion, which was the denouement of the civil-military crisis in the 1970s.[53]

The debate over the equipment of Canada's forces in Europe was largely limited to the army and the revisionists in this era, particularly Macdonald, Trudeau, and Head, and it raises difficult questions about civil-military relations. Some authors, like Doug Bland, argue that the army came very close to outright disobedience of the civilian government in its attempts to keep a tank, especially in the early 1970s, although he does not note any specific examples. He also contends that although Hellyer and Trudeau tried to recast defence policy, the services always promoted their own interests.[54] Head and Trudeau later wrote that their plan to ensure that Canadian army units be based on national interests, and therefore be light, "never did materialize ... so insistent were the land forces on retaining heavy armour."[55]

In *A National Force,* Kasurak argues that Cadieux, Allard, and other senior officials at DND fooled Trudeau and Cabinet by conspiring to keep the force on the Central Front: they had no intention of tasking it to AMF and NATO's northern flank. This effectively forced Trudeau and Macdonald to buy tanks as criticism from allies mounted. He also maintains that the army stalled in adopting the new airmobile structure and was fixated on building a mechanized army. Kasurak concludes that the army initiated the crisis in civil-military relations, which peaked during the writing of the 1971 White Paper.[56]

Kasurak is right to argue that the army subverted the revisionists, but he has identified the wrong figures and the wrong time. Allard had nothing to do with undermining policy. A proponent of light forces, he was persistent in his agenda of moving the Canadian brigade south and making it a light, airmobile force. It is also unlikely that Cadieux attempted to fool Cabinet. He was angered by the review and by Head's report, but he initiated planning to retire Canada's tanks and always expressed his opposition immediately and strongly during the review. He stated in an interview with Peter Stursberg that "when he [Trudeau] accepted that short phrase which I wrote down [planned and phased reduction], then it was obvious to me that, that, you know, we were all right."[57]

It is also unlikely that Cadieux and Allard tried to fool Cabinet by the placement of the force. It was always going to be in southwest Germany, close to the Iron Curtain, even if it was tasked to AMF. The Norwegians would not have accepted pre-positioned Canadian troops, or even equipment, and Lahr was close to existing Canadian air bases. It is likely that Goodpaster seized upon the opportunity to task the force as a reserve for the Central Front and keep Canadians near the front line, and Allard agreed once he began to realize that the AMF option was impractical. Cadieux's report in 1971 that he considered the final configuration of 4 CMBG to be contingent upon further study matches his message to Goodpaster in September 1969. Finally, there is no evidence that Macdonald or Trudeau held the two responsible for subverting Cabinet. In Macdonald's analysis in 1971, he blamed Allard for the AMF confusion but attributed it to a bad idea, not to deceit. He also did not critique Cadieux. Macdonald did not mention the AMF episode in his angry letter criticizing the planned purchase of tanks in 1975; rather, he saved his venom for NATO allies and barely mentioned DND or the army. Kasurak contends that "Trudeau used the occasion of the discussion of the White Paper in Cabinet to have Macdonald report Cadieux's failure to follow direction."[58] Trudeau was frustrated, but this is stretching the minutes, which read as follows:

> The Minister of National Defence described that Cabinet decision as the result of a proposal by the then CDS. He believed from his study of the record that further consideration by the Defence Staff led to the conclusion that the plan was too costly (involving expenditures of about $500 million) and impracticable. The then Minister of National Defence had apparently not consulted Cabinet on the reversing of this decision because he had planned to wait until new arrangements could be worked out to replace the interim land force role.[59]

The most likely suspects who buried the AMF option were the deputy minister of national defence from 1967 to 1971, Elgin Armstrong, and Lieutenant-General Mike Dare, VCDS from 1969 to 1972. There is no evidence to suggest that Armstrong wanted to undermine Cabinet, but he was on the committee, in April and May 1969, that developed the AMF option, and he was in a position to exercise continual oversight over plans, unlike officials in the Privy Council Office or Treasury Board. Dare, Allard's right-hand man during the summer of 1969, was also in a position of power to stymie Cabinet by delaying the implementation of plans and stifling the flow of information. Gordon Smith, who was familiar with Dare and present at some of the key meetings, recalled that Dare did not like the April 1969 decision and resisted the retirement of tanks, but he made no secret of it.[60] This matches the historical record: Dare continually argued that Canada should keep its tanks. His resistance to policy, however, did not mean that he buried the airmobile option or stopped the army from examining it. It is possible that Armstrong and Dare purposefully ignored the AMF option in the hope of subverting the revisionists or because they thought it was a foolish idea.

The real crisis in civil-military relations occurred after the publication of the White Paper; there was little possibility for reconciliation between the two groups. On the one hand, the revisionists had asserted Canada's interests in 1969 by withdrawing the tank. By 1973, this had become a point of enforcing civilian control of defence policy, and retreat in the face of service interests was unthinkable. On the other hand, the army, entrusted with the defence of a small part of West Germany against a heavily armoured foe, thought that the government was foolish for planning to deploy a light force in Central Europe.

The revisionists' anger at the AMF episode was justified, but their attempt to discipline the army was flawed. The decision to replace the Centurion with a DFSV did not punish those responsible in the highest echelons of command, nor did it bolster the credibility of the civilian government. Allies were perplexed by it, and soldiers did not understand the rationale for the militarily questionable decision. There was a groundswell of criticism of this policy in the officer corps, the army's planning began to diverge dramatically from government expectations for the land force, and the army made the case for tanks whenever it could.

Regardless, the army begrudgingly made plans to field a light force in Europe that would be compatible with the army at home and to buy the Scorpion to replace the Centurion. The greatest subversion of civilian control came from Dextraze. When the army was ready to buy and field the Scorpion, Dextraze undermined that plan in the hope that sooner or later, the government would change its policy. Although he could not convince the government to change on his own, he would gain a powerful ally in 1975.

7
Tanks, Trade, and Strategy
Trudeau Relents

Given the present fiscal framework and low priority which Trudeau has attached to Canada's defense effort since becoming prime minister in 1968, no one, either privately or publicly, believes that this government would allocate the necessary funds to permit the Canadian Armed Forces to maintain the status quo in strength and tasks.

– US Ambassador William Porter to the Department of State, 18 October 1974

I have come here, Mr. Chairman, for three reasons. The first is to state clearly and unequivocally Canada's belief in the concept of collective security, Canada's support for NATO, and Canada's pledge to maintain a NATO force level which is accepted by our allies as being adequate in size and effective in character.

– Pierre Trudeau, speech at the NATO heads-of-government summit, 30 May 1975

The army's case for tanks was weakened by the October, or Yom Kippur, War in 1973. After their total defeat in the Six-Day War of 1967, Egypt and Syria began planning a campaign to recover lost territories from Israel. Amply supplied by the Soviet Union with vehicles, rocket-propelled grenades, and anti-tank and surface-to-air missiles, Syria attacked the Golan Heights on 6 October 1973, and Egyptian forces broke through Israeli defences in the Sinai at the Suez Canal. Instead of continuing the advance, the Egyptian army set up strong anti-tank and anti-air defences, and Soviet-supplied missiles took a heavy toll on Israeli tanks and aircraft. An emergency resupply of vehicles by the United States allowed Israel to commit its reserves and push the Syrians back in the north, and to break through Egyptian defences in the Sinai, thus driving into Egypt proper. The war finally ended on 27 October, and although Israel had regained the upper hand, the conflict had been costly.[1]

It did not take long for armies around the world and defence analysts to start gleaning lessons from the war and evaluating the performance of Western hardware, operated by Israel, against Soviet hardware, operated by Egypt and Syria. The war saw some of the largest tank battles since the Second World War, as well as the widespread use of missiles and rocket-propelled grenades, which were used particularly effectively by Egypt and took a heavy toll on Israeli tanks, poorly supported by infantry and artillery in the early stages of the war.[2] The US army was particularly interested in the war as it rebuilt after Vietnam, analyzing it exhaustively.[3] In Canada, the analysis of the war played out on the pages of *Canadian Defence Quarterly* and regimental journals. In the spring of 1974, retired colonel J. Clarkson wrote an article that outlined some preliminary observations on the conflict. He noted the prevalence of Egyptian and Syrian missiles and the losses they inflicted on Israeli tanks and aircraft, noting that "under certain conditions the defensive power of the anti-tank guided missile is close to decisive," although tanks operating outside of missile range could still inflict heavy losses on opponents. He concluded by highlighting the defensive power of anti-tank missiles and the danger for NATO armies, since the Soviets were leaders in this technology and had fielded large numbers of missiles in Europe.[4]

This view did not go uncontested. In the next issue, two captains, L.W. Bentley and D.C. McKinnon, argued that anti-tank missiles were effective but could only devastate "scattered, over-extended daylight thrusts." They noted that after the initial heavy losses of tanks, Israeli armour, infantry, and artillery started to cooperate as an all-arms team to suppress enemy infantry armed with anti-tank weapons, reducing their effectiveness. They did note that Egyptian success in defending positions with missiles might influence Soviet thinking for an attack in Central Europe. They concluded that "it would be rash to dismiss the capabilities of armour because of the proven effect of the ATGWs [anti-tank guided weapons]" and that "no new tactical doctrines or weapon systems appeared in the Yom Kippur War to radically change the conduct of conventional mobile warfare."[5]

Most in the army thought that although the October War had exhibited the lethality and capability of modern weaponry, land warfare had not fundamentally changed. This was at odds with some analysts or officials who looked at the loss of roughly three thousand tanks during the three weeks of the war, more than the entire US army tank inventory in Europe, and concluded that the army needed to explain to skeptical officials why tanks were still needed.[6] James Richardson toured the Middle East after the war and, after discussion with some Israelis, stated that missiles had eclipsed the effectiveness of the tank.[7] He also reportedly asked the German defence minister, Georg Leber, if tanks were obsolete.[8] To challenge this perception, the Royal Canadian Armoured Corps Association, a group of retired and serving members of the armoured corps, brought in Israeli General Avraham Adan, a distinguished tank commander, to talk about the need for tanks, and the association sponsored other talks as well.[9] It also tried direct appeals to Trudeau. In November 1974, Lieutenant-Colonel M.A. Stevenson, president of the association, sent a letter to the prime minister, attaching a paper titled "Why the Canadian Armed Forces Need Tanks." He challenged the assertion that the October War proved that the tank was obsolete; rather, he argued, it exhibited the need for better cooperation among armour, infantry, and artillery. Light mobile forces with lightly armoured tanks were of little use, and he suggested a purchase of the Leopard or a retrofitted Centurion. Trudeau very likely did not draft the reply, but he signed it and thanked Stevenson for his interest. He affirmed the defence priorities from April 1969, stating that a review of policy was underway.[10]

That review was a product of the October War. The Organization of the Petroleum Exporting Countries and other nations put an oil embargo on the United States and other countries for supporting Israel, which resulted in a global economic slowdown that finally ended the post–Second World War economic boom.[11] Despite the slowdown, inflation remained high, even spiking to 12 percent in November 1974.[12] Formula financing's 7 percent annual increase could not contend with "stagflation," which would not only devastate a still anemic capital budget but also force significant personnel cuts.

Dextraze would not countenance this, stating that further reductions would seriously degrade combat capability. After Richardson asked for more money in September 1974 and Cabinet denied his request, Dextraze and the minister had a heated exchange during a meeting of the Defence Council. The general argued that the military should tell the government how much its commitments would cost and the government should pay them, while Richardson argued that the military had 10 percent of the federal budget and 2.5 percent of GDP and should design a force within those parameters. Richardson, however, was willing to go back to Cabinet and make a case for extra funds.[13] In November 1974, he submitted a memo to Cabinet that explained the ramifications of the funding crisis. DND was facing an enormous shortfall, and the only way it could stay under the budget ceiling was by reducing to a strength of seventy-three thousand. This entailed cutting Canada's NATO commitment, which "clearly would have massive policy implications" and damage relationships with allies.[14] The military could pare six thousand troops from the forces at home, but it would take years to replace the knowledge and capabilities of those departed personnel, and massive cuts would damage Canada's relationship with the United States. DND asked for an extra $227 million for the 1975–76 fiscal year to forestall these cuts, but there was no flexibility in the federal budget for this sizable sum of money, so the Cabinet Committee on External Policy and Defence and the Treasury Board suggested a policy review.[15]

On 28 November 1974, Cabinet met to discuss the problem, and the Defence Structure Review (DSR) began. There were three phases to the review. The first, from November 1974 to April 1975, determined the military's tasks in light of the priorities established by *Defence in the 70s*. After Cabinet approved these, fifty-five in total, the second phase involved consultation with allies and the selection of force structures to meet these tasks. This second phase ended in November 1975, resulting in the promise of tanks for the troops in Europe, a plan to buy a long-range patrol aircraft as soon as possible, plans to buy new fighters and ships, and increased defence spending to pay for all this new equipment. The third and final phase involved the purchase of new equipment to re-equip the forces.

Trudeau and Head were sensitive to the possibility that the DSR might undermine the 1969 defence priorities confirmed in the 1971 White Paper, particularly the retirement of the Centurion. In November 1974, Head commented, "One of those roles – heavy armour on the central NATO front – has been the subject of subsequent Cabinet consideration precisely because tanks are incompatible with use in any other task. They are not air-portable; they are of no use within Canada; they are not employed in peacekeeping assignments."[16] A few months later, he added: "DND is arguing that we will be 'letting down the side,' will 'not be paying our dues in the club,' 'will not be meeting our international commitments' if we fail to meet adequately the tasks assigned to us by our NATO and NORAD allies." He gave a conditional yes to the question of maintaining Canadian troops in Europe but skirted the tank issue. As the DSR proceeded from tasks to force structure, Trudeau and the government were confident that close adherence to the four priorities would prevent service or allied interests from dictating policy.[17] Unlike during the revision of defence policy in 1969, Trudeau was willing to listen to allies, a willingness that flowed from a growing appreciation of NATO but was primarily related to Canada's efforts to negotiate a trade link with the EEC.

In the wake of American efforts to reduce the drain on its balance of payments and resolve other economic problems in 1971, often termed the "Nixon shock," Canadian economists and diplomats became even more worried about Canada's dependence on the United States. In a special issue of *International Perspectives,* Mitchell Sharp, with the help of Klaus Goldschlag, laid out the options. Canada could continue in the present relationship, move to closer integration with the United States, or pursue a "comprehensive long-term strategy to develop and strengthen the Canadian economy and other aspects of its national life and in the process to reduce the present Canadian vulnerability." This alternative, which became known as the Third Option, was about diversification rather than anti-Americanism.[18] Attempts to foster a contractual link with the EEC began in earnest in 1973 and picked up in 1974.[19] It quickly became apparent that the Europeans were still resentful of the reduction in 1969. As Trudeau and Head recall,

> Marcel Cadieux, then ambassador to the EEC, had reported the existence of some criticism of the Canadian initiative [to create an official link with the EEC]

on the part of diplomats displeased with the 1969 reduction of Canadian forces in Europe: "Canada should not expect favours from Europe if it is not prepared to shoulder its defence burden" was the message.[20]

In late 1974, a working group composed of CDS Dextraze, Cabinet ministers, and officials from DND, External Affairs, the Treasury Board, and the Privy Council Office began identifying DND's tasks and the required military capabilities to discharge them. During this stage, Richardson argued that because of Canada's isolation and security, the government should focus on air and naval power, maintain ground troops as an aid to the civil power, and bring the troops in Europe home. Donald Macdonald supported this position, arguing that Canada's only commitment to NATO's forces in Europe should be flyover aircraft in case of war. Richardson's Mackenzie King–like proposal was his alone: it was not suggested by DND officials or anyone else in Cabinet. Trudeau retorted that because Canada was immune from attack, it was possible to take a diametrically opposed position and argue that "other considerations should prevail in establishing the structure of the armed forces." Trudeau's advisers recommended that he resolve the matter quickly: either quash Richardson's proposal or establish it as policy. Two major problems with the proposal were that it would devastate the army's morale and esprit de corps if it became merely an aid to the civil power and, more important, that NATO allies would be furious.[21] Richardson's proposal was rejected and Canadian troops would remain in Europe.

News of the review filtered through to allies, who feared the worst. The US ambassador to Canada, William Porter, reported: "Given the present fiscal framework and low priority which Trudeau has attached to Canada's defense effort since becoming prime minister in 1968, no one, either privately or publicly, believes that this government would allocate the necessary funds to permit the Canadian Armed Forces to maintain the status quo in strength and tasks."[22] In early December, Trudeau met with the American president, Gerald Ford. The president spoke about the difficulties for NATO in this era, declaring that the United States would not reduce its forces. Trudeau affirmed that Canada would not leave either NATO or NORAD but was seeking the best value for its defence dollar.[23]

The Americans continued to apply pressure on the Canadians to increase defence spending and support for NATO in light of the Soviet buildup. In February 1975, the deputy secretary of defense, Robert Ellsworth, met with two senior Canadian officials – John Halstead, from External Affairs, and D.H. Kirkwood, from National Defence. Ellsworth expressed hope that Canada could increase its defence efforts and increase and modernize its NATO contribution. Halstead responded that although Canada was committed to collective defence and could certainly do more in Europe, the government had set its priorities in 1969. Kirkwood added that the government was conducting a review of its forces with a view to modernizing them, although he did not think defence spending would vary dramatically. Ellsworth asked to be kept abreast of the review and said he hoped that 4 CMBG could be upgraded. Cabinet was considering the options, replied Kirkwood, and would have to focus on the replacement of the tank.[24]

While the first phase continued, Trudeau travelled to Bonn in March 1975 and met with Helmut Schmidt, now the chancellor. German support for Canada's link with the EEC was essential, because without the blessing of Europe's most powerful economy, the seeds of the Third Option would fall on stony ground. A briefing note for Trudeau's visit to Bonn highlighted Schmidt's interest in Canada and the importance that West Germany placed on defence cooperation.[25] Schmidt was frustrated that he had not met Trudeau earlier, but they became fast friends and remained so until Trudeau's death.[26] External Affairs noted, with some satisfaction, that Trudeau had a very successful visit; in the two-hour discussion, the prime minister affirmed Canada's commitment to the alliance, which pleased Schmidt. The chancellor was also happy that his efforts to improve the bilateral defence relationship between the two countries had been effective. Trudeau explained that he saw the "sought-after contractual link with [E]EC as complementary to our membership in NATO."[27] The German records confirm that Trudeau described the economic field and the military commitment in Europe as complementary.[28] The matter of tanks also came up, and in *The Canadian Way,* Trudeau and Head recount Schmidt's comments and their effect on Trudeau:

> "A German farmer is not able to detect the identity of NATO aircraft flying overhead as their contrails stream behind them. Besides, he knows that those airplanes can flee westward as quickly as they can fly eastward. He recognizes the maple leaf on tanks and infantry vehicles, however, and knows that there is no escape for them in the event of war. These units are reassuring and important, whether or not there is a persuasive military role for them." This kind of straight talk, intellectually and politically credible, was wholly attractive to Trudeau.

They also note that Schmidt was fearful of "(i) an exchange of nuclear munitions, which would reduce Europe to an uninhabitable wasteland, and (ii) the disappearance of allied forces, which were of such psychological significance."[29] Trudeau would see Schmidt two more times during 1975, and the chancellor would continue to press the matter of maintaining Canadian tanks in Europe.[30]

Although Trudeau's opinion on the importance of Canadian tanks was changing, it is apparent that this information did not permeate External Affairs. A few weeks after Trudeau and Schmidt's first meeting, the outgoing German ambassador, Rupprecht von Keller, paid a farewell visit to H.B. Robinson. After exchanging pleasantries, Robinson asked von Keller if the Canadian contingent in Europe might be more useful in the neglected Canadian North. What would West Germany's response be in case of withdrawal? Von Keller said this would be a "severe blow" *(ein harter Schlag)*. He emphasized the military value of Canadian troops, as well as the political and psychological consequences of withdrawal. It would contribute to the erosion of NATO and would be interpreted as a loss of interest in Europe. Robinson replied that although no decision had been made, there were considerations for an improved defence of the Canadian North. A few days later, von Keller met with Trudeau and, in a short conversation, impressed upon him the importance of Canadian troops. Trudeau said that the government had no intention of withdrawing or reducing in the foreseeable future, but despite this reassurance, von Keller was not convinced that withdrawal or reduction was out of the question.

The German foreign ministry directed the embassy to tell Robinson that his remarks had worried the Federal Republic. The Germans thought that during Trudeau's March visit, a common understanding of security threats had been reached, which "included the deployment of Canadian troops in the centre of the Federal Republic of Germany" *(Dazu gehöre zentral die Stationierung kanadischer Truppen in der Bundesrepublik Deutschland)*. A reduction in Canada's strength during the buildup of the Warsaw Pact would weaken NATO and the prospects for détente; it would also "affect Canada's political participation in the alliance, to which we attach great importance" *(auf die politische Mitsprache Kanadas in der Allianz auswirken, auf die wir großen Wert legen)*. Robinson directed the German envoy to Canada, Rudolf Wolff, to clarify the matter with Halstead, who stated that although withdrawal was not an option, the breakdown of the force's air and ground components was under examination.[31]

The American ambassador, Porter, took a more aggressive tack. In his annual policy assessment of Canada in April 1975, he wrote,

> A mature Canada should be willing to bear its fair share of the mutual defense burden. Every appropriate opportunity that offers itself should be seized upon by US officials to impress upon Canadians that a prosperous, strong (and mature) Canada is able and willing to contribute to the common defense on a per capita basis significantly higher than the present level, which approximates that of Luxembourg. We may not succeed in getting the GOC [Government of Canada] to contribute more, but if they don't we should make them as sheepish about it as possible.[32]

Schlesinger, who in 1973 had taken an interest in the Canadian brigade as part of his efforts to strengthen NATO's conventional forces, would become more forthright, perhaps because of Porter's counsel or because he was generally heavy-handed.

Dextraze met Trudeau at some point during the DSR and made his case for tanks. He later recalled that during his five years as CDS, he had only five meetings with Trudeau, but in one of them, he gave Trudeau a mini tactical lesson on tanks and why Canada's army needed them.[33] He told Trudeau, perhaps in the same meeting, that if Canada did not have tanks in Central Europe, 4 CMBG should be withdrawn from that theatre.[34] C.R. Nixon recalled that Dextraze also dropped off a letter arguing for tanks at 24 Sussex Drive, the prime minister's residence.[35]

The general also discussed the Centurion replacement with James Richardson. In April 1975, Dextraze reiterated the same point he had made to Trudeau, stating that "as long as Canada wanted a fighting formation on the European Central Front, a tank would be required." If Canada did not want to operate tanks, it could rely on other nations to provide them under Canadian command, and "if Cabinet desires otherwise, then he [Dextraze] is prepared to offer advice on alternative organizations for Europe, but he stressed the point that a land fighting formation has three basic components, infantry, artillery and armour, and all three must be present to maintain a fighting capability." Richardson responded that the 1971 White Paper called for a light force without tanks and that the ministers at that time must not have understood that point. The CDS stated that there was some confusion about that matter, but he was "gratified by the progress now being made to clarify the issue." Because the Centurion would be difficult to keep in service past 1976, Dextraze said, it was necessary for Cabinet to decide quickly on whether the army would keep tanks.[36]

This question came to Cabinet on 17 April 1975, when the working group established in late 1974 presented its assessment of the full range of the military's tasks, fifty-five in total. The next stage was to develop a range of force structures for each task, varying in cost and capability, from which Cabinet could then pick and choose based on needs and costs. The group's paper outlined five major questions that needed resolution, one of them being the equipment of Canada's NATO contribution. The preamble asked, "While it is current policy to station combat forces in the central part of Western Europe, what kind of forces should they be in light of their exposure to a threat of attack quite different in character from anything to which our forces in Canada are exposed?"[37] Just as in the policy reviews of 1963–64, 1968–69, and 1971, the question of whether Canada's troops in Europe should be heavy or light came to the fore.

The detailed section analyzing Canadian land forces in Europe emphasized that this military contribution needed to be taken seriously, which meant that those forces had to be prepared to fight the Warsaw Pact's sizable armies and tactical air forces. The first option was for a unit of anti-tank and anti-aircraft units, which had originally been suggested in the land force policy review of 1973–74. While these would be effective, they would be incompatible with forces at home. They would also be expensive and would be parcelled out among allied units, reducing the distinctiveness of Canada's NATO contribution. The other option was a mechanized force that would lack strategic mobility and be specialized, but it would be more compatible with units at home and cheaper than air and anti-tank units. A mechanized force needed tanks, and the working group's assessment refuted the assertion that anti-tank missiles in the October War had made tanks obsolete. To the contrary, the paper argued that tanks were a vital component of a modern army and were needed in Europe to deter the Warsaw Pact.[38] The option of a light tactical reconnaissance formation, which had been government policy since 1971, was no longer on the table. The principle of compatibility of army units at home and abroad, although recognized as desirable, was discarded in favour of the military requirements of the Central Front.

The discussion of this paper in Cabinet was vague, but Trudeau affirmed that one of the crucial elements in the report was linking Canada's force contribution in Europe to social, political, and economic developments on the continent. This was a thinly veiled reference to the Third Option, as well as to ongoing negotiations to reduce tensions in Europe, particularly those related to the Mutual and Balanced Force Reductions and the Conference on Security and Cooperation in Europe. Trudeau was also keenly interested in the type of war that might arise in Central Europe and the role that Canada might play in it.[39]

After this Cabinet meeting, two important items were added to the agenda of the May 1975 NATO summit in Brussels: a meeting of the Defence Planning Committee and a NATO heads-of-government meeting. The committee was going to discuss defence planning for the next seven years and provide a "long range defence planning concept for the Alliance as a whole." This was largely at the behest of the United States and Schlesinger, but some European nations, including West Germany, pressed for it as well. There was also pressure, especially from the Americans and Germans, to have countries that were contributing below the NATO European average to increase defence spending by a rate of 3 to 5 percent. The Cabinet Committee on External Policy and Defence rejected any increases, stating that Canada's commitments and any modifications to the defence budget would be decided after the DSR.[40]

At the meeting of the Defence Planning Committee, the German defence minister, Georg Leber, drew attention to reports that Canada was considering withdrawal from Europe. He asserted that a Canadian contingent in Europe, equipped with tanks, was important. Richardson responded that no decisions had been made as yet, and any changes would be discussed with NATO allies. Schlesinger stated that since Europe was the most vulnerable area, all allied forces in Europe were necessary: Canadian tanks were indispensable. Canada was also examining commitments in other areas, replied Richardson, to which Schlesinger countered that it would be a mistake to replace tanks with infantry.[41]

Although the Defence Planning Committee got off to a rough start, the heads-of-government meeting went much better. Trudeau, thoroughly delighted by it, suggested more frequent summits for NATO leaders, which surprised many allies, but little came of his proposal.[42] His satisfaction with the summit contributed to a more favourable assessment of the alliance and built upon his positive experience at the meeting, in October 1974, of the North Atlantic Council, in which he discarded his prepared speaking notes in favour of a free-ranging discussion. Trudeau, however, still thought that the allies, primarily the Europeans, should contribute more: he stated during the 1974 meeting, "If other allies do more, this would help Canada to play a larger military role."[43]

While at the NATO summit in Brussels, Trudeau and Allan MacEachen met with Ford, Kissinger, and other American advisers. Noting that Schlesinger "took us on" at the Defence Planning Committee meeting, Trudeau said, "We want to assure you that any decision from our defense review won't lessen our commitment. We will retain at least our present commitment in real terms." However, he stressed that the military's preparations for convoy protection was flawed and then expressed his skepticism about alliance strategy: "Flexible response was never defined. Massive retaliation and trip wire are more obvious."[44]

That same day, Schmidt took another opportunity to talk to Trudeau. He said he was concerned that the DSR would lead to withdrawal of Canada's tanks. The diplomatic cable noted that "he [Schmidt] wanted to point out that it was military view and his own view that tanks were essential for an effective Canadian presence in Germany." Trudeau responded that Canada could not do everything and needed to establish priorities and make the most effective use of limited resources. Of course, Canada would consider strategic imperatives, military requirements, and the views of allies. Schmidt repeated that Canada needed tanks to have an effective presence in Europe. When Trudeau asked what he thought of light mobile troop carriers, Schmidt declared that they would be useless against Soviet tanks and would not have the same psychological weight as tanks. He proposed that representatives from the Federal Republic of Germany and Canada should meet to study the issue of Canadian forces in Europe. Trudeau agreed to this proposal and announced it in a press conference at the end of the summit.[45] Gordon Crean, Canadian ambassador to West Germany, referred to the discussions as "intimate," and Arthur Menzies, the Canadian ambassador to NATO, in recalling the meeting later, stated that "he [Schmidt] would feel a good deal easier about the Canadian forces remaining in Europe if we were to get some new heavy main battle tanks."[46] On that same day, Trudeau delivered a speech in which he reassured allies that Canada was committed to collective security and the alliance and would "maintain a NATO force level which is accepted by our allies as being adequate in size and effective in character."[47] This was not stirring rhetoric, but it encouraged allies, who referred to it over the course of the summer, accustomed to Trudeau's lack of enthusiasm for the alliance.

The Germans kept up the pressure on the Canadians for a new tank. In June, Leber visited Canada and told MacEachen, Richardson, and Trudeau that Canada should retain properly equipped troops in Germany. This was code for tanks, but the Canadians were cagey and did not make a commitment.[48] The next month, Gordon Crean, who was leaving his post, paid a farewell call to Schmidt. The chancellor inquired if Donald Macdonald was still opposed to tanks, and Crean surmised that Schmidt was trying to ferret out the source of opposition to new tanks. In a message sent directly to Trudeau, Crean reported: "I summed up by saying that I was satisfied that if Prime Minister was convinced that Canadian forces in Europe should remain with a mixed configuration, including a tank element which Mr. Leber had pleaded for, then those forces would indeed remain in that form."[49]

The consultations with allies that Trudeau had promised at Brussels in May 1975 took place the following month. The Canadians sent a paper to the Americans and Germans on 18 June 1975 with a list of options for Canada's forces in Europe. Focusing primarily on the ground contribution, the paper suggested six options for the land force and included every proposal for restructuring that had been made since 1969. The first option was to retain the armoured regiment and either replace or modernize the Centurion, and the second was to withdraw the Canadian tanks and replace them with foreign vehicles under Canadian command. The third and fourth options, respectively, were to replace the Centurion with a loaned tank or a DFSV. The fifth option was a conversion of the brigade into an anti-tank formation, while the final option was to convert it into an airmobile formation with attack helicopters. The Canadians could maintain the air-land contribution at its present strength in these varying guises, convert to an all-land formation and maintain personnel at brigade strength (roughly six thousand), or become an all-air formation.[50]

The Germans responded quickly. They attached enormous importance to the political and military significance of the Canadian contribution, stating that it was in Canada's interest for NATO to be a link between Europe and North

America rather than simply between the United States and Europe. "To both the allies and a potential aggressor, the Canadian forces in Germany are the visible proof of Atlantic solidarity," the German document noted. "As such, they are firmly rooted in the minds of the German people, in particular in the area where they are stationed." The Germans did not want any real change in the organization or equipment of the Canadian contribution and emphasized that the formation needed tanks in order to be effective. They also wanted a "clearly identifiable Canadian military formation in Europe with capability to carry out its own assigned task." As Canada's delegate to the North Atlantic Council, Menzies, reported, "In last analysis any option that involved retention of tanks by Canadian forces in Europe would be acceptable." The Germans concluded by saying that they could make Leopard 1 tanks available for purchase or rent within two years, which would be helpful because the United States was low on tanks after the massive resupply of Israel during the October War, and production was behind schedule.[51]

Robert Ingersoll, deputy secretary of state, reviewed the document written by the American mission to NATO as a response to Canada's list of options. Ingersoll was aware of Trudeau's discussions with Schmidt and the importance of Canadian forces for the trade talks with the EEC, and he knew that the time was favourable to press the government to improve its contributions in Europe without diminishing its effort elsewhere. The State Department revised the paper with the "aim of providing Trudeau with best possible rationale to persuade Canadian Cabinet of importance of Canada's NATO contribution."[52] When the Americans and Canadians met on 26 June 1975 at NATO headquarters, Menzies explained how inflation had initiated the review and outlined the background to the policy to replace the Centurion with a light vehicle.[53] David Bruce, Menzies's American counterpart, noted that "the Canadian participants pressed strongly for written U.S. comments on the options which would give Canadian officials leverage with their ministers on replacement of Centurion tanks and F-104 aircraft."[54] The Americans' final written response to the Canadians, coordinated with the Germans, cautioned against any reductions, noting that NATO was already spread thin and that a drastic Canadian restructuring would be a bad example for other alliance members.[55] The closing comments stated that the United States favoured maintaining the current Canadian contribution, although modernized with new or upgraded tanks. They stated: "Since most disadvantageous disparity confronting NATO is WSAW [Warsaw] Pact's impressive armored superiority, this Canadian reserve must contain first class tank formation that can move rapidly to meet a breakthrough anywhere along army group front. This function cannot be performed by lighter mechanized vehicles, air-mobile units, or light anti-armor formations."[56] In early August,

Menzies summed up the results of his discussions with the Americans and Germans. He noted that although *Defence in the 70s* had called for the replacement of the Centurion with a light DFSV, conditions since 1971 had changed considerably. The Warsaw Pact had improved its armoured forces in Central Europe, and the Germans wanted tanks to demonstrate Canada's commitment to the alliance, while the United States wanted them in order to counterattack and blunt any Soviet breakthroughs. Menzies stated that the Germans wanted the Canadians to have a vehicle that was at least as capable as the M60 or the Leopard and that a rebuilt Centurion would probably be inadequate. He recommended renting or purchasing Leopards based on the German offer from June.[57]

The culminating meeting of the summer of 1975 was between Schmidt and Trudeau in Helsinki. Trudeau was attending the signing ceremony of the Conference on Security and Cooperation in Europe, and Trudeau and Schmidt met for breakfast on 31 July at the German embassy. Trudeau began by thanking Schmidt for supporting Canada's attempts to forge trade links with the EEC, to which Schmidt replied, "We have to." The chancellor quickly asked how the DSR was progressing. Trudeau summarized the consultations and stated that he expected a resolution by September, but he did not want to prejudge a decision on tanks. He stated that "because our allies considered them so important he thought we would probably keep them. It did not make much sense in terms of Canada's overall defence posture but we must take our allies' views into account." According to the German records, Trudeau said that if Canada decided to keep tanks, it would be because of the Germans' intense pressure.

Trudeau "wished he could find answers to the questions about the sort of war we should expect. Would it be quick? Perhaps there were no answers." He asked for Schmidt's appraisal, but "he could in any case assure the Chancellor that his point about the importance of tanks in Central Europe had been taken aboard." Schmidt and Trudeau discussed the different scenarios and responses, and the prime minister questioned Schmidt on the use of tactical nuclear weapons and the efficacy of conventional forces. The chancellor emphasized that although he would never allow the use of nuclear weapons in Germany, they were useful because the Soviets thought that NATO would use them. Schmidt summed up his thinking "in a nutshell": "We needed nuclear weapons to deter the Russians from aggression or adventure but we needed conventional forces to actually stop the enemy if he tried to advance." This seemed to satisfy Trudeau, who responded

> that Canadian participation in NATO was predicated on what our allies wanted us to do. Our choice regarding the structure of our forces would therefore be essentially political, tailored to accommodate within our budget the most

> efficient forces and equipment required to do the job. The choices were not easy, however, because while our NATO allies wanted us to maintain tanks in Europe, the USA wanted us to maintain the LRPA [long-range patrol aircraft] in the North Atlantic.

Schmidt stressed the "psycho-political element" of Canada's participation in the alliance and of NATO itself: "In the Chancellor's view the Canadian presence in Europe was primarily of political importance and the effectiveness of NATO was primarily political rather than military." According to the German records of the discussion, Schmidt highlighted that without Canadian troops on the continent, Canada could not have been in the Conference on Security and Cooperation in Europe, to which Trudeau responded that this was a strong argument for Canada's participation in NATO. The prime minister stated that Canada had no intention of reducing the presence in Germany and that he did not think its composition would be changed in view of the German and American opinions on the matter. Schmidt said that the West Germans also "welcomed the Canadian presence in Lahr because they wanted to show the Russians and others that the NATO forces in Germany were not all German or American."

Schmidt asked if there was any opposition from the Canadian public to maintaining tanks in Germany but did not press Trudeau. Trudeau responded that "Canadians were not against tanks in Germany, but that they were against letting the Americans do all the surveillance in Canadian air and sea space. It was this problem of doing more for the protection of Canadian sovereignty in addition to maintaining our presence in Europe which caused the real difficulty." He added that the NATO contribution was good politics in Canada and "made the Canadian military feel they were performing a useful role." Schmidt concluded by stating that if Canada ever felt it had to reduce its tanks, it must do so under the MBFR (Mutual and Balanced Force Reductions) formula; otherwise, it would be seen as a unilateral move. The German records note that Schmidt emphasized the words "mutual" and "balanced" in discussion with Trudeau. The two leaders then discussed other topics, such as nuclear nonproliferation, and Trudeau extended an open invitation for Schmidt to visit Canada, which he did in 1976.[58]

Schlesinger was due to visit Ottawa in September, and Dextraze "sent word to Schlesinger's office to suggest in effect that the Secretary's presentation be reasonably low key, apparently with a view to ensuring that the prime minister not be antagonized."[59] The American ambassador, William Porter, took the opposite tack, notifying Washington that a "forceful presentation on defence matters, not seen as DND-engineered, made to Trudeau by person of SECDEF's [secretary of defense's] stature, could have important impact at critical point in Canadian defence policy decision-making process."[60]

Schlesinger made his presentation to James Richardson and some parliamentarians on 15 September and took Porter's, not Dextraze's, advice. Richardson noted that Canada was reviewing its defence posture to determine the relative emphasis on land forces in NATO, antisubmarine warfare, and North American air defence, and Schlesinger responded with a long statement in which he emphasized the need for conventional forces and stressed that any reductions by Canada would have a "far-reaching psychological effect." He noted the need for Canadian tanks in Europe, which was the first priority; antisubmarine warfare was the second, followed by air defence, a distant third. When someone questioned him on the marginal value of a Canadian improvement of its armour, Schlesinger reiterated that NATO's greatest weakness was in its ground forces and that "the most cost effective effort for Canada would be to upgrade its tank force in NATO. It would make a far greater impact on Europeans than anything else Canada could do now."

In the presentation to Cabinet, Schlesinger was forceful. He emphasized a number of times that NATO needed a credible ground force in Central Europe as well as the ability to support it. Macdonald was put off by Schlesinger's approach and, perhaps to prod him,

> suggested that Canada might be better off to withdraw totally from NATO and put its resources into ASW [antisubmarine warfare] since even if Canada quadrupled its NATO capability, it would not weigh very much in the total balance. He said that the Alliance is basically a bilateral one between the US and Europe and that Canada did not have much influence.

Schlesinger responded that this would lead to the reduction in strength of the smaller NATO powers and the eventual disintegration of the alliance: "If Canada went back to its prior level of forces, it would have a dramatic effect on the Alliance – and perhaps stimulate Soviet response to MBFR." Trudeau was unsatisfied, contending that "it was more urgent to convince the Europeans than Canadians of the threat. He did not believe that Europeans had the same perception of danger as did the US, otherwise they would be doing more." A Canadian increase would probably have little effect on the Soviets in regard to the Mutual and Balanced Force Reductions. Schlesinger emphasized, among a number of other items, that Canada should maintain its current ground commitment to NATO and consider increasing it to the previous level; its defence priorities, he said, should be NATO ground forces, defence of the Atlantic sea lanes, and then air defence.[61] In his report on the discussion, Porter noted

Macdonald's objections but pointed out that he was isolated and that the presentation had had the intended effect.[62] Schlesinger later recalled:

> I went up to Ottawa and I suggested to the prime minister and members of the cabinet, "suppose Western Europe were not protected, suppose Western Europe indeed fell under control of the Soviet Union, and suppose the United States was thereby slowly forced back into the Western hemisphere, how would Canadians like being locked up here in the North American continent with an America that felt defeated and mean-spirited? I don't think the Canadians would feel very comfortable under those circumstances." That was, perhaps, a point with a touch of malice, but I think they got the point.[63]

By October, allies were impatiently awaiting the results of the review, and delegates to NATO's Defence Review Committee, noting that Canada's responses to the defence planning questionnaire were incomplete, pressed for an increased contribution. The Canadian delegation was guarded but noted that there were "grounds for 'cautious optimism.'"[64]

In early November, Ivan Head went over to Europe with Dextraze to discuss the results of the DSR with senior American officers and SACEUR, now General Alexander Haig. Head reported that SACEUR had stated unequivocally that politicians from European countries had told him of a link between Canada's NATO involvement and the search for a contractual link with the EEC. Haig might have been instructed to say this by NATO allies, or even by members of Canada's military such as Dextraze in a call upon the "fraternity of the uniform."[65] However, Marcel Cadieux, Canadian ambassador to the EEC, confirmed this connection: "European governmental representatives ... made no secret of the fact that Canada's NATO contributions were employed by their governments as a measurement of Canada's earnestness for an enhanced relationship with the Community." Head submitted a lengthy report on his recommendations for the DSR and, with some convoluted logic, justified keeping tanks in Europe. He noted that the Western Europeans valued Canadian tanks and suggested that Canada's contribution to European defence was political resolve, not actual military need. Canada did not need to alter its preference for the compatibility of its army units, but it could agree with allies that tanks were the proper expression of that political resolve. Although the plan to replace the Centurion with a DFSV made military sense for Canada, allies had not accepted it. He noted that "a political decision is now required: whether to accept the views of those allies that the presence on German soil of Canadian tanks represents important evidence of the cohesiveness of the alliance – the political 'resolve' – to be seen by German peasants and Warsaw Pact observers alike." Head did not elaborate further on the reasons for staying in Central Europe and keeping tanks, nor did he address his steadfast defence of the decision to go light in 1973. He laid out the options for a new tank with some help from a report by Dextraze, produced in June. A refitted Centurion would be cheap, about $60 million, and it would be a first-class vehicle. It would be slow, however, and Canada would be the only member of NATO to use it as a front-line tank, so spare parts would be more expensive. Head's preferred option was to take up the German offer from June 1975 and lease or rent Leopards. He liked this option: it was cheap, it gave Canada flexibility, and six NATO allies used the Leopard. Furthermore, if the vehicles were owned by the Germans, there would be no need to transport them from Europe to Canada, and Canada could maintain a semblance of compatibility between the troops in Canada and Europe. Head counselled that Canada should retain tanks and replace the Centurion with the Leopard on a lease or rental basis.[66]

The paper that finally came to Cabinet in November 1975 and concluded the second phase of the DSR addressed a whole host of issues – including, notably, the purchase of new aircraft and ships – but the first item on the agenda was whether Canadian troops in Europe would have a tank. The document noted that consultations with the United States and Germany "made it abundantly clear that both governments attach very great importance to (a) the continued stationing, and if possible the strengthening, of Canadian forces in central Europe, and (b) the maintenance in such a stationed contribution, and if possible, the strengthening, of a land force equipped with tanks." Both allies made it clear that they wanted air and land forces, "although their most vital concerns focused upon the land component." The paper summed up *Defence in the 70s* and the rationale therein for replacing the Centurion with a DFSV, but it noted that "since then it has proved impossible, both in consultations with the NATO military authorities and in those with the German and U.S. governments, to identify any role in which a more lightly equipped force of the kind previously envisaged could credibly contribute to the conventional deterrent posture of the NATO forces in the key Central European region." After noting Trudeau's speech in Brussels in May 1975, in which he said that Canada would maintain forces that were "accepted by our allies as being adequate in size and effective in character," the paper concluded that Canada should maintain tanks in Europe and decide immediately on whether to retrofit or replace the Centurion. The Centurions would not last longer than the spring of 1976, so the new tank decision was needed immediately.

There were two major options on the table. The estimate for a Centurion retrofit was $75 to $100 million, while new Leopards would cost from $185 to $240 million. The purchase of a tank was cheap compared to new aircraft or ships and could be accommodated by the defence budget. The paper recommended purchasing the Leopard, despite its expense, for its military and political benefits, but leasing the Leopard was still an option.[67] In broader terms, the paper recommended that the defence budget should increase at the rate of inflation to prevent personnel cuts; in addition, to finance the re-equipment program, the capital budget should increase at a rate of 12 percent per year starting in 1976–77.[68]

The Cabinet Committee on Priorities and Planning reviewed this paper on 12 November 1975 and approved the use of tanks by a full Canadian tank regiment in Europe – fifty-seven gun tanks and eight support tanks. These tanks would either be retrofitted Centurions or leased or purchased Leopards. That same day, Macdonald sent a lengthy letter to Trudeau, putting his critiques of the DSR on paper because he could not attend the meeting. Macdonald thought that the review and the equipment purchases had reordered the defence priorities of 3 April 1969, to which someone wrote "No" in the margin. He was opposed to the emphasis on European defence, particularly the tank: "I most strongly object to the attempt to re-introduce the heavy tank role because it is unnecessary and wasteful of Canadian resources, and rather more fundamentally because it represents an attempt on the part of the armed forces to dictate our military involvement in the face of the contrary decision by Cabinet." He proceeded to outline the decision to replace the Centurion and to emphasize mobility and air-transportability for Canada's land forces, both of which had been accepted by NATO authorities. Macdonald stated: "I am aware that that decision was not happily accepted by all elements, past and present, then interested in Canadian defence policy, but it was our decision founded upon Canadian defence staff advice. I have no doubt that N.A.T.O. and U.S. and German authorities would force upon us other defence decisions if they can." He wrote that if Canada reaffirmed its decision to eliminate the tank, NATO would find the force useful after all, to which someone again wrote "No." Macdonald concluded his letter by asking that in any matters related to the defence budget, expenditure, or procurement, the "concurrence of the Minister of Finance be required," and someone noted this paragraph with an exclamation mark, perhaps noting the consequences if Macdonald wielded veto power.[69] Macdonald, still in possession of substantial power from his position at the Department of Finance, was fighting to the end.

Five days later, on 17 November, Head weighed in. He said that the equipment priorities did not represent a reordering of *Defence in the 70s* and countered Macdonald's assertion that the tank was incompatible with an airmobile army. Leasing German tanks would reduce the potency of that argument. He recounted Schmidt's assessment that tanks, not light vehicles, were needed on the Central

Front, but regardless, it would be worthwhile to emphasize the political rather than military value of the tanks.[70]

Macdonald's objections came to naught, and Cabinet confirmed the recommendations of the paper on 20 November, instructing James Richardson to start working on the purchase immediately.[71] The military also began the work of purchasing new ships, fighters, and patrol aircraft, and thus began the wholesale recapitalization of the Canadian Armed Forces, much of which remains in service today. Most of this equipment went to bolster Canada's commitments to the Cold War, and the revisionists' attempts to reorient Canadian defence policy on domestic needs alone finally faltered. Stiff opposition from allies and the military eventually forced him to return to the status quo of the early 1950s commitments, albeit greatly reduced. The DSR attempted to put a veneer of rational planning on Canada's defence posture and its commitments, but it cut the pattern to fit the cloth.

Most accounts of the DSR and the decision to buy tanks make note of Schmidt's influence, although in general terms. Two other figures have claimed, or been assigned credit, for changing Trudeau's mind and convincing him to allow the army to keep its tanks.[72] The first is Dextraze, who was instrumental in undermining the Scorpion purchase and continually pressed the issue of the tank. Despite the general's persistence, he was unable to change Trudeau's mind on the matter by himself, his greatest success being in delaying the replacement of the Centurion. It is likely that Trudeau understood the limitations of light vehicles from a tactical perspective, but after 1973, the elimination of the tank had become an assertion of national interests and the civilian control of defence policy. Trudeau's final statement in Cabinet in 1973 that it "was not open for re-consideration" was evidence that he was prepared to ignore the professional advice of his military and of senior NATO leadership. Schlesinger has sometimes been credited with changing Trudeau's mind, and he also took credit for the tanks.[73] He emphasized the military rationale for tanks and, in his characteristically blunt fashion, pressed the Canadians to keep them. Trudeau, however, was noticeably cool towards his entreaties; it is unclear if Schlesinger's pressure was supported by any other major American figures, although there is some suggestion that Kissinger, in his discussion with Trudeau in October 1975, supported Schlesinger's views.[74] No references to tanks, however, were made in discussions between Ford and Trudeau, and a far more important bilateral concern was the Canadian purchase of the long-range patrol aircraft.[75]

It was politics, not tactics, that changed Trudeau's mind, and, as other authors have noted, Schmidt was the primary influence. Accounts diverge somewhat as to how Schmidt convinced Trudeau to relent. Some note that the chancellor was subtle and that he told Trudeau that the success of Canada's negotiations for the trade link was predicated on an improvement in Canada's contributions to NATO. Others claim that Schmidt effectively told Trudeau, in a short and admirably pithy linkage of foreign and defence policy, "No tanks, no trade."

One of the analyses in the second category notes that Schmidt lectured Trudeau on the need for Canada to improve its defences, particularly in the form of new tanks for Canadian troops in Europe, and that he "personally advised Trudeau to 'pull up Canada's military socks' if the country wished to discuss any increase in trade deals."[76] R.B. Byers puts it more delicately, stating that Schmidt, the German foreign minister, and the NATO secretary general, Joseph Luns, criticized Canada's military contributions and asserted that the desired contractual link with Western Europe was based on an improvement in Canada's military performance.[77] J.L. Granatstein and Robert Bothwell, in *Pirouette,* argue that it was a combined operation by Jacques Dextraze, Deputy Minister of Defence Sylvain Cloutier, and the chancellor. Schmidt gave Trudeau a lesson in European security, and the prime minister was eager to please the Germans, so he agreed to the purchase of tanks.[78] Head and Trudeau duck the matter of increased support for NATO in their 1995 foreign policy memoir *The Canadian Way.*[79] However, Roy Rempel, in *Counterweights,* is adamant that the Germans linked trade and defence policy.[80] The illustrated history of the Royal Canadian Armoured Corps notes the "no tanks, no trade doctrine" and adds that a "'walk in the woods' with Helmut Schmidt has been credited with changing Trudeau's mind on the matter of a Canadian tank."[81] In *Alliance and Illusion,* Robert Bothwell makes a passing reference to the purchase of tanks and, in a footnote, cites a Canadian diplomat who noted that the tanks and the Third Option were linked.[82]

Although the "no tanks, no trade" diktat is entertaining, it is likely false: there is no reference to it in the archival record. It could be argued that such a frank exchange would not make it into official dispatches, but it appears that the link between tanks and trade was more implied than explicit. Ramsey Withers offered the most likely germ of the story, recalling that the report of the Helsinki conference was that Chancellor Schmidt told Trudeau that Canada should pull its weight in the alliance or lose trade with Germany.[83] However, John Halstead recalled the connection as more implied than stated:

> Some people have suggested that in fact the Europeans exercised blackmail over us; that when we came, when the Prime Minister came, and said we would like to have a contractual link with you, with the European Community, the Europeans said: "Well, you'd better do something about your defence if you want that." I was present at two tête-à-tête meetings between Trudeau and Schmidt

> and at numerous other meetings. I accompanied Trudeau on his visits to all the European capitals during that campaign, 1974-75, it started in the fall of '74 with visits to Paris and to Brussels and it went on in '75 with visits to all the other capitals. And not once was that said or anything near it, but nevertheless, you know, it was a sort of unstated assumption in the background, because it was obvious to everyone that we couldn't be credible in our professions [with] a desire to broaden and deepen our relations with Europe in some areas and leave security out of it.[84]

The "no tanks, no trade" diktat is entirely at odds with Schmidt's approach to Canada beginning in the early 1970s, which was accommodating and conciliatory when military relations between Canada and its allies were perhaps at their lowest ebb. He also supported Canada's efforts to implement the Third Option in the summer of 1975, well before the government's final decision on tanks, and the following year, Schmidt's support, combined with American pressure, was essential to Canada's inclusion in the Group of Six, against the opposition of French president Valéry Giscard d'Estaing.[85]

Whether the chancellor was subtle or overt appears to have been irrelevant to the outcome: Schmidt put pressure on Trudeau to buy tanks, and the prime minister bought them. However, Schmidt's efforts to build links with Canada and help the government achieve its foreign policy goals were unique. Many authors, especially Roy Rempel, have criticized Canada for its defence policy blunders during the Cold War. Rempel correctly argues that Canadian policymakers never fully understood the value of the mechanized brigade, and consequently, they failed to link foreign and defence policy.[86] There is no more embarrassing example than the lack of connection between the defence policy review of 1969, which angered the Europeans, and Mitchell Sharp's 1972 "Canada-U.S. Relations: Options for the Future," which announced the goal of fostering trade links with Europe.

The focus on Canada's failings, however, obscures European mistakes. Europe expected Canada to maintain 10 percent of its armed forces thousands of kilometres from home for nothing in return but the vague promise of influence and the threat of disapproval. Canada had devoted enormous resources to help liberate and rebuild Europe, and Europeans were overjoyed to see first-rate Canadian soldiers on the Iron Curtain in the 1950s. This did not, however, translate into any tangible thanks, no trade deals or closer ties between Canada and European countries. Canada, in contrast to the United States and the United Kingdom, paid its own way in Europe, receiving no money or trade preferences to offset the drain on the balance of payments. Even after Europe's postwar recovery, the EEC built tariff walls that priced out many Canadian exports, particularly agricultural products, while China and the Soviet Union bought large quantities of Canadian grain.[87] Even Ross Campbell stated that he could not document an example of Canada's role as a "good ally" in the 1950s or 1960s winning it some tangible benefit.[88] Karl Carstens, who occupied a number of key posts in Germany's foreign and defence ministries in the 1960s, stated that "he sympathized with Cdn [Canadian] complaints we are unloved despite our contributions to Europe and he agreed we were taken for granted. Europe discussed with the US and then hoped Canada would go along."[89]

To be fair, Canada's allies had never been serious about Article 2 of the NATO treaty – the "Canadian article," so called because of the persistence of its Canadian proponents – which called for cooperation, particularly in economic matters, between alliance members. In the 1950s and 1960s, the allies probably saw economic relations as a province of other international organizations, such as the General Agreement on Tariffs and Trade, and saw no reason to link trade and defence. Furthermore, the Europeans had built the EEC for European interests, not to harmonize relationships with allies. This, however, did not prevent them, in 1974 and 1975, from specifying, or at least implying, that trade and defence were intertwined.

The only European to really break this mould was Helmut Schmidt, and this partially explains the success of his appeals to Trudeau. He wielded enormous power as the leader of Europe's strongest economy and had the status to indeed lecture Trudeau, but he reached out to him as a generous and accommodating ally. He wanted Canadian tanks in Europe but was willing to offer considerable West German support for Canada's initiatives in return; he showed Trudeau that the alliance was not a relic of 1950s internationalism but could serve Canadian interests. In short, Schmidt showed Trudeau that it was worth it to be part of the NATO "club," and if the dues were tanks, so be it.[90]

While this might explain the purchase of tanks, it does not explain Trudeau's growing support for the alliance, which manifested itself in later controversies such as cruise missile testing. Axworthy commented that NATO was probably much more appealing to Trudeau in 1975 than it had been earlier, because it led Western Europe's efforts during the Conference on Security and Cooperation in Europe, which successfully resolved Europe's postwar boundaries.[91] After his discussions with Schmidt in 1975, Trudeau also came to recognize the importance of the alliance's conventional forces, especially Canada's small contributions, in maintaining the balance of power in Europe and the solidarity of the alliance. He was always skeptical of flexible response, and rightfully so. NATO members struggled to develop a clear statement of the forces required for deterrence, an exceedingly difficult, if not impossible, task, and there was little inclination, particularly on Europe's part, to build up NATO's ground forces to match the real or imagined power of the Warsaw Pact. Trudeau realized that no one knew what a war in Central Europe would look like, and Canada had no ability to prompt a revision of strategy on its own. More importantly, the array of forces was driven more by intra-alliance politics than by a statement of military need. Despite its military shortcomings, flexible response was an effective political strategy that did hold the alliance together, and Canada's commitment, however small, reinforced alliance cohesion and solidarity. As François Richard, an officer posted to the Privy Council Office in the 1970s, stated years later, "Trudeau believes that the alliance works to prevent war; but he is also convinced that flexible response is for the birds. He's ready to put money on deterrence, but not on waging war."[92] This still left the enduring question of the Cold War – How much is enough? – and Canada had some latitude in answering it because of NATO's flexibility. Trudeau was able to reduce the brigade and move it in 1969, despite the protests of allies, and there were no real long-term consequences for the plan to field a half-strength unit of light vehicles instead of a full mechanized brigade with tanks.

After Canada decided to buy tanks, Trudeau asked Schmidt if he was concerned about the Soviet Union's growing military power. Schmidt responded that he

> thought the situation in Europe was stabilized and that the Russians did not intend to start any serious trouble there. To this, the Prime Minister asked, half jokingly, why if such were the case the Chancellor had attached so much importance to Canada's re-equipping its forces in Europe with the new tanks. The Chancellor replied that the important thing was for NATO to maintain the balance of power in Europe. As long as it did so, the situation there would remain stabilized.[93]

Schmidt's emphasis on the political value of the alliance and its role in maintaining the balance of power appealed to Trudeau. Axworthy commented that Trudeau did not like monopolies of power or ideas and always wanted effective balances and countervails, so Schmidt's emphasis on NATO's role in balancing relations between East and West probably had traction with Trudeau.[94] The leaders in the Kremlin were never going to try and launch a first strike and seize Western Europe, but they were tough negotiators and would exploit any advantage to the fullest, from bilateral relations to multilateral summits on arms control. In a speech to NATO some years later, Trudeau stated:

> We cannot wait for the Soviet Union to develop such a preponderance of military capability that the balance will swing strongly in its favour enabling it to achieve security on its own terms. The Soviets' assurance of complete security cannot be bought at the cost of our incapacity to protect ourselves. That would

> be no basis either for security or for détente. In seeking to improve the reality of our security we must maintain the balance of deterrent strength. But our security problem will not be solved simply by the reactive policy of trying to match the military capacity of the potential adversary. We must also pursue with vigour, at every opportunity and along every avenue open to us, the goals of a meaningful policy of détente and of a genuine reduction in our mutual capacity to wage war.[95]

The question of whether Canada's forces in Europe would have tanks or DFSVs, a recurrent problem since 1963, had been resolved. The problem now was to determine which one to buy.

8

"From a Beetle to a Porsche"

The Purchase of the Leopard

The first Leopard came in. It was off-loaded from the tank transporter in Lahr. A young trooper got in to drive it up to the unit and he was nailed by the military police for speeding. Speeding in a 30 kilometre zone. He must have been doing round about 55 to 60 kilometres an hour. That speeding ticket is now, or was, affixed to the wall in Lahr.

– Terry Seeley, Interview with J.R. MacDougall, July 2004

From our point of view I would like to add that the number of tanks is not important. What is decisive is and will remain the demonstration of practical solidarity within the alliance as it has again and again been generally urgently sought.

– State Secretary Helmut Fingerhut, October 1976

Although it was November 1975 by the time the government decided to keep tanks in Europe, Dextraze directed his staff to start investigating a Centurion modernization or replacement as early as May 1975. The army had never stopped collecting information on new tanks, and Mac Campbell had an unnamed folder in his filing cabinet that was the clandestine drop-box for all information on what was unofficially referred to as the tank replacement project.[1] By June 1975, the head of Chief Land Doctrine and Operations, Major-General G.G. Brown, submitted a report to Dextraze on the options for new vehicles. The army would need 113 tanks to equip the forces in Europe, flesh out war stocks, and provide a training complement at home. The candidates had not changed dramatically since the late 1960s, although two new contenders had arrived on the scene, both arising from the cancelled MBT-70. The West Germans were developing the Leopard 2, which would enter service in 1979, and the Americans were developing the M1 Abrams, which would enter service in 1980. These vehicles eventually incorporated the latest technological advances – a 120 mm gun, composite armour, and improved fire control – and were the best in the world, although the Abrams suffered from significant teething problems. The army discounted these tanks because they would not be in service for at least four years, so Canada would probably only start receiving them in the mid-1980s, after the Germans and Americans had equipped their armies. The Centurion would not last that long without another rebuild, and, more importantly, the government could change its mind. The army would need a vehicle that was already in service, and Brown's report ranked the Leopard as the most effective, followed by the British Chieftain, and finally, the American M60. A modernization of the Centurion with a new engine, transmission, improved suspension, and new fire control system was also on the table. Other tanks, such as the Swiss Pz 68 or the French AMX-30, were ruled out for technical reasons.

Rejecting the Chieftain because it was too slow, the army was left with three options: a modernized Centurion, the Leopard 1, and the M60. A hundred and thirteen modernized Centurions would cost about $58 million; 113 Leopard 1s, $146 million; and 113 M60s, $94.1 million. The high price of the Leopard was due to German labour prices having risen dramatically during the economic slowdown: a Leopard cost $350,000 in September 1972 but $850,000 by May 1975. Major-General Brown recommended the Centurion upgrade because it was the cheapest, and he advised that they be modernized immediately before the tanks were totally worn out.[2] Dextraze passed this memo on to Ivan Head, emphasizing that a modernized Centurion was a first-class tank, even though the hulls were over twenty-five years old.[3]

This preference disquieted External Affairs officers, who feared that NATO allies would scoff at a modernization and that Canada would squander the political benefits from the decision to keep tanks, especially with the ongoing negotiations with the EEC. In late August 1975, Gordon Riddell, from the Bureau of Defence and Arms Control Affairs, in External Affairs, sent a note to H.B. Robinson regarding Canadian forces in Europe. He noted the meetings in Brussels and Helsinki, where Trudeau had effectively promised a new tank for Canadian forces in Europe but expressed concern about the army's preference for a Centurion retrofit. Riddell stated that Major-General Ramsey Withers, the deputy to the ADM – Policy, thought a retrofitted Centurion was qualitatively superior to the M60 or the Leopard and would also be much cheaper than a new tank. Drawing from the report produced in June, DND estimated the cost of a new Leopard at $850,000 each, an M60 at $515,000, and a retrofitted Centurion at $279,000. Withers had suggested that the Dutch company that had done the rebuild in 1973–74 could do the work, using Israeli upgrade kits to replace the engine and drivetrain. Riddell was worried that DND was dramatically underestimating the cost of this refurbishment and that trouble would ensue in Cabinet and the media if cost overruns occurred. Another concern was that there would be some pressure to have work done in Canada, especially with high unemployment. Riddell also thought that the Germans might supply some discounted vehicles given their interest in having Canadian tanks in Europe.

Riddell's biggest concern was that a rebuilt Centurion would not fully convince Europeans of Canada's commitment to Europe. Canada would be going against the grain of alliance standardization, and the logistical and maintenance arrangements of a retrofitted Centurion would be inferior to those of a US or German tank. He suggested that Robinson bring this matter up with Dextraze, being sure to emphasize that he was not judging the effectiveness of the Centurion versus the Leopard or M60 but addressing the foreign policy implications of the purchase. Riddell advised Robinson to gently approach the issue of whether the retrofitted Centurion was really superior or whether Dextraze had decided that it was the most palatable option for Trudeau and Cabinet, as well as the other services. If it was the latter, Riddell concluded,

> there is a danger that the Prime Minister, having been converted to the need for an effective tank in Europe to meet the preoccupations of our allies, will persuade Ministers to adopt the retrofit option in the belief that it was a militarily defensible option when in fact it may not be. The net result would be that our allies would be unimpressed and we would lose the political benefits in Europe of the Prime Minister's decision to maintain the tank.[4]

After duly meeting with Dextraze over lunch, Robinson reported that the general's mind was still open about the tank. Dextraze's first choice was the Leopard 2, but it would not be in production for at least three years and would lock Canada into the tank role for at least the next twenty-five years; he doubted the government would accept this. His next choice was for a Centurion retrofit, which he said was superior to both the Leopard 1 and M60 and would be much cheaper. When Robinson raised the possibility of renting Leopard tanks, Dextraze replied that this was "lacking in dignity and self-respect for Canada," although he would accept it if there were no other alternatives. The final option was to carry on with the Centurion until a decision was made on a replacement, possibly for another four or five years.[5]

This discussion, and other army investigations, probably prompted Dextraze to explore other options. The army preferred the Leopard despite its cost; the assessment of some officers was that modernizing the Centurion, although feasible, would have numerous problems. Not only would it take years to actually produce and test the prototypes, but it would be difficult to maintain a tank that no other NATO armies were using.[6] In the fall of 1975, Dextraze sent the deputy chief of the defence staff and a key bureaucrat from the ADM – Materiel office to Germany to discuss the acquisition of the Leopard. They received general cost information, as well as notice that it would be twenty-two months before the Canadians could receive their own vehicles, but the Germans could loan them thirty to thirty-five tanks as an interim measure.[7] Dextraze later recalled that he persuaded the head of the German armed forces to arrange a meeting between himself and the German defence minister, Leber, from whom he requested about a hundred new Leopards. According to Dextraze, he "got him [Leber] to agree by stressing that PET was usually in disagreement with everything, but that he had agreed to a new tank."[8]

On 21 October 1975, DND allocated funds for 113 tanks, either new vehicles or modernized Centurions, and on 27 November 1975, the requirement rose to 128 tanks.[9] The army had a paper that justified the need for 128 tanks to maintain the regiment in Germany and supply a training school in Canada, but some in the army were now talking about purchasing 156. Dextraze was infuriated, fearing that the higher number would ruin his credibility with Trudeau and Head. The CDS brought in senior members of the requirements staff and the armoured corps, lined them up in a conference room, and shouted that they were embarrassing him, since he had already passed the number of 128 to his political masters. He then picked up a heavy ashtray and threw it at the wall (the ashtray did not break) and asked each officer whether the number was 128 or 156. Each officer said 128.[10] In December 1975, the army formed a Project Management Office to look at the three possibilities: a Centurion modernization, a long-term lease of tanks, or a new purchase.

The key figures in the purchase were the project manager, Lieutenant-Colonel Dave Hampson, and Robert Bradshaw, from the Marine and Industrial Machine Products section at DSS. Bradshaw, Hampson's civilian counterpart, was responsible for negotiations. The project director in charge of operational requirements was Major Ken Black, who was assisted by Major Jim Gervais, tasked to the project in 1977. The deputy project manager and project engineer was Major Mac Campbell, replaced by Major Gerry Koeller in 1978. Major Larry Brownrigg managed and tracked expenditures, and the representative from the Department of Industry, Trade, and Commerce was W.E. Grant.[11] John Killick, a senior official who held the post of chief of supply in the ADM – Materiel office, kept the project team small by using the matrix management system. A small group of soldiers was directly tasked to the project, bringing in other technical and logistics experts as required. For example, if the team was working on manuals or on weapons systems, it would bring in a soldier with experience in that field until the work was done and then return him. Those soldiers could contribute to other projects rather than being tasked to one acquisition for years.[12] Their work was reviewed by a steering committee, and the most important oversight was from the Senior Review Board.[13] This board of high-ranking officers and bureaucrats was composed of John Killick; Major-General G. Brown, later replaced by Brigadier-General M. Pitts, from Chief Land Operations; and the director general of Marine and Industrial Machinery Products from DSS, W.B. Christie.[14]

Brownrigg recounted that he, Dextraze, Jim Fox (Director Armour / Land Plans), Hampson, and some other armoured corps and RCEME (Royal Canadian Electrical and Mechanical Engineers) officers met to discuss the plans. Dextraze asked if Fox could live with a rebuilt Centurion, to which Fox answered yes. Dextraze then said that a new tank might be a possibility and that he wanted the options on his desk in less than three weeks. Using a huge chart spread around a room, the team charted out when the various tanks would be available, the support and logistics required for each option, and the risks at each stage of the purchase. The team, under Hampson's direction, visited tank manufacturers in Germany, France, and the United Kingdom and received news that they could probably secure the loan of a few dozen tanks to replace the Centurions and bridge the gap until their own tanks were ready.[15]

The team's analysis of tank options did not vary significantly from that produced in June 1975. They ruled out the M1 and Leopard 2 because they would not be available for some time, and they also ruled out the French AMX-30 and the British Chieftain. Of the two remaining vehicles, the Leopard 1 and M60, the team preferred the Leopard 1 for several reasons. It was newer than the M60 and was relatively light, forty-two tonnes to the Centurion's fifty-two.[16] Although it had less armour, it was fast and reliable and was armed with the same 105 mm gun as the Centurion. The Germans had agreed to loan Canada some tanks until KM could produce Leopard 1s for the Canadian army, probably in 1978. The army, especially Dextraze, had little interest in Head's pet project of leasing or renting tanks from the Germans on a permanent basis. Long-term leasing was an unattractive option because of both cost and legal and political ramifications.[17] The team concluded that the best option was to rent tanks from the German army temporarily so the Centurions could finally be retired and then to acquire the Leopard 1s in 1978. The team's first choice was the Leopard 1A4, but only about 250 of these were in service, so about an hour before presenting their findings to the Senior Review Board, they changed their recommendation to Leopard 1A3s. Thousands of these were in service with Germany, Belgium, Denmark, Australia, and the Netherlands, so spare parts and support from allies would be plentiful.[18]

The Leopard 1A3 was also currently in production, and KM would not have to retool its lines. The Australian army had tested the M60 against the Leopard 1 in 1972 and 1973 and had decided to purchase 101 Leopards, which were produced from 1976 to 1978. The Australian Leopard, the AS1, was very similar to the German army's variant, and the Canadian plan was to buy the Australian variant with only minor alterations so as to avoid significant retooling or developmental charges.[19] The Canadian army, however, incorporated three major additions, referred to as the "three beauties": an image-intensification viewer for the driver; the American AN/VVS-2, a searchlight produced by Varian in California; and a low-light sight for the main gun, the German Panzer-Ziel-und-Beobachtungsgerät 200. These would allow the Canadians to fight effectively at night, which was necessary because Soviet doctrine was to attack twenty-four hours a day.[20] The Defence Management Committee approved the proposal, with minor revisions, on 5 April 1976.[21]

Cabinet met to discuss the tank purchase just a few weeks later, on 20 May 1976, seven years to the day after it had approved Allard's ill-fated plan. The project team's memo that the ministers read compared the modernization of the Centurion to the purchase of the new Leopard 1. The team had investigated three proposals to modernize the Centurion, one from KM and two from the British firm Vickers. Because neither of these companies had actually undertaken a Centurion modernization in quantity, the project was filled with unknowns, but the army chose one of the proposals from Vickers as the most realistic option.

Vickers estimated that it could deliver refurbished Centurions starting in April 1980 and could finish the program by January 1982, but this would necessitate a rebuild to squeeze a few more years out of Canada's existing tanks. The army's estimate for the overhaul of 128 Centurions was $65 million, close to the estimate from the summer of 1975 of $60 million for 113 Centurions, but the total project costs had risen to roughly $150 million. The major increase was due to a contingency fund of more than $20 million, logistics support of roughly $25 million, and a $16-million rebuild of Centurions to keep them running until the overhauled tanks came into service in 1980. Vickers also promised $10 million worth of industrial and regional benefits (IRBs), a contractual obligation to buy Canadian products in order to offset the costs of the purchase. Logistics support would be difficult and spare parts costly because Canada would be the sole operator of refurbished Centurions in Europe. The modernization was possible – the Israeli army had used their modified Centurions quite effectively in the October War – but the Canadians had little information on their program, and the whole project held many technical risks.

The memo argued that the Leopard was a much more attractive alternative for many reasons. It met Canada's need at a reasonable cost, and it would be easier to field and maintain. Not only was it reliable, but spare parts would be plentiful and cheap because the tank was in service with six other NATO countries. Although the Centurion and the Leopard had the same gun and the Centurion had better armour, the memo noted that the army needed the Leopard's excellent mobility on the European battlefield more than it needed armour. However, the Leopard was more expensive: 128 new tanks would cost about $160 million. The tanks could start arriving in January 1978, with the order completed by April 1979.

If Canada chose to purchase Leopards from Germany, it could get $3.5 million from KM for the old Centurion fleet, and the company, which had a good reputation for fulfilling offset obligations, could offer IRBs worth 30 to 50 percent of the value of the contract. Although allies would probably be happy with either option, buying Leopards from KM would obviously help German-Canadian relations, and it would be less risky than the Centurion modernization. The paper concluded that the government should buy 128 Leopard 1s and negotiate to dispose of the Centurion fleet through KM.[22]

Cabinet was already prepared to accept this recommendation, so there was a minimum of discussion on the matter. The foreign minister, Allan MacEachen, sent a message from Europe that he was being criticized by NATO allies for the recent cancellation of Lockheed's bid for the long-range patrol aircraft program. He wanted to deflect this with a firm statement on Canada's plans for new tanks for Canadian forces in Central Europe. Most ministers were sympathetic but did not want to prejudice negotiations with the manufacturer. Trudeau was adamant that the "final decision on procurement of the Leopard be subject to the successful conclusion of iron-clad undertakings on the part of the suppliers, particularly with respect to offsets [IRBs]." Cabinet agreed that the military could purchase 128 Leopards and rent thirty-five tanks as an interim measure; word was then sent to MacEachen that he could announce this decision to NATO allies.[23]

The Treasury Board approved the purchase on 3 June 1976, and the contract went to DSS for negotiations on 14 June. National Defence wanted to finalize the deal by late September, with a guarantee that its order could be squeezed in before KM retooled its lines to produce Leopard 2s for the German army.[24] The negotiations took place at KM's main plant during the summer shutdown. Every report on the negotiation from multiple government offices noted that it had gone smoothly and that the relationship between the Canadians and the Germans was cordial.[25] In one report, Hampson commented that "they [KM] negotiated as very tough and knowledgeable businessmen, but once an agreement was reached the firms were dedicated to achieving their contract obligations."[26] Mac Campbell stated that there was real trust between the Canadians and Germans as they negotiated, and no significant problems arose. The Canadians were impressed by the company's professionalism and intimate knowledge of the vehicle and were able to talk directly to the firm's design and engineering staff. On a lighter note, Campbell recalled that for the first few days of negotiations, the Germans would take the Canadians out for long lunches, often involving multiple beers. To avoid having the negotiations drawn out by these long lunches, Campbell suggested that they bring sandwiches and coffee to the plant instead.[27] They completed negotiations by 6 August 1976 and signed the contract on 12 October 1976.[28]

The only real hiccup during negotiations was German hesitation over the Canadian Financial Administration Act. By law, the government allocated funds on an annual basis, and if the government were to run out of money during a major, multiyear purchase, there would be no legal redress for the contractor. Deputy Minister of National Defence C.R. Nixon wrote:

> Although Parliament has authorized the Department to enter into contracts which obligate it to make payments in future years, Section 33 of the Financial Administration Act prevents these contracts from being legally binding by making future payments subject to future Appropriation Acts. For some reason, Canadian corporations have been willing to accept this situation. I suspect that most, if not all of them, do not fully understand that the Financial Administration Act makes the contracts "not worth the paper they are written on" insofar as future payments are concerned.

Since the Germans were understandably hesitant to sign a contract subject to this clause, a compromise was made: DND agreed to relinquish all rights to equipment under production if Canada failed to make a payment because of Section 33.[29] Brownrigg also noted that the Canadians agreed to extract concessions from the manufacturers of the three supplementary items and get them to cover any delays or problems with that materiel instead of KM being responsible.[30]

One additional feature of the negotiations was the purchase of spare parts. A modern tank requires thousands of different parts, ranging from washers to entire engines, as well as specialized test equipment to verify the operation of components on the vehicle. The German army's supply catalogue listed 15,500 different line items for spare parts for the Leopard.[31] For each vehicle, RCEME, responsible for maintaining vehicles, developed a policy that specified both the required maintenance to keep the vehicle running and the required supplies of spare parts. This policy is essential to ensure that the depots are fully stocked, because larger and more complex parts, such as engines, have a longer lead time than small items, such as washers. The team signed the contract for major components in December 1976 and then addressed the smaller items with a series of seventy-eight amendments to the original contract and fifty-three new contracts.[32] The army developed its estimates for the required spare parts from the army's Maintenance Policy, input from Director Procurement Supply Support, the contractor's advice, and information from other armies using the Leopard. Although the Canadians negotiated a contract in January 1978 for smaller spare parts, there would be some delay in delivery, and the Canadian supply depots would not be fully stocked upon arrival of the Canadian tanks, termed Leopard C1s. To accommodate the delay, Hampson secured a guarantee from KM that it would support the tank and that Canadian supply officers could buy spare parts directly from one of KM's companies if there was an emergency.[33] The Canadians also secured the promise that they would receive the entire package of technical drawings for the Leopard and its spare parts, which was kept in a sealed vault in Switzerland in case of emergency or war.[34]

The last hurdle arose in early October. When the Treasury Board reviewed the contract, it did not find justification for the "three beauties": the driver's image-intensification viewer, the search-light, and the night-sight. The board estimated the costs at $5 to $20 million, so it instructed DND to put the items on hold until the army prepared another submission justifying the purchase of the three special items.[35] The army resolved the problem quickly and the Treasury Board approved the three extra items.[36]

The first German rental tanks, Leopard 1A2s, started arriving in late 1976, and the full complement of thirty-five arrived by April 1977.[37] In a ceremony on 2 June 1977, which Dextraze attended, Canada's Centurions in Europe were finally retired from service.[38] Gesellschaft für Logistischen Service, one of KM's holdings, handled disposal of the Centurion fleet; there was some delay in selling them because External Affairs insisted on stringent requirements on the sale of the Centurion, and it took nearly a year and half for the department to establish acceptable end-user certificates to prevent the tanks from falling into unsavoury hands. Once this was achieved, disposal of the tanks in Europe went quickly, but they brought in little money. Twenty-one complete tanks were sold to Switzerland, seven bridge layers went to Denmark, and the turrets of the remaining sixty-eight were sold to Austria as static border defences and the hulls cut for scrap. The remainder of Canada's Centurion spare parts were sold to Denmark. Of the Centurions located in Canada, sixty served as monuments or hard targets and the rest were sold.[39] By 1979, all of Canada's Centurions and spare parts had been sold or disposed of.[40]

The army had hoped that the sale of the Centurions in Europe would bring in $5 to $6 million, but the total value was only $1.25 million.[41] Hampson noted that there was little incentive for Gesellschaft für Logistischen Service to seek out the best deal and recommended that Crown Assets Disposal Canada should handle disposal in future projects.[42] In 1982, the Treasury Board assessed the Leopard purchase, noting that the sale of the total Centurion fleet, on both continents, had brought in only $2 million rather than the expected $16 million. The report recommended, like Hampson, that disposal of existing equipment should be handled separately.[43]

To bridge the gap between the Centurions and the new Canadian tanks, the Germans scrounged for Leopard 1A2s to equip 4 CMBG, even taking some from a training range in Wales, and supplied thirty-two gun tanks, two recovery tanks, and one bridge layer. The total cost of the rental of thirty-five tanks for approximately two years was $2.7 million, a bargain price that basically covered the cost of inspecting and repairing the tanks after the Canadians had returned them.[44] The Canadian embassy in Bonn and Canadian Forces Europe handled the rental negotiations, which were cooperative and straightforward.[45]

When the 1A2s started arriving, Clive Milner, the commanding officer of Canada's armoured regiment in Europe, the Royal Canadian Dragoons (RCDs), recalled that when he asked Technical Services in Ottawa to translate the Leopard manuals, they responded that it would take two years. The army obviously could not wait this long, so the RCDs sent some officers to the German armour school in Münster in October 1976 to develop training materials and an instructor cadre for the rest of the unit. Milner noted that an officer named Harry Mohr was instrumental in helping the regiment adapt to the Leopards.[46] Mohr's parents were Sudeten Germans who had immigrated to Canada in 1956, when he was eleven, so Mohr could speak German. He and some other soldiers literally cut and pasted from the German manuals as they developed materials to train Canadian troops, including adaptation courses in gunnery, driving and maintenance, communications, and a course for crew commanders.[47] Four CMBG ran these courses in January 1977; although the training was rushed, it worked, and the brigade was operational with the rental Leopards in mid-1977.[48]

The Germans supplied six sergeants experienced in supply and maintenance to help keep the tanks running. They also gave the Canadians access to the German supply system and to spare parts, fuels, and lubricants during the loan period.[49] Later reports, and every interview, confirmed that relations between the two armies in terms of supply and maintenance were good.[50] Clive Milner and Jim Fox commented that the Germans helped out immensely with the rental Leopards and that technicians from the German army or KM would come down at the slightest hint of a problem. Milner also noted that the Canadians did everything they could to ensure they were maintaining the tanks properly.[51] The rental agreement included a limit of 1,450 kilometres for gun tanks for the first year and 1,200 for subsequent years.[52]

Terry Seeley, the regimental second-in-command from 1977 to 1979, stated: "On one or two exercises ... we were well in excess of 1200 to 2000 kilometres on the vehicle. Not with the Centurion. You were lucky on an exercise using the Centurion to get any more than about maybe 100 kilometres, 150, 200 kilometres out of it."[53] The turret and crew compartment of the Leopard was smaller than the Centurion, but the Leopard was almost twice as fast.[54] Although the Centurion retained its edge in armour, this made the tank so heavy that it could not cross some bridges, and its tracks would rip up the asphalt on roads. Milner also noted that the brigade's tactics changed with the Leopards and that the infantry in armoured personnel carriers did not have to wait for the slow Centurions to catch up. It was, he said, "like going from a Beetle to a Porsche."[55] The Leopard was also much easier to maintain. An engine change on the Centurion could take up to forty-eight hours, but, according to Seeley, a good crew could change an engine on a Leopard in fourteen minutes.[56] This might have been a record, but every soldier attested to the tank's reliability and ease of maintenance.[57] The Leopard engine also used diesel, not gas like the Centurion, so it was easier to get fuel from German or American stocks.[58]

One of the highlights during the rental period was winning the Canadian Army Trophy in 1977. Canada originally sponsored the trophy in 1963 to improve tank gunnery in the armies in Central Europe and won in the centennial year of 1967. Canada withdrew from the competition from 1971 to 1975, and the RCDs were unsure if they would compete in 1977, given that they had just fielded rental tanks. At the insistence of the colonel of the regiment, Merritt "Bomber" Bateman, a Second World War veteran, the Canadians submitted a team drawn from the RCDs.[59] Participating countries supplied twelve tanks with crews to go on a simulated battle run, and each tank had ten rounds of main gun ammunition and a hundred rounds of machine gun ammunition. A troop of three tanks would advance and fire at fifteen moving and static targets with the main gun at ranges up to two kilometres, as well as at six groups of ten machine gun targets at closer range. The judges assessed the performance of each troop based on its speed of completion and use of ammunition.[60] The Canadians were a Cinderella team, but as Clive Milner noted in his pre-tournament speech, "Cinderella had a lot of ugly step-sisters too." Ramsey Withers, commander of Canadian Forces Europe, presented the victorious RCDs with a case of champagne on the firing pad.[61]

The first batch of Leopard C1s rolled off KM's lines in July 1978 and arrived at the Combat Arms School in Gagetown in August, where they replaced Canada's last Centurions still being used for training.[62] When the first four Leopards arrived, KM's representative, August Feigel, wanted to take them around the perimeter of Gagetown, something the venerable Centurion could not do without breaking down multiple times. The Canadians were frustrated, thinking that they would have to set up recovery vehicles to repair the Leopards, but to their surprise, the four Leopards were still in good repair after completing the circuit.[63]

The school sent driving and maintenance instructors to the RCDs in Germany, and some gunnery instructors went to a NATO armour school in Belgium.[64] Bill Coupland, chief instructor at the armour school in Gagetown from 1977 to

1979, recounted that the manuals needed to be completely rewritten. The driving and maintenance manual took eight months to produce and had to be translated into "Canadianese," and the French manual was also difficult. The soldiers at the armour school did this work in-house at the school.[65] In the interim, they relied on manuals developed during the rental period and on Australian manuals.[66] The manuals were still not completed by 1981, when the Project Management Office closed and the Leopard project fell under the authority of the life cycle materiel manager.[67]

The manual problem was a small one in the grand scheme of the purchase, and once the crews and instructors had adapted to the tank, things ran smoothly. With the tanks at Gagetown being run nearly twenty-four hours a day upon arrival, there was fear of wearing them out.[68] The army also built a new five-kilometre closed driving circuit for the Leopards. While the Centurion had been so slow that the instructor could easily stop the vehicle in time if there was danger of hitting another tank, the Leopard was too fast and therefore needed a longer circuit.[69]

The Canadians in Europe received their first C1s in late 1978 and returned the rentals, four a time, as the new tanks came in. The two-year rental of the Leopard 1A2s had provided good training and preparation for the arrival of the C1s, and the army put the new tanks through their paces with two major exercises in late 1979.[70] Koeller commented that the introduction was smooth and that, unlike some other pieces of equipment, the Leopard 1s were fully operational upon delivery.[71] There were some minor changes to the tank, and the armoured corps also insisted that the turret contain a cooker to boil water for soup or tea, which posed some difficulties for KM's engineers. For minor modifications such as the location of brackets in the turret, KM had an exact wooden mock-up of a turret at its main plant. If there was a change, a soldier from the RCDs would travel down and confer with KM's engineers, who would tape up the bracket or change and then fold it into production.[72] The major differences between the rental 1A2s and the C1s were that the latter had a larger turret with spaced armour and the Belgian SABCA fire control system with a laser range-finder. Jim Gervais commented that the SABCA was the most advanced system in service on Leopard tanks, and it was accurate and quick.[73] It had seven sensors that accounted for wind speed or temperature and automatically adjusted the gun, but it experienced a few glitches.[74] In one instance, the system did not account for the heat expansion of the turret during repeated firing, so at long distances, rounds would miss just over their targets.[75] On sunny days in the summer, the top of the gun barrel would droop slightly because of the heat, causing rounds to miss just below the target.[76] These unanticipated problems, common to all nations that used the SABCA system, were resolved after some consultation with the manufacturer.[77]

According to Seeley, the arrival of the Leopard, despite these problems, improved morale dramatically because of its speed and manoeuvrability compared to the "clapped-out" Centurion. "You could disperse it and bring it together rapidly," said Seeley, "and use the entire regiment as a hammer."[78] The Leopard's major advantages over the Centurion were its speed and reliability. An army report from 1982 noted, "The mechanical performance of the fleet to date has been good and is an outstanding improvement over the Centurion." The Leopard, it went on, was "a fairly simple, effective MBT, with a simple durable and well designed engine and powertrain."[79] Lieutenant-Colonel Hampson noted that personnel worked overtime to make the introduction a success, and maintenance, logistics, and training personnel had a hard time keeping up with demand. Overall, eighty-seven Leopards were in Europe as part of 4 CMBG's complement for a full regiment with war stocks; thirty-one went to Canadian Forces Base Gagetown for training, with nineteen tanks and one armoured recovery vehicle forming a squadron of tanks for training and the rest being used at the Combat Arms School; five were for logistic stocks in Canada; four were in Canadian Forces Base Borden for technician training; and one went to Land Engineering Test Establishment in Ottawa.[80]

Once the C1s entered service, they were under warranty for six months or two thousand kilometres of use. KM also provided six field service representatives, three in Canada and three in Europe, to help with the introduction of the tanks and to assess warranty claims. The company also guaranteed that it would help keep the tanks running in an emergency. Army reports noted that the three representatives in Canada spoke good English, had a good rapport with the army, and supported most warranty claims. The representatives in Europe were also good but did not speak English, were not always on site, and frequently denied warranty claims, blaming the operator for mistakes.[81]

The Germans also established the Leopard Club, an organization for the exchange of information on training, logistics, and operational use. Three major sub-groups of the Leopard Club – Combat Improvement, Training, and Logistics – would meet twice a year at meetings coordinated by the Germans.[82] Canada joined the Leopard Club in early 1977, and these meetings produced reams of data, some of it very technical, such as a panzer brigade's test of a new type of oil.[83] Since this kind of detailed discussion allowed the army to quickly resolve many problems and adopt the best practices from other countries, the army saw the Leopard Club as very beneficial.[84] Bill Coupland, the Canadian representative on the training group, concurred.[85]

The Leopard Club also facilitated the supply of spare parts and repairs for the Leopard fleet. Each year, member nations would submit their requests for spare parts and rebuilt assemblies to the German Ministry of Defence, and the

Germans would make spare parts available for pickup at their supply depots. The Canadians in Europe picked up their spare parts at a German army depot at Herbolzheim, eighteen kilometres from the major base at Lahr. Other countries could submit to have their manufacturers included in the production of spare parts, but otherwise, all the contracts were done through the German Ministry of Defence. Canada joined this arrangement in 1977, the only wrinkle being that the Canadians needed longer lead times for spare parts for the Leopard fleet in Canada, which took time to arrive by sea.[86] Gerry Koeller commented that this arrangement worked effectively.[87]

Army and Treasury Board reports after the purchase noted problems in acquiring sufficient stocks of spare parts, tools, and test equipment, which sometimes slowed training.[88] The Canadian liaison officer in Munich noted that greater coordination was needed early on in the provision of tools, test equipment, manuals, spare parts, and training.[89] Soldiers who served in Europe and Canada commented that there were no notable delays in the supply of spare parts and no degradation of training or combat capability.[90] It is likely that the Leopard's reliability, especially compared to the Centurion, masked many problems as well. Gerry Koeller noted that while the supply of spare parts in Germany was good, some unexpected problems arose at Gagetown because the terrain was less forgiving than that of Central Europe. The final drive was bolted onto a housing on the vehicle, but the shale and stone in New Brunswick wore off the one-and-a-half-inch-thick heads of the bolts so much that the crew could not get a wrench or socket on them. The project officers could not anticipate such problems, and it was difficult to quickly restock Gagetown because it was so far from the German supply depots.[91]

A Treasury Board report noted with disapproval that Canada had no facilities that could produce spare parts for the tank and was therefore totally reliant upon KM and its subcontractors.[92] This criticism was legitimate but unrealistic, given that Canadian self-sufficiency would be exceedingly expensive and that there was no guarantee of the reliability of parts. The decision to rely on the Leopard Club and the German army simplified logistics and meant that the army did not need to cobble together a supply system from both sides of the Atlantic.

One of the central features of the purchase was the IRB program, which Trudeau had emphasized in Cabinet. The procurement of the Leopard C1 was the first major program to require foreign contractors to spend a proportion of the contract's value in Canada. Despite KM's hesitation, the Canadians secured contractual obligations for KM to spend 40 percent of the contract's value in Canada within ten years and a "best efforts" clause to get to 60 percent. The criteria were entirely quantitative, with no requirements for licence production of parts or assemblies in Canada or technology transfers. Only manufactured products counted as offsets, although some semi-processed materials were acceptable. The value of the offset was determined by the Canadian content of the product, whether it was labour, raw materials, or transportation. KM negotiated the provision that any purchases by its holdings or associated companies would count against the offset targets, as long as there was some proof that it had occurred because of the efforts of the contractor.[93] Canadian wine served on Lufthansa and KLM (Royal Dutch Airlines) flights, as well as Nova Scotia lobster served in Munich, counted as offsets in the Leopard program because the companies that bought these products were associated with KM.[94] The cost for administering the offset program amounted to roughly $1.3 million, which was folded into the price of each vehicle.[95]

In the summer of 1976, representatives from KM's subcontractors visited Canada for several months to canvass possible Canadian companies for offsets. They showed interest in electronics, as well as fine castings and wood products, but none of these purchases was likely to be directly related to the production of the Leopard. The German company Diehl was interested in establishing a factory in southwestern Ontario to assemble track for armoured vehicles; it eventually did so, although the plant is no longer in operation.[96] By January 1978, KM had $19 million worth of orders in Canada, of which $10 million had been backed up by formal contracts, representing 28 percent of the commitment.[97] By November 1979, it had met 40.5 percent of the total offset commitment, and four years after the contract was signed, KM had reached 54 percent of its obligation for offsets in the ten-year period.[98] However, 80 percent of the money went to Ontario and Quebec for manufactured components, with New Brunswick, British Columbia, and Manitoba only supplying some plywood and agricultural products.[99] To resolve this, the Department of Industry, Trade, and Commerce sponsored a trip in May 1980 for sixteen representatives from twelve German firms to come to the Maritimes and the West to show off 175 Canadian companies. The trip report was hopeful, noting that feedback from the participants was good and that the Germans were optimistic about opportunities for Canadian industry.[100] By 1982, KM was close to the contract requirement, having spent 32 percent of the entire contract value in Canada, and the offset program was declared a success.[101]

The final feature of the purchase was the fluctuating exchange rate. The estimated cost of the purchase at April 1975 exchange rates was $184.9 million, but by November 1979, the rising exchange rate had increased the cost to $261.5 million. Costs in 1978–79 rose at a rate of 41.6 percent and at a further 20 percent in 1979–80.[102] C.R. Nixon tried to move funds forward to avoid the escalating exchange rate; in a handwritten note attached to a submission asking for

$55 million to cover escalation in 1978, he wrote: "P.S. Minister, it is particularly disappointing that we were stymied about 2 years by T.B. Secretariat *and* Mr. Goyer when we attempted to advance some payments in order to regulate our cash flow ... Had we been successful, some of the extra $55 million would not have been required" (emphasis in original).[103] There was nothing that the contractor or the army could do about it, and the Treasury Board approved all the increases caused by the exchange rate. Apart from that expense, the deal actually ended up under budget by $850,000.[104]

The Leopard certainly helped German-Canadian relations: the Germans were delighted that the Canadians had purchased their vehicle. The German defence minister, Georg Leber, who had pressed the Canadians for tanks, expressed his happiness to Halstead in January 1977 about the improving defence relationship between the two countries and said he wanted to visit the Canadian troops in Lahr.[105] The Leopard also played a large part in the close relations between Leber and James Richardson's successor as defence minister, Barney Danson.[106]

Despite this, there was some criticism that Canada was getting an old tank. It is true that Canada received some of the last Leopard 1s to be produced, and the generation of tanks fielded by allies in the early 1980s – the M1 Abrams, Leopard 2, and the Challenger – were significantly better than the Leopard 1.[107] The Soviets also improved their armoured forces, with factories in the Urals continuing to churn out new tanks. By the late 1980s, analysts were discussing the Leopard C1's vulnerability to the latest Soviet tanks and the need for a new vehicle.[108] In meetings of the Standing Committee on External Affairs and National Defence, Conservatives Allan McKinnon and Robert Coates continually pressed military officers and James Richardson – later, Barney Danson – about why Canada had purchased the Leopard when allies were on the cusp of introducing new tanks with larger guns.[109] In December 1975, Andrew Brewin, defence critic for the NDP, asked Dextraze if it would not be better to refit the Centurion and buy a state-of-the-art tank ten years down the road rather than buying the Leopard 1. The general responded with some homespun wisdom: "My father used to say, wait for two years and you will get a much better car; when the two years were up he would say, wait another two years because it's going to be even better then."[110] But Dextraze knew that the window of opportunity, both fiscal and political, might not be open for long.

These imperatives set the stage for a successful procurement. The need to field a limited number of serviceable tanks with a limited budget forced the army to adopt modest objectives, so the team wisely bought a vehicle that was in production and in service, with a minimum of alterations and modest IRBs. The German company had produced thousands of Leopards since 1965 for various customers, and Canada effectively bought "off the shelf." There were no major teething troubles for the C1, unlike the M1 Abrams introduced in the early 1980s, and the project had little technical risk. Only one major engineering change to the vehicle was necessary, and consequently, there was little fluctuation in the cost of the actual tanks: the estimate for the Leopards was $110,099,500, and the actual cost was $114,010,700.[111] Although Canada did not develop any facilities to produce sophisticated components for the Leopard or acquire any technology transfers, it was a reasonable choice. The Canadian army's needs were too small to support any nascent industries, and Canada's ability to compete with European sources and their well-established networks and proximity to the Leopard fleet was questionable.

Political support for the project was also essential. In many analyses of procurement, the criticism is that politics, whether in the form of favouritism with contractors or arbitrary decisions made without regard for professional military advice, makes acquisitions more costly and endangers soldiers in the field. This was not the case with the Leopard, where politics was not a liability but an asset. Trudeau did not want to buy the tanks, but he had been convinced that they were necessary to facilitate Canada's broader foreign policy objectives, so every soldier, bureaucrat, and member of Cabinet knew that they were a priority. Less than a year after the military earmarked funds for the tanks, there was a signed contract.

The Germans were also accommodating at all levels of government, industry, and military, which was not surprising given their country's interest in keeping Canadian forces in Europe equipped with tanks. They did their best to ensure that the purchase moved along quickly and did not take advantage of the Canadians, despite being the sole source. The German government and army assisted the Canadians with the bargain price for rental tanks and ensured that the Canadians were trained and had enough spare parts and technical knowledge to keep the tanks running. The cooperation between the two armies did not end once the C1s arrived, and the Leopard Club allowed Canada to draw on the resources of Germany and other nations that operated the tank.

This is not to diminish the achievements of the Project Management Office. A small team of five officers directly tasked to the project and one civilian negotiator effectively managed one of the largest programs for the army during the Cold War, in terms of time and money, and delivered a first-class armoured vehicle.[112] Lieutenant-General Ramsey Withers, VCDS, noted "that this was a very successful project and commended Col Hampson and the SRB [Senior Review Board] on their efforts. The project was launched rapidly, carried out expeditiously, on time and within cost."[113] The Office of the Auditor-General was also favourable: in its 1984 report, it pronounced the acquisition of the Leopard a success, declaring that it was executed with "due regard for economy and efficiency."[114]

Conclusion

FROM 1963 TO 1975, the maintenance of a few thousand soldiers in Europe posed a difficult problem for Canadian policy-makers. Not only was the brigade expensive to equip and maintain; it ate up a large proportion of the army's strength while constituting a tiny percentage of NATO's forces. Canada's allies, however, wanted it to remain in Europe. Although there was some talk of withdrawal, the main debate centred on whether the brigade would have heavy or light vehicles, and each option acquired significance far beyond the thickness of the armour or the calibre of the gun. For some soldiers in the 1960s, light vehicles were the future of land warfare, and for the revisionists, they were a symbol of Canadian interests in 1969 and an assertion of the civilian control of defence policy in the early 1970s. For allies, Canadian diplomats, and the traditionalists, heavy vehicles remained the physical manifestation of Canada's commitment to Europe and its allies, and for most soldiers, they were a critical component of a modern army. By late 1975, Canada's allies had convinced a skeptical Trudeau of the political rationale for tanks, but the matter faded in importance the following year as the government's attention shifted to the battle for Canadian unity after the election of René Lévesque's Parti Québécois. There was some talk in the mid-1980s of putting Canada's forces on the flanks to support Norway, but not enough political support could be garnered to push this idea past the protests of the army and NATO allies.[1] Ironically, the 1987 DND White Paper announced that Canada would go back to a commitment of a two-brigade division for the Central Front, but there was no political will to implement this plan. The White Paper was so out of sync with the strategic climate and the fiscal situation in Canada that it was a dead letter by 1989. Canadian troops finally came home from Europe in 1994.

The present analysis of the defence policy debate over Canadian troops in Europe and the Leopard C1 sheds some light on the army's many difficulties during this period. But like other recent works, it undermines the "Golden Age" narrative of the Canadian army, according to which the army suffered a slow decline from a peacetime high in the 1950s until disaster in the 1990s.[2] Many authors have noted the stresses caused by the frequent restructurings and the budget freeze from 1963 to 1975, stresses that were quite apparent while the army struggled to equip and structure itself. But after 1975, the army had the stable funding and personnel levels needed to rebuild a settled, if reduced, organization with a clear mission and some important pieces of new equipment, primarily the Leopard. This continued until 1989 and should cause more questioning of the narrative of decline and neglect of the Cold War military.[3] The second half of the Cold War should also be judged on its own merits, not on the supposed peak of the 1950s, when a volatile international climate, the fresh memories of the Second World War, and an unprecedented foreign policy consensus in Canada allowed for high defence spending and a clear defence policy.

There was another dynamic as the army struggled to balance itself between the demands of Central Europe, which called for a mechanized army with tanks, and the demands of the rest of the world, including Canada, which called for light deployable forces with DFSVs. The 1964 Defence Department White Paper started the process of shifting the army away from Europe, and this accelerated with the renegotiation of NATO commitments in 1967. The Trudeau government made it a point to wrench the army from Europe and base its planning on domestic needs, symbolized by the withdrawal of the Centurion, but the army became disenchanted with this plan. By 1975, it had defeated this challenge, with the assistance of allies, and for the rest of the Cold War, its planning was based on the possibility of a large-scale war in Central Europe.[4] Future work on the army could use a periodization based on 1963 to 1975 as the era when the army turned its eye from Europe to develop forces for use around the world and then, at the revisionists' instigation, turned inward. From 1975 to 1989, the focus, as it had been in the 1950s and early 1960s, returned to Europe.

Although the military's lot improved, Canada's relationship with NATO remained frustrating. Henry Kissinger captured this in his sole substantial reference to Canada in *The White House Years,* using words that could have been applied directly to the tank issue:

> Unlike the European countries, it [Canada] was not directly threatened; unlike the United States, it could not be decisive in the common defense; the Canadian defense contribution would be marginal compared with that of the major European powers or the United States. Canada's ties, therefore, had above all a strong symbolic character. ... Canada, in fact, was beset by ambivalences which, while different from those of Europe, created their own complexities. ... Its instinct in favor of common defense conflicted with the temptation to stay above the battle as a kind of international arbiter.[5]

As Kissinger noted, Canadian contributions were never going to be decisive and probably never will be; therefore, Canada will never have much influence in the formation of strategy, although it might enjoy some limited tactical influence.

Whether Canadian contributions can win sway with specific allies in the pursuit of foreign policy goals is contingent upon varying circumstances, but generally, the influence purchased by Canada's military commitments is limited. During the Cold War, NATO offered few opportunities for Canada to resist the inexorable economic and cultural pull of the United States, and Canada's voice counted for little in the chanceries of the European capitals. Although Canada had legitimate security interests in preserving peace on a continent with nearly a hundred thousand Canadian graves, it is apparent that Canada's military contributions were maintained, and from time to time qualitatively improved, primarily out of concern for the negative consequences of not doing so, not for their positive value in enhancing Canada's economic prospects or influence. They were the "club dues" that maintained good relationships with allies; they won little else but a place at the table.[6]

This book shows that for a brief moment, Canadian troops in Europe were indeed an entry to Europe, but this flowed primarily from Helmut Schmidt's unique approach to Canada; closer West German–Canadian relations in the late 1970s and early 1980s were based on the friendship between the two leaders.[7] The purchase of tanks very likely helped Canada's negotiations with the EEC that produced the contractual link in July 1976, but the Third Option amounted to little, and the Canada-US relationship intensified. There might be some situations when Canada can win some influence with its contributions, but it should have modest expectations of its military contributions to NATO: despite its skill and competence, the Canadian military will never be decisive, and consequently, its influence will generally be limited. More research is required to examine the value of Canada's "club dues" in the post–Cold War era – particularly its contributions to the peacekeeping and humanitarian operations of the 1990s, the war in Afghanistan, and other alliance operations.

Although Canada's relationship with NATO rarely gains the attention of the public, defence procurement makes the headlines more frequently. Many Canadian pundits and authors argue that the procurement process is overly politicized or too slow and is stifled by cumbersome bureaucracies and red tape. In the United States, there is significant criticism of the Pentagon's oversight of bungled or cancelled programs, and since the 1960s, many commentators have argued that the military-industrial complex has siphoned off billions of taxpayer dollars.[8] There is even a dark comedy – *The Pentagon Wars*, starring Kelsey Grammer and Cary Elwes – about the intrigue surrounding the development of the M2/M3 Bradley vehicle.[9]

For smaller countries like Canada, struggling to balance cost and the need for technologically advanced equipment, it is tempting to try and distill the lessons of the successful Leopard procurement and apply them to other projects, and there are some. The first is the importance of clear and reasonable objectives imparted by political and fiscal limits. The team responsible for purchasing the vehicle knew they needed to field a limited number of tanks quickly and at a reasonable cost, so they had modest objectives. This did not mean that the Canadians bought the cheapest option or an unsatisfactory tank: the Leopard C1 was the most expensive option of in-service tanks and a good vehicle. The second is the importance of politics, which can never be separated from procurement. Indeed, successful procurement requires political support. Few projects, even if they are essential or well managed, can prevail against skeptical politicians who control the purse strings and do not see the political utility of major projects. Although it was begrudging, the Leopard C1 had this support, as did the other major procurement projects in this era – the long-range patrol aircraft, the CF-18, the Armoured Vehicle General Purpose, and the City Class frigates. None of these went as smoothly as the Leopard procurement – all of them suffering their share of delays, setbacks, and mounting costs – but they were all ultimately successful because they had the political support, won through the DSR or by other means, to see them through.

The conclusions from the Leopard purchase cannot be taken too far, however. Although buying the Leopard off the shelf with few modifications and modest IRB requirements was a good decision, it does not mean that Canada and other small powers should apply this to all projects. The other major purchase of armoured vehicles in 1976, the Armoured Vehicle General Purpose, involved significant alterations to the original Swiss vehicle and an agreement to produce it under licence in Canada. The complexity of this deal did not undermine it; to the contrary, it led to the development of one of Canada's biggest defence export successes, the Light Armoured Vehicle. Each procurement project has its own imperatives, constraints, and opportunities, and although all must have clear political and fiscal limits, each must be judged individually. In his comprehensive history of US aircraft procurement in the Second World War, I.B. Holley, a major figure in technological and procurement history, stresses the uniqueness of each procurement process:

> In sum, effective procurement for national defense calls for a high order of leadership. Those who buy the nation's armament must develop sound political insight, a keen understanding of the arts of organization, and, not less than the officer who leads troops in the field, must display unusual courage. But they would do well to remember that there is simply no set of rules governing military procurement. To pretend to have found any such certainty is to court disaster. Continuing and unremitting study is the only alternative.[10]

More research on the major projects in this era would broaden the historical knowledge of the opportunities and perils of procurement.

Another area that requires more research is Trudeau's defence policy. He has been heavily criticized for his handling of the defence file, and some of this is justified. The attempt to recast defence policy in the late 1960s and early 1970s angered allies with little appreciable benefit, and the frozen budget ensured that the military's strength would continue to diminish. However, his critiques of flexible response and Canada's relationship with NATO were well founded, and the frozen defence budget, a legacy of the Pearson Cabinet, had been in place since 1963. There was little incentive to change it during détente and when allies were reducing spending.

By the mid-1970s, however, Trudeau had addressed these problems. The debate over the brigade in Europe was one of the "classrooms" for Trudeau's education in international affairs in which he learned the importance of Canada's small, but significant, military assets.[11] The second major change was the increase in defence spending. Some accounts emphasize Deputy Minister of National Defence Sylvain Cloutier's efforts to increase the defence budget; while it is true that these attempts were critical, they are sometimes portrayed as skilful bureaucratic manoeuvring that forced a recalcitrant Trudeau and Cabinet to increase spending.[12] This explanation, like "no tanks, no trade," is far too narrow: it is unlikely that the reason the defence budget doubled from 1976 to 1984 and a wholesale rearmament program began was because Trudeau was forced into it by threats from other leaders or that he was hoodwinked by his bureaucrats.

An anecdote from 1978 sheds more light on the matter. In August of that year, Trudeau returned from an economic summit in Europe and announced cuts of $2.5 billion to the federal budget to contend with inflation. The prospects for the defence budget were grim, and massive cuts would probably devastate the new procurement programs. In his memoirs, Barney Danson, the minister of defence at the time, recalls going to see Trudeau at night to plead with him to lessen the burden on defence and only impose a cut of $100 million for one year, even though other departments would suffer proportionally larger annual cuts. Trudeau agreed, although Danson knew there was going to be a fight in Cabinet as the ministers defended their territory. Danson's recollections from the Cabinet meeting are striking:

> Bob [president of the Treasury Board] read the press release itemizing the planned cuts, and as he neared the part on Defence, I anxiously peered at my notes. Then, when he read the paragraph on Defence I had given him, the room exploded in rage. If I wanted a friend under these circumstances, I would have to fetch my dog. Before I could begin my arguments, the prime minister spoke

> up and the room was suddenly silent. I wish I had a transcript of his exact words, but in essence he said that I had worked this out with him and that he was in full agreement. He went on to say that the military had, in effect, taken a budget cut every year for ten years by having its budget frozen while inflation took its toll. He reminded everyone that Defence was finally catching up and he was not going to see it fall behind again. I crumpled up my notepaper, tossed it under the table, and somehow restrained myself from crying with joy, kissing the prime minister, or even smiling smugly as my colleagues glowered at me. "OK, Bob. What's next?" asked the prime minister, as I said a silent prayer of gratitude.[13]

This episode and other questions in this era – namely, antisubmarine warfare, North American air defence, and the support for NATO in the late 1970s and early 1980s – require more examination, but researchers should no longer consider the Trudeau era as entirely a "long dark night of the spirit" for the armed forces.[14]

Some might argue, with justification, that Canadian security is too vital an issue to serve as an education for prime ministers in defence policy. This is true, but few countries have unblemished records, and Trudeau strove to understand the military problems that NATO faced, whether it was the tactics of tanks or how long a war would last. He did not simply accept or reject the professional advice of his bureaucracies; rather, he questioned and prodded his subordinates, did not hesitate to seek out alternative sources of advice, and realized when he needed to adjust course.[15] He made mistakes, but after 1975, he was a far better prime minister for defence than scholarship or public opinion would suggest, and his defence policy has been unfairly criticized. The military began to rebuild after more than a decade of turmoil, and the purchase of the Leopards was accompanied by the commitment of billions for new aircraft, ships, and other vehicles. Many historians have identified these changes, but they argue that Trudeau was forced into them despite his pacifist or anti-NATO inclinations. These assertions are false: If Trudeau had run roughshod over allies, DND, and External Affairs from 1969 to 1972, why would this not have continued? It is also at odds with Trudeau's character as a politician. He was not an opportunist and did not shy away from conflict or making people angry. Once convinced, his determination was an asset as he supported the Armed Forces when it was not politically expedient and when there were no more points to be scored with allies.

Notes

Introduction

1 Because most participants in this policy discussion used the term *tank* instead of the more accurate *main battle tank (MBT)*, I use the former term in this book.

2 See Chapter 1 of Aaron Plamondon, *The Politics of Procurement: Military Acquisition in Canada and the Sea King Helicopter* (Vancouver: UBC Press, 2010), and Randall Wakelam, *Cold War Fighters: Canadian Aircraft Procurement, 1945–54* (Vancouver: UBC Press, 2012), ix. Godefroy notes that the army's current process is "Conceive, Design, Build, and Manage." Andrew Godefroy, "Chasing the Silver Bullet," *Canadian Military Journal* 8, 1 (2007): 63. See also Robert Addinall, "To Transform an Army: The Canadian Interpretation of the RMA and the Transformation of Armoured Vehicle Design, 1992–2008 – The Case of the LAV III" (PhD diss., War Studies, Royal Military College, Kingston, ON, 2011), and Peter Kasurak, *A National Force* (Vancouver: UBC Press, 2013).

3 Some of the key programmatic works about this method are Trevor J. Pinch and Wiebe E. Bijker, "The Social Construction of Facts and Artefacts: Or How the Sociology of Science and the Sociology of Technology Might Benefit Each Other," *Social Studies of Science* 14, 3 (1984): 399–411, and Wiebe E. Bijker, Thomas P. Hughes, and Trevor J. Pinch, eds., *The Social Construction of Technological Systems: New Directions in the Sociology and History of Technology* (Cambridge, MA: MIT Press, 1987). See also Trevor Pinch, "The Social Construction of Technology: A Review," in *Technological Change: Methods and Themes in the History of Technology*, edited by Robert Fox (Amsterdam: Harwood Academic Press, 1996), 23–24; Paul Rosen, "The Social Construction of Mountain Bikes: Technology and Postmodernity in the Cycle Industry," *Social Studies of Science* 23, 3 (1993): 481–82; and Wiebe E. Bijker, *Of Bicycles, Bakelites, and Bulbs: Toward a Theory of Sociotechnical Change* (Cambridge, MA: MIT Press, 1995). For other applications of this methodology, see Donald Mackenzie, *Inventing Accuracy: A Historical Sociology of Nuclear Missile Guidance* (Cambridge, MA: MIT Press, 1990); Gabrielle Hecht, *The Radiance of France: Nuclear Power and National Identity after World War II* (Cambridge, MA: MIT Press, 1998); and Tiina Männistö-Funk, "The Crossroads of Technology and Tradition: Vernacular Bicycles in Rural Finland, 1880–1910," *Technology and Culture* 52, 4 (2011): 733–56. See also Glen Norcliffe, "G-COT: The Geographical Construction of Technology," *Science, Technology, and Human Values* 34, 4 (2009): 449–75.

4 See Michel Fortmann, Martin Larose, and Susan M. Murphy, "An Emerging Strategic Counterculture? Pierre Elliott Trudeau, Canadian Intellectuals and the Revision of Liberal Defence Policy concerning NATO (1968–1969)," *International Journal* 59, 3 (2004): 537–56.

5 "Supreme Allied Commander Europe (SACEUR)," *NATO*, 2016, http://www.nato.int/cps/en/natolive/topics_50110.htm.

6 The army legally ceased to exist in 1968 when the three services were formally abolished and the army's units and offices were parcelled out to Mobile Command in St. Hubert, Quebec, and to what eventually became Chief Land Doctrine and Operations in Ottawa. For simplicity's sake, this study will refer to the organizations overseeing Canada's land forces as the "army."

7 See Andrew Richter, *Avoiding Armageddon: Canadian Military Strategy and Nuclear Weapons, 1950–63* (Vancouver: UBC Press, 2002); Sean Maloney, *Learning to Love the Bomb* (Washington, DC: Potomac Books, 2007); and John Clearwater, *Canadian Nuclear Weapons* (Toronto: Dundurn Press, 1998), *"Just Dummies": Cruise Missile Testing in Canada* (Calgary: University of Calgary Press, 2006), and *U.S. Nuclear Weapons in Canada* (Toronto: Dundurn Press, 1999). For work on the Arctic, see Whitney P. Lackenbauer, Franklyn Griffiths, and Rob Huebert, *Canada and the Changing Arctic: Sovereignty, Security and Stewardship*, forewords by Bill Graham and Hugh Segal (Waterloo, ON: Wilfrid Laurier University Press, 2011), and Whitney P. Lackenbauer and Peter Kikkert's collection of primary sources, *The Canadian Forces and Arctic Sovereignty* (Waterloo, ON: Wilfrid Laurier University Press, 2010).

8 John English, *Just Watch Me: The Life of Pierre Elliott Trudeau* (Toronto: Knopf, 2009), 584–86.

9 Michael Hart notes in general terms how the reduction in 1969 and Trudeau's inattention to Europe in the early years of his time in office confused the Europeans when the Canadians abruptly reversed policy and tried to implement the Third Option, which never got off the ground. Michael Hart, *A Trading Nation: Canadian Trade Policy from Colonialism to Globalization* (Vancouver: UBC Press, 2002), 291–92.

10 Isabel Campbell, *Unlikely Diplomats: The Canadian Brigade in Germany, 1951–64* (Vancouver: UBC Press, 2013), 188–89.

11 In recent years, a number of reports have sought to ameliorate a defence procurement system in Canada that many argue is dysfunctional. See Alan S. Williams, *Reinventing Canadian Defence Procurement: A View from the Inside* (Montreal and Kingston: McGill-Queen's University Press, 2006); J.C. Stone, *A Separate Defence Procurement Agency: Will It Actually Make a Difference?* (Ottawa: Canadian International Council and Canadian Defence and Foreign Affairs Institute, 2012); Michael Byers and Stewart Webb, *That Sinking Feeling: Canada's Submarine Program Springs a Leak* (Ottawa: Canadian Centre for Policy Alternatives and Rideau Institute, 2013); Tom Jenkins, *Canada First: Leveraging Defence Procurement through Key Industrial Capabilities – Report of the Special Adviser to the Minister of Public Works and Government Services*, February 2013, http://www.tpsgc-pwgsc.gc.ca/app-acq/documents/eam-lmp-eng.pdf; Richard Shimooka, *Towards an International Model for Canadian Defence Procurement* (Ottawa: Conference of Defence Associations Institute, 2013); and Ross Fetterly, "Arming Canada: Defence Procurement for the Twenty-First Century" (PhD diss., War Studies, Royal Military College, Kingston, ON, 2011).

12 Sean Maloney, "The Royal Canadian Armoured Corps: An Illustrated History," Accessed May 14, 2012. http://www.seanmmaloney.com/canadian-armed-forces-operations/the-royal-canadian-armoured-corps-an-illustrated-history-co-authored-with-john-marteinson-and-michael-mcnorgan-foreword-by-desmond-morton-toronto-robin-brass-200/.

13 See Godefroy, "Chasing the Silver Bullet," and Andrew Godefroy, *In Peace Prepared* (Vancouver: UBC Press, 2015).

14 See Wakelam, *Cold War Fighters*, ix, for a succinct definition of "force structure."

15 When quoting from diplomatic cables, this study will not retain all upper case and will replace the "not/not" or "no/no" convention with "not" or "no." Apart from that, there will be no changes.

Chapter 1: The 1964 *White Paper on Defence*

1 G.S. Foggo, "The Army Council: Minutes of the 63/33 Meeting," 29 July 1963, file 1725, Robert Lewis Raymont fonds, 73-1223, series 3, box 83, Directorate of History and Heritage, National Defence Headquarters, Ottawa (hereafter DHH).

2 P.C. Dobell to D. Kirkwood and H. Robinson, "Future Disposition of the Balance of the Division Earmarked as Part of SACEUR's Strategic Reserve," 3 November 1965, file 27-4-NATO-1-SACEUR, Records of the Department of External Affairs, RG 25, vol. 11399, Library and Archives Canada, Ottawa (hereafter LAC); meeting of Special Committee on Defence, 18 June 1963, accessed at Canadian Command and Staff College, Fort Frontenac Library, Kingston, ON (hereafter FFL).
3 Meeting of Special Committee on Defence, 11 July 1963, FFL.
4 John Marteinson and Michael McNorgan, *The Royal Canadian Armoured Corps: An Illustrated History,* with Sean M. Maloney, foreword by Desmond Morton (Toronto: Canadian Royal Armoured Corps Association and Canadian War Museum, 2000), 346. Christopher F. Foss, ed., *Jane's Armour and Artillery: 1990–1991* (London: Jane's Information Group, 1991), 133.
5 Marteinson and McNorgan, *Royal Canadian Armoured Corps,* 366, and Foss, *Jane's Armour and Artillery: 1990–1991,* 131, 133.
6 Meeting of Special Committee on Defence, 16 November 1963, FFL.
7 Adrian Lewis, *The American Culture of War* (New York: Routledge, 2007), 162.
8 John Duffield, *Power Rules: The Evolution of NATO's Conventional Force Posture* (Palo Alto, CA: Stanford University Press, 1995), 112–13.
9 Lewis, *American Culture of War,* 199, 209.
10 "Report of the Ad Hoc Committee on Defence Policy," 30 September 1963, 28, file 12, Pierre Elliott Trudeau fonds, MG 26, series O11, vol. 2, LAC.
11 Ibid., 87–88.
12 Ibid., 94.
13 Ibid., 101–4.
14 Ibid., 106–16.
15 Ibid., 161.
16 Meeting of Special Committee on Defence, 22 October 1963, FFL.
17 Copy of "Paul Hellyer to the Chiefs of Staff Committee," 27 August 1963, Annex I of "Interim Report of the Study on a Mobile Force," November 1963, file CSC 2447–1, part 1, Records of the Department of National Defence, RG 24, vol. 21811, LAC.
18 "Interim Report of the Study on a Mobile Force," November 1963, 1–3, file CSC 2447–1, part 1, RG 24, vol. 21811, LAC.
19 Appendix A to Annex III of "Interim Report of the Study on a Mobile Force," 2, November 1963, file CSC 2447–1, part 1, RG 24, vol. 21811, LAC; R.G. Herbert, "Minutes of the 28th Meeting of the Joint Service Study Group," 1 November 1963, 1, file CSC 2447–1, part 1, RG 24, vol. 21811, LAC; Army Planning Group, "Army Division – Mobile Force," 22 October 1963, 3, file CSC 2447–1, part 1, RG 24, vol. 21811, LAC. Foss, *Jane's Armour and Artillery: 1990–1991,* 191.
20 "Interim Report of the Study on a Mobile Force," 45.
21 Paul Hellyer, interview with author, 7 July 2014.
22 Frank Miller, on behalf of Paul Hellyer, to Air Officer Commanding 1 Air Division, to be passed to Lucien Cardin, 11 November 1963, file 2531, 73–1223, series 5, box 114, DHH.
23 C.J. Marshall to Arthur Menzies, "Canadian Brigade in Europe," 21 November 1963, file 27–16–3-3, RG 25, vol. 10376, LAC.
24 Meeting of Special Committee on Defence, 17 and 18 December 1963, FFL.
25 "Suggested Amendments of the Draft White Paper on Defence dated February 8 1964, submitted by the Department of External Affairs," [February?] 1964, 3–4, file 8000–05, part 1, Records of the Department of Finance, RG 19, vol. 4889, LAC.
26 Ross Campbell to Frank Miller, 6 February 1964, 3, file 759, 73–1223, series 1, box 43, DHH.

27 Canada, Department of National Defence, *White Paper on Defence* (Ottawa: Queen's Printer, 1964), 12–16, 19.
28 Ibid., 21–22, 24.
29 Ibid., 24.
30 G. Walsh to P. Hellyer, "Organization of the Field Force," 7 May 1964, file 112.1.009 (D37), DHH.
31 R.J. Sutherland, "Minutes of the 129th Meeting of the Defence Council," 2 November 1964, file 1407, 73–1223, series 3, box 69, DHH.
32 Paul T. Hellyer, Memorandum to the Cabinet: "National Defence Equipment Programme, 1965–66 to 1969–70," 16 November 1964, file 3135–280/C3–5, part 1, RG 24, accession 1994–95/725, box 3, LAC.
33 "IDP Data Form, Major Equipment, Light Reconnaissance Tank," 15 July 1965, file 3136–5-L0690, RG 24, accession 1993–94/257, box 27, LAC.
34 Foss, *Jane's Armour and Artillery: 1990–91*, 267, 290, 602.
35 Paul Hellyer and Lucien Cardin, "New Equipment for Armed Forces," *Canadian Army Journal* 43, 3 (1964): 6, FFL.
36 Charles J. Gauthier, "Chapter VII: Important Equipment Acquisitions during the 1970–1990 Period," 12–13, files 59 and 60, Charles J. Gauthier fonds, 92–228, series 3, DHH.
37 J.A. Charles, "Concept of Operations for the Mobile Force," 25 February 1965, file 3185–100, part 1, RG 24, accession 1986–87/165, box 5, LAC.
38 ATOB, "Appreciation and Proposed Options for the Structure of the Canadian Army Field Force, 1965–70 Period," 1965, Annex J, 11, Director General Land Force Development fonds, 96–26, box 1, DHH.
39 Ibid., 4–5.
40 Ibid., Annex H, Factor 8, Administration and Logistics, 1.
41 Ibid., Annex E, Factor 5, Finance and Equipment, 2.
42 Secretary of State of Canada, *Organization of the Government of Canada*, 9th ed. (Ottawa: Queen's Printer, 1978), 344–45.
43 Douglas L. Bland, *Chiefs of Defence: Government and the Unified Command of the Canadian Armed Forces* (Toronto: Canadian Institute of Strategic Studies, 1995), 79.
44 J.G. DeProse, ed. "Governor General Opens Mobile Command HQ," *Sentinel* 1, 2 (1965): 25, FFL.
45 Andrew Godefroy, "Chasing the Silver Bullet: The Evolution of Capability Development in the Canadian Army," *Canadian Military Journal* 8, 1 (2007): 53–66.
46 P.W. Holloway, "Minutes of Chief of Defence Staff – Staff Meeting 37/65," 2 December 1965, file 1559, 73–1223, series 3, box 79, DHH.
47 L. Lemnitzer to Frank Miller, 10 January 1966, file 2526A, 73–1223, series 5, box 113, DHH.
48 Frank Miller to L. Lemnitzer, 18 January 1966, file 2526A, 73–1223, series 5, box 113, DHH.
49 L. Lemnitzer to Frank Miller, 22 February 1966, file 2526A, 73–1223, series 5, box 113, DHH.
50 Paul Hellyer, interview with author, 7 July 2014.
51 J.L. Wilson, "MOBCOM Briefing," *Sentinel* 3, 2 (1967): 1–4, FFL; R.J. Sutherland, "Minutes of the 169th Meeting of the Defence Council," 1 and 2 February 1966, 2–10, file 1450, 73–1223, series 3, box 73, DHH.
52 Standing Committee on National Defence, 28 February and 1 March 1967, FFL.
53 R.J. Sutherland, "Minutes of the 194th Meeting of the Defence Council," 15 August 1966, file 1391, 73–1223, series 3, box 68, DHH; R.J. Sutherland, "Minutes of the 205th Meeting of the Defence Council," 29 November 1966, file 1391, 73–1223, series 3, box 68, DHH.

Chapter 2: The Traditionalists at Work

1 H.A. Porter, "Memorandum: FRR Priority Listings – Land Forces," 1 April 1968, file 3136–10, part 1, RG 24, accession 1994–95/725, box 3, LAC.
2 DERL3 [Director Equipment Requirements Land], "OER L-14/66, Direct Fire Support Vehicle 1971-80," May 1968, 1–3, file S-3500-L14/66, RG 24, box 8022, LAC.
3 Sean M. Maloney, "'A Proportion of their Cavalry Shall Be Converted': Light Armoured Force Development in Canada's Army, 1952–1976," *Army Doctrine and Training Bulletin* 2, 4 (1999): 96.
4 DERL3 [Director Equipment Requirements Land], "OER L-14/66, Direct Fire Support Vehicle 1971-80," May 1968, Annex A – Mobility, file S-3500-L14/66, RG 24, box 8022, LAC.
5 Ibid., Annex B – Firepower.
6 Ibid., Annex C – Protection.
7 Ibid., 10.
8 Steven J. Zaloga, *M551 Sheridan: US Airmobile Tanks 1941–2001* (Oxford: Osprey, 2009), 16–17, 42.
9 D.A.G. Waldock, "IDP-67 – Future Capital Requirements," 20 May 1966, file 3136–10, part 1, RG 24, accession 1994–95/725, box 3, LAC.
10 Bill Coupland, email to author, 20 January 2014; Don Dingwall, *The Centurion in Canadian Service* (Ottawa: Service, 2005), 15.
11 W. Finan to R. Rowley, "Battle Efficiency – The Royal Canadian Dragoons," 15 November 1966, file 2140–1, part 1, RG 24, vol. 22412, LAC.
12 K.R. Ward, "Comments on Draft Report: Reliability of Centurion Tank," 26 November 1965, file 7101-Tanks/C1, part 30, RG 24, vol. 31754, LAC.
13 N.G. Wilson-Smith, "Main Battle Tanks," 31 May 1967, file 1611, 73–1223, series 3, box 80, DHH.
14 Paul Hellyer to Robert McNamara, 30 May 1964, and Robert McNamara to Paul Hellyer, 18 June 1964, file 140, 73–1223, series 1, box 9, DHH.
15 "Report on US/FRG Co-operative Tank Development Program," 29 July 1965, file 142, 73–1223, series 1, box 9, DHH.
16 D.A.G. Waldock, "IDP-67 – Future Capital Requirements, LAC," 20 May 1966, file 3136–10, part 1, RG 24, accession 1994–95/725, box 3, LAC.
17 N.G. Wilson-Smith, "Main Battle Tanks," 31 May 1967, file 1611, 73–1223, series 3, box 80, DHH.
18 P.W. Holloway, "Minutes of Chief of Defence Staff – Special Staff Meeting," 21 July 1967, file 1611, 73–1223, series 3, box 80, DHH.
19 Zaloga, *M551 Sheridan*, 22–23, 32.
20 Walter J. Spielberger, *The Leopard 1 and Leopard 2 Weapon Systems* (Stuttgart: Motorbuch Verlag, 2000), 208.
21 "Integrated Defence Program – 1967," 12 July 1966, 6–8, file 6, Department of National Defence Estimates Collection, 75–457, series 1, box 21, DHH.
22 Aide-Memoire to the Government of Canada from the Embassy of the United States of America to Canada, 24 September 1968, Annex A, file 27–4-NATO-1, part 7, RG 25, vol. 10289, LAC.
23 "Future Resource Requirements (FRRs)," November 1969, file 3136–10, part 1, RG 24, accession 1994–95/725, box 3, LAC.
24 H.B. Robinson, "Future of NATO," 17 May 1966, Paul Martin fonds, MG 32, vol. 226, file 16, LAC.
25 Cabinet of the Government of Canada, "France and NATO," Privy Council Office, 31 March 1966, Cabinet Conclusions Database, LAC.

26 Lester Pearson, "NATO, 1966," 20 April 1966, MG 26, series N6, vol. 9, LAC.

27 Paul Martin to Lester Pearson, "Comments on Your Notes on NATO," 6 May 1966, and Paul Martin to Lester Pearson, "NATO Forces in Europe," 7 May 1967, file 27-4-NATO-3-1-CDA, RG 25, vol. 10295, LAC. See John English, "Problems in Middle Life," in *Canada and NATO: Uneasy Past, Uncertain Future,* edited by Margaret MacMillan and David Sorenson (Waterloo, ON: University of Waterloo Press, 1990), 47–66.

28 H.B. Robinson, interview by R. Bothwell and J.L. Granatstein, 5 August 1987, 2, file 144, box 9, J.L. Granatstein fonds, F0316, accession 1989–036, Clara Thomas Archives and Special Collections at York University, Toronto (hereafter CTASC).

29 Cabinet of the Government of Canada, "Canada's Military Contribution in Europe – Redeployment of R.C.A.F. Units in Europe," Privy Council Office, 14 July 1966, Cabinet Conclusions Database, LAC.

30 Rufus Z. Smith, "Memorandum of Conversation," 21 August 1966, in *Western Europe Region,* vol. 13 of *Foreign Relations of the United States, 1964–1968,* ed. Charles S. Sampson (Washington, DC: Government Printing Office, 1995), 452–53.

31 Frederick Sharp to Jean Victor Allard, "Optional Contributions to NATO," 14 June 1967, file 1612, 73–1223, series 3, box 80, DHH.

32 D.H. Ross to DC Plans, "Optional Contributions to NATO," 14 July 1967, file 2525, 73–1223, series 5, box 113, DHH.

33 P.W. Holloway, "Chief of the Defence Staff – CDS Staff Meeting 16/67," 14 June 1967, file 1612, 73–1223, series 3, box 80, DHH.

34 Paul Hellyer, "Canada's Military Contribution to NATO 1968–1972," 8 September 1967, Cabinet Document 553–67, Records of the Privy Council Office's Collection of Cabinet Documents, RG 2-B-2, vol. 6328, LAC; Paul Martin, "Canada and Collective Security," 5 September 1967, Cabinet Document 555–67, RG 2-B-2, vol. 6328, LAC; Paul Martin, "Canada and NATO," 5 September 1967, Cabinet Document 557–67, RG 2-B-2, vol. 6328, LAC; P.M. Pitfield, "Canada, Collective Security and NATO," 11 September 1967, Cabinet Document 560–67, RG 2-B-2, vol. 6328, LAC.

35 Cabinet of the Government of Canada, "Collective Security and NATO," Privy Council Office, 12 September 1967, Cabinet Conclusions Database, LAC. See Chapter 4 of Greg Donaghy, *Tolerant Allies: Canada and the United States, 1963–1968* (Montreal and Kingston: McGill-Queen's University Press, 2002).

36 See "Questions Regarding DC Ops Paper on Main Battle Tank," 19 July 1967, and [R. L. Raymont?], "Re: DC Ops Paper on Main Battle Tank," file 2521, 73–1223, series 5, box 113, DHH; R.M. Aldwinckle to the VCDS, "Main Battle Tanks," 14 July 1967, file 142, 73–1223, series 1, box 9, DHH.

37 P. Holloway, "Minutes of Chief of the Defence Staff – Staff Meeting 17/67," 26 July 1967, file 1613, 73–1223, series 3–4, box 80, DHH.

38 R.J. Hauser, "Aide Memoire: Visit of Officials of Krauss-Maffai [sic] Fahrzeuge Munich Germany, December 4, 1967," file 142, 73–1223, series 1, box 9, DHH.

39 L. Lilley, "Modification of Centurion Tanks, Netherlands Army," 15 May 1968, file 142, 73–1223, series 1, box 9, DHH.

40 R.J. Sutherland, "Minutes of the 230th Meeting of the Defence Council," 9 January 1968, file 1392, 73–1223, series 3, box 68, DHH.

41 C. Ritchie (ambassador to the United Kingdom), "Proposed Move of 4 CIBG to South Germany," 31 October 1967, R. Bower (ambassador to West Germany), "Proposed Move of 4 CIBG to South Germany," 25 October 1967, A.E. Ritchie (ambassador to the United States), "Proposed Move of 4 CIBG to South Germany," 31 October 1967, file 27–16–3-3, RG 25, vol. 10376, LAC.

42 Ross Campbell (ambassador to NATO), "Proposed Move of 4 CIBG to South Germany," 24 October 1967, file 27–16–3-3, RG 25, vol. 10376, LAC.
43 "Re-Location of 4 CIBG: Foreign Policy Implications," [February 1967?], file 27–16–3-3, RG 25, vol. 10376, LAC.
44 Léo Cadieux, "Policy Guidance: 1968–1974," 6 February 1968, file 2101, 73–1223, series 4, box 105, DHH.
45 Jean Victor Allard to Léo Cadieux, "Optional Roles for 4 CIBG," 14 February 1968, file 2531, 73–1223, series 5, box 114, DHH.
46 Jean Victor Allard, 14 February 1968, file 2531, 73–1223, series 5, box 114, DHH.
47 Jean Victor Allard to H.B. Robinson, 19 February 1968, file 27–4-NATO-1-SACEUR, RG 25, vol. 11399, LAC. In the letter to Robinson, Allard attached a draft of his proposed letter to SACEUR, still Lyman Lemnitzer. Jean Victor Allard to Ross Campbell, 21 February 1968, file 2531, 73–1223, series 5, box 114, DHH.
48 Ross Campbell to Jean Victor Allard, 27 February 1968, file 2531, 73–1223, series 5, box 114, DHH.
49 Jean Victor Allard, "Relocation of 4 CIBG in Allied Command Europe," sent by R.W. Timbrell to N.G. Wilson-Smith, 15 March 1968, file 2531, 73–1223, series 5, box 114, DHH.
50 N.G. Wilson-Smith to Jean Victor Allard, "Discussions Concerning Role and Re-Location of Canadian Forces Europe," 26 March 1968, file 2531, 73–1223, series 5, box 114, DHH.
51 R.J. Sutherland, "Minutes of the 237th Meeting of the Defence Council," 9 January 1968, file 1392, 73–1223, series 3, box 68, DHH.
52 Charles J. Gauthier, "Chapter VII: Important Equipment Acquisitions during the 1970–1990 Period," 5, files 59 and 60, 92–228, series 3, DHH.
53 "Doctrinal Planning Guidance for Mobile Command, 1970–1975," February 1968, file 5, William B.S. Sutherland fonds, 79–527, box 2, DHH.
54 Andrew Godefroy, "Chasing the Silver Bullet: The Evolution of Capability Development in the Canadian Army," *Canadian Military Journal* 8, 1 (2007): 53–66.

Chapter 3: Trudeau Takes the Reins

1 Tom Axworthy, interview with author, 4 September 2013, confirmed in email to author, 23 January 2014.
2 Wilhelm Grewe, "3 Ministersitzung der Nuklearen Planungsgruppe (NPG) in Den Haag am 18./19. April 1968," 19 April 1968, in *Akten zur Auswärtigen Politik der Bundesrepublik Deutschland 1968, 1. Januar bis 30. Juni*, ed. Mechthild Lindemann and Matthias Peter (Munich: R. Oldenbourg, 1999), 472–76; see 473n4.
3 "Canada and NATO," [April 1968?], file 27–4-NATO-3, part 1, RG 25, vol. 10295, LAC.
4 J.L. Granatstein and Robert Bothwell, *Pirouette: Pierre Trudeau and Canadian Foreign Policy* (Toronto: University of Toronto Press, 1990), 11. See J.L. Granatstein, *A Man of Influence* (Ottawa: Deneau, 1981), 375–79, for an overview of the drafting of the paper and its limited impact.
5 Mitchell Sharp to Pierre Trudeau, "Review of Foreign Policy," 27 May 1968, Mitchell Sharp fonds, R 4515, vol. 37, LAC.
6 Tom Axworthy.
7 Jean V. Allard, *The Memoirs of General Jean V. Allard*, with Serge Bernier (Vancouver: UBC Press, 1988), 291.
8 Ross Campbell, interview by Roger Hill, 13 and 16 April 1987, transcript part of *In Alliance: An Oral History of Canadian Involvement in NATO*, Canadian Institute for International Peace and Security, December 1991 (hereafter *In Alliance*), 344, file 1, John

Halstead fonds, vol. 1, LAC; "The Prime Minister's Remarks at the December 9th Meeting," December 1968, file 2104, 73–1223, series 4, box 105, DHH.

9 Allan Gotlieb, email to author, 20 January 2014.

10 "Extracts from Prime Minister's Press Conference, Winnipeg Manitoba, 24 May 1968," file 27-4-NATO-1, RG 25, vol. 10289, LAC.

11 Allan Gotlieb and Max Yalden, "Some Reflections on Canadian Foreign Policy," 1968, file 4, Max Yalden fonds, R 11847, vol. 1, LAC.

12 "Rationale for Canadian Defence Forces," [April?] 1968, file 832, 73–1223, series 2, box 45, DHH.

13 R.L. Raymont, 1 April 1968, file 832, 73–1223, series 2, box 45, DHH.

14 A.E. Ritchie, interview by R. Bothwell and J.L. Granatstein, 15 March 1988, notes of interview, 2, file 29, box 6, Robert Bothwell fonds, accession 1988–0074, University of Toronto Archives.

15 See Hubert Zimmerman's *Money and Security: Troops, Monetary Policy and West Germany's Relations with the United States and Britain, 1950–1971* (Cambridge: Cambridge University Press, 2002).

16 John Duffield, *Power Rules: The Evolution of NATO's Conventional Force Posture* (Palo Alto, CA: Stanford University Press, 1995), 165–66, 179–81.

17 See Francis Gavin, "The Myth of Flexible Response," Chapter 2 in *Nuclear Statecraft: History and Strategy in America's Atomic Age* (Ithaca, NY: Cornell University Press, 2012).

18 This discussion took place at a meeting of the National Security Council on 14 February 1969, and the document is based on Alexander Haig's handwritten notes. "Parity, Safeguard, and the SS-9 Controversy (Documents 1–57): 7. Notes of National Security Council Meeting," 14 February 1969, in M. Todd Bennett, ed., *National Security Policy, 1969–1972,* vol. 34 of *Foreign Relations of the United States, 1969–1976* (Washington, DC: Government Printing Office, 2011), 20–21. https://history.state.gov/historicaldocuments/frus1969-76v34/d7.

19 Ivan Head and Pierre Trudeau, *The Canadian Way: Shaping Canada's Foreign Policy, 1968–1984* (Toronto: McClelland and Stewart, 1995), 77.

20 Léo Cadieux, "Re: Defence Review," 30 April 1968, Cabinet Document 196–68, RG 2-B-2, vol. 6332, LAC.

21 M.A. Crowe, "Defence Review," 13 May 1968, Cabinet Document 233–68, RG 2-B-2, vol. 6332, LAC.

22 Cabinet of the Government of Canada, "Defence Review," Privy Council Office, 15 May 1968, Cabinet Conclusions Database, LAC.

23 Charles J. Gauthier, "Introduction: The Legacy of the 1960s," 16–7, file 53, part 2, 92–228, series 3, DHH.

24 Cabinet of the Government of Canada, "NATO," Privy Council Office, 26 September 1968, Cabinet Conclusions Database, LAC.

25 Cabinet of the Government of Canada, "Report on the NATO Ministerial Meeting," Privy Council Office, 21 November 1968, Cabinet Conclusions Database, LAC.

26 Hans Ruete, "NATO-Ministerkonferenz Herbst 1968," 14 November 1968, in *Akten zur Auswärtigen Politik der Bundesrepublik Deutschland 1968, 1. Juli bis 31. Dezember,* ed. Mechthild Lindemann und Matthias Peter (Munich: R. Oldenbourg, 1999), 1460–63.

27 John Halstead, interview by R. Bothwell and J.L. Granatstein, 9 December 1987, 2, file 142, box 9, F0316, accession 1989–036, CTASC.

28 Michael Shenstone, interview by R. Bothwell and J.L. Granatstein, 2 February 1989, 2, file 148, box 10, F0316, accession 1989–036, CTASC.

29 Special Task Force on Europe, "Canada and Europe: Report of the Special Task Force on Europe," February 1969, 89–106, Cabinet Document 158–69, RG 2-B-2, vol. 6342, LAC.

30 "The Defence Policy Review," February 1969, 44–49, Cabinet Document 157–69, RG 2-B-2, vol. 6342, LAC.
31 Hume Wright, "Report of the Cabinet Committee on External Policy and Defence on Its Discussions of the *Report of the Task Force on Europe* and the *Defence Policy Review*," 27 March 1969, Cabinet Document 302–69, RG 2-B-2, vol. 6344, LAC.
32 Head and Trudeau, *Canadian Way*, 77–81.
33 H.B. Robinson, interview by R. Bothwell and J.L. Granatstein, 5 August 1987, 2, file 144, box 9, F0316, accession 1989–036, CTASC.
34 Although "Canadian Defence Policy: A Study" is generally attributed to Head, M.A. Crowe, one of the members of the Non-Group, later recalled that Hume Wright, from the Privy Council Office, was its principal drafter.
35 Ivan Head, "Canadian Defence Policy: A Study," [March 1969?], 1–5, MG 26, file 11, series O11, vol. 2, LAC.
36 Ibid., 7.
37 Ibid., 3, 5.
38 Pierre Elliott Trudeau, "The Relation of Foreign Policy to Defence Policy," 12 April 1969, in *Canadian Foreign Policy 1966–1976: Selected Speeches and Documents*, ed. Arthur E. Blanchette (Montreal and Kingston: McGill-Queen's University Press, 1980), 344.
39 Head, "Canadian Defence Policy," Appendix 1.
40 Head and Trudeau, *Canadian Way*, 79.
41 J.H. Warren to Jean-Luc Pepin, "Defence Policy Review," 28 March 1969, file 8000–05, part 2, RG 19, vol. 4889, LAC.
42 Ross Campbell, interview by Roger Hill, 13 and 16 April 1987, *In Alliance*, 347.
43 Henry Kissinger to Richard Nixon, "Your Final Meeting with Prime Minister Trudeau," 25 March 1969, in *Western Europe, 1969–1972*, vol. 41 of *Foreign Relations of the United States, 1969–1976*, ed. James E. Miller and Laurie Van Hook (Washington, DC: Government Printing Office, 2012), 387–88.
44 Harold H. Saunders, "Memorandum of Conversation," 27 March 1969, in *Middle East Region and Arabian Peninsula, 1969–1972; Jordan, September 1970*, vol. 24 of *Foreign Relations of the United States, 1969–1976*, ed. Linda W. Qaimmaqami and Adam M. Howard (Washington, DC: Government Printing Office, 2014), 24–26.
45 Granatstein and Bothwell, *Pirouette*, 5.
46 Cabinet of the Government of Canada, "The Defence Policy Review and the Report of the Special Task Force on Europe," Privy Council Office, 29 March 1969, 2, Cabinet Conclusions Database, LAC.
47 Ibid.
48 Ibid., 5.
49 Ibid., 7.
50 Ibid., 6.
51 Mitchell Sharp, *Which Reminds Me ... : A Memoir* (Toronto: University of Toronto Press, 1994), 174–76.
52 Cabinet of the Government of Canada, "The Defence Policy Review and the Report of the Special Task Force on Europe," Privy Council Office, 1 April 1969, 2, Cabinet Conclusions Database, LAC.
53 H.B. Robinson, interview by R. Bothwell and J.L. Granatstein, 11 August 1987, 1, file 144, box 9, F0316, accession 1989–036, CTASC.
54 Gordon Smith, email to author, 17 January 2014.
55 Léo Cadieux, interview by R. Bothwell and J.L. Granatstein, 9 December 1987, 2, file 141, box 9, F0316, accession 1989–036, CTASC. See also Granatstein and Bothwell, *Pirouette*, 25.

56 Cabinet of the Government of Canada, "The Defence Policy Review and the Report of the Special Task Force on Europe," Privy Council Office, 1 April 1969, 3, Cabinet Conclusions Database, LAC.
57 Charles J. Gauthier, "Chapter I: Preface," 35, file 53, 92–228, series 3, DHH.
58 Hans Ruete, "Unterredung des Bundesaußenministers mit Secretary of State Rogers," 9 April 1969, in *Akten zur Auswärtigen Politik der Bundesrepublik Deutschland 1969, 1. Januar bis 30. Juni,* ed. Franz Eibl and Hubert Zimmermann (Munich: R. Oldenbourg, 2000), 459–61.
59 Cabinet of the Government of Canada, "Report on the NATO Ministerial Meeting in Washington, 10–11 April, 1969," Privy Council Office, 17 April 1969, 3, Cabinet Conclusions Database, LAC.
60 R.B. Byers, "Defence and Foreign Policy in the 1970s: The Demise of the Trudeau Doctrine," *International Journal* 33, 2 (1978): 312. http://dx.doi.org/10.1177/002070207803300203.
61 J.L. Granatstein and Robert Bothwell, "Pierre Trudeau on His Foreign Policy: A Conversation in 1988," *International Journal* 88, 1 (2010–11): 174.
62 Head and Trudeau, *Canadian Way,* 77.

Chapter 4: The Summer of 1969

1 L. Lemnitzer to Jean Victor Allard, "Future Role and Location of 4 CIBG and 1SCA Air Division Canadian Armed Forces," March 1969, file 823, 73–1223, series 1–2, box 212, DHH.
2 "Defence Policy Review – Phase II, Report by Interdepartmental Working Group," 30 April 1969, Cabinet Document 430–69, RG 2-B-2, vol. 6346, LAC.
3 Sean M. Maloney, "'A Proportion of their Cavalry Shall Be Converted': Light Armoured Force Development in Canada's Army, 1952–1976," *Army Doctrine and Training Bulletin* 2, 4 (1999): 95–96.
4 "Defence Policy Review – Phase II, Report by Interdepartmental Working Group," Annex C, 1.
5 Ibid., 14.
6 For an overview of the development and rationale of the force, see Sean M. Maloney, "Fire Brigade or Tocsin? NATO's ACE Mobile Force, Flexible Response and the Cold War," *Journal of Strategic Studies* 27, 4 (2004): 585–613. http://dx.doi.org/10.1080/1362369042000314529.
7 "Defence Policy Review – Phase II, Report by Interdepartmental Working Group."
8 Cabinet of the Government of Canada, "Report on Defence Policy Review – Phase II," Privy Council Office, 20 May 1969, Cabinet Conclusions Database, LAC.
9 Henry Kissinger, *The White House Years* (Boston: Little Brown, 1979), 392–93, 948–49.
10 "Report of the Ad Hoc Committee on Defence Policy," 30 September 1963, 29, file 12, MG 26, series O11, vol. 2, LAC.
11 Ross Campbell, interview by Roger Hill, 13 and 16 April 1987, *In Alliance*, 346.
12 Ross Campbell, "Ministerial DPC: Private Consultation with Central Region Defence Ministers," 28 May 1969, file 18, MG 26, series O11, vol. 24, LAC.
13 "Verbatim Record of a Meeting of the Defence Planning Committee Held on Wednesday, 28th May, 1969 at 3.30 p.m. at NATO Headquarters, 39," 28 May 1969, 13, file DPC-VR(69)10, North Atlantic Council fonds, Defence Planning Committee series.
14 Henry Kissinger to Richard Nixon, "A Strategic Overview," n.d. (attachment, "The Modern World, A Single 'Strategic Theater,'" is dated 29 September 1969), in *Foundations of Foreign Policy, 1969–1972*, vol. 1 of *Foreign Relations of the United States, 1969–1976*, ed.

Louis J. Smith and David H. Herschler (Washington, DC: Government Printing Office, 2003), 110–21.

15 John Duffield, *Power Rules: The Evolution of NATO's Conventional Force Posture* (Palo Alto, CA: Stanford University Press, 1995), 196.

16 Henry Kissinger to Richard Nixon, "NATO Defense Planning Committee Meeting," 23 May 1969, in *Western Europe; NATO, 1969–1972*, vol. 41 of *Foreign Relations of the United States, 1969–1976*, ed. James E. Miller and Laurie Van Hook (Washington, DC: Government Printing Office, 2012), 62–64.

17 Helmut Sonnenfeldt to Henry Kissinger, "State Department Démarche on Canadian Defense Plan," 28 May 1969, in Miller and Hook, *Western Europe; NATO, 1969–1972*, 391–92.

18 G. Duckwitz, 27 May 1969, in *Akten zur Auswärtigen Politik der Bundesrepublik Deutschland 1969, 1. Januar bis 30. Juni*, ed. Franz Eibl and Hubert Zimmermann (Munich: R. Oldenbourg, 2000), 645.

19 H.C.F. Elliott, "Canadian and NATO Consultations on Canada's Proposed Force Reductions," 10 June 1969, 4–6 of the attached transcript of Rear-Admiral R.W. Timbrell's presentation, 29 May 1969, file 1392, 73–1223, series 5, box 113, DHH. Foss, *Jane's Armour and Artillery: 1990–1991*, 267.

20 Ibid., 9, 18.

21 H.C.F. Elliott, "Canadian and NATO Consultations on Canada's Proposed Force Reductions," 10 June 1969, 2–3 of the attached transcript of Rear-Admiral R.W. Timbrell's presentation, 5 June 1969, file 1392, 73–1223, series 5, box 113, DHH.

22 G. Duckwitz, 27 May 1969, in *Akten zur Auswärtigen Politik der Bundesrepublik Deutschland 1969, 1. Januar bis 30. Juni*, ed. Franz Eibl and Hubert Zimmermann (Munich: R. Oldenbourg, 2000), 645n11.

23 J.R. Chisholm, "Minutes of the 267th Meeting of the Defence Council," 16 June 1969, file 1393, 73–1223, series 3, box 68, DHH.

24 "Land Forces Canada," June 1969, file 18, 79–527, box 2, DHH.

25 Frederick Sharp to Donald Macdonald, "Canadian Force Commitments to NATO Europe Including the Air Sea Transportable Combat Group to AFNorth," 1 February 1971, file 2530, 73–1223, series 5, box 114, DHH.

26 "Chronological Resume Concerning Canadian Land Force," January 1971, file 2530, 73–1223, series 5, box 114, DHH.

27 "Gespräch des Bundeskanzlers Kiesinger mit Generalsekretär Brosio, NATO," 6 June 1969, in *Akten zur Auswärtigen Politik der Bundesrepublik Deutschland 1969, 1. Januar bis 30. Juni*, ed. Franz Eibl and Hubert Zimmermann (Munich: R. Oldenbourg, 2000), 684, 684n5.

28 "Summary Record of a Meeting of the Committee Held at the NATO Headquarters, Brussels, 39 on Friday, 13th June at 10.15 a.m.," 27 June 1969, file DPC-R(69)10, North Atlantic Council fonds, Defence Planning Committee series.

29 "Gespräch des Bundeskanzlers Kiesinger mit Generalsekretär Brosio, NATO," 684, 684n5.

30 Charles J. Gauthier, "Chapter I: Preface," 39–40, file 53, 92–228, series 3, DHH.

31 Cabinet of the Government of Canada, "NATO Policy," 6, Privy Council Office, 24 July 1969, Cabinet Conclusions Database, LAC.

32 Andrew Goodpaster to Léo Cadieux, 3 August 1969, file 2530, 73–1223, series 5, box 114, DHH.

33 T.R. Milton, "Memorandum for NATO's Military Committee – 'Canadian Force Reductions,'" 6 August 1969, includes message from SACEUR Andrew Goodpaster to Léo Cadieux, 3 August 1969, and Supreme Headquarters Allied Powers Europe's counterproposal of 3 August 1969, 2–6, file 2519, 73–1223, series 5, box 113, DHH.

34 Harold Linder to the Department of State, "Canadian Force Reductions," 7 July 1969, in Miller and Hook, *Western Europe; NATO, 1969–1972*, 393–96.
35 M. Dare to Jean Victor Allard, "Summary of SACEUR Proposals, Canadian Forces Europe," 7 August 1969, file 2519, 73–1223, series 5, box 113, DHH.
36 Jean Victor Allard to Doug Bland, "La mise en place des composantes et le quartier géneral," [1988 or 1989], file 224, Jean Victor Allard fonds, 84–126.
37 M. Dare to Jean Victor Allard, "Summary of SACEUR Proposals."
38 Cabinet of the Government of Canada, "Canadian NATO Force Proposals," Privy Council Office, 13 August 1969, Cabinet Conclusions Database, LAC. It is unclear where Trudeau got the number of forty-three hundred or forty-four hundred.
39 B.V. Genge, "Summary Record of Discussion held on 15 August, 1969 between General JV Allard, CDS and General HM Wade, Chief of Staff, SHAPE [Supreme Headquarters Allied Powers Europe]," 28 August 1969, file 2530, 73–1223, series 5, box 114, DHH.
40 External Affairs (Ottawa) to Ross Campbell, "CDN [Canadian] NATO Force Proposals," 15 August 1969, 1–2, file 3342, 73–1223, series 9, box 139, DHH.
41 Ross Campbell, "CDN [Canadian] NATO Force Proposals," 22 August 1969, 3, file 3342, 73–1223, series 9, box 139, DHH.
42 DND (Cadieux) to SACEUR (Goodpaster), "Reconfiguration of Canadian Forces in Europe," 2 September 1969, file 3342, 73–1223, series 9, box 139, DHH.
43 Cabinet of the Government of Canada, "Defence Review – Announcement of Force Changes," Privy Council Office, 11 September 1969, Cabinet Conclusions Database, LAC.
44 Ross Campbell, "CDN [Canadian] NATO Force Proposals," 4 September 1969, 3, file 3342, 73–1223, series 9, box 139, DHH.
45 Ross Campbell, "CDN [Canadian] NATO Force Proposals," 9 September 1969, 3, file 3342, 73–1223, series 9, box 139, DHH.
46 F.T. Harris to Canadian Land Forces Command and Staff College, "Presentation by Colonel Harris," 10 March 1971, Canadian Forces Headquarters, Director of Combat Development, 80–499, DHH.
47 Hans Ruete, "Außenpolitische Tendenzen in Ottawa," 12 September 1969, in *Akten zur Auswärtigen Politik der Bundesrepublik Deutschland 1969, 1. Juli bis 31. Dezember*, ed. Franz Eibl and Hubert Zimmermann (Munich: R. Oldenbourg, 2000), 995–99.
48 Sean Maloney, "Sean M. Maloney.com – The Royal Canadian Armoured Corps: An Illustrated History," Accessed May 14, 2012. http://www.seanmmaloney.com/canadian-armed-forces-operations/the-royal-canadian-armoured-corps-an-illustrated-history-co-authored-with-john-marteinson-and-michael-mcnorgan-foreword-by-desmond-morton-toronto-robin-brass-200/.
49 Douglas L. Bland, *Chiefs of Defence: Government and the Unified Command of the Canadian Armed Forces* (Toronto: Canadian Institute of Strategic Studies, 1995), 190.
50 For example, *ARMOR*, a publication of the United States Army Armor Branch, contained a number of articles in the late 1960s and 1970s on the continued relevance of tanks. See N.A. Shackleton, "Will the Tank Go the Way of the Horse?" *ARMOR* 77, 5 (1968): 4–8; Warren W. Lennon, "The Death of the Tank," *ARMOR* 81, 1 (1972): 4–14; and William R. Kraft Jr., "Why Tank Heavy Forces in Europe?" *ARMOR* 82, 1 (1973): 8–10. All accessed at FFL.

Chapter 5: The Revisionists Assert Control

1 J.M. Shoemaker to Pierre Trudeau, "The Department of National Defence," 21 September 1970, file 8, MG 26, series O11, vol. 2, LAC.
2 Marc Lalonde, email to author, 17 January 2014.

3 Donald Macdonald, interview by R. Bothwell and J.L. Granatstein, 5 April 1988, 2, file 143, box 9, F0316, accession 1989-036, CTASC.
4 Directorate of Land Operational Research, "Preliminary Report: Quick Response Research War Games Bronze Nimbus IV and V," 20 March 1970, 1–2, 9, and Annex A, file 44, 79-527, box 3, DHH.
5 F.T. Harris to Canadian Land Forces Command and Staff College, "Presentation by Colonel Harris," 10 March 1971, Canadian Forces Headquarters, Director of Combat Development, 80-499, DHH. The letter includes Colonel Harris's presentation.
6 J.R. Chisholm, "Minutes of the 301st Meeting of the Defence Council," 21 December 1970, file 1397, 73-1223, series 3, box 69, DHH.
7 Charles J. Gauthier, "Chapter I: Preface," 28, file 53, 92-228, series 3, DHH.
8 Ross Campbell, "Questions on the Canadian Reply to DPQ (70)," 18 September 1970, and H. Tellier, "Canadian Reply to DPQ (70)," 5 October 1970, file 27-4-NATO-1-9 1970, RG 25, vol. 10291, LAC.
9 P. Walker, "Meeting with Mr. Campbell, Officers of OMP and Officers from DND on Various Military Topics, November 2, 1970," 10 November 1970, file 27-4-NATO-3-1-CDA, part 2, RG 25, vol. 11397, LAC.
10 J.R. Chisholm, "Minutes of the 301st Meeting of the Defence Council," 21 December 1970, file 1397, 73-1223, series 3, box 69, DHH.
11 Smith did not recall the controversy over Canada's forces in Europe. Gordon Smith, email to author, 10 February 2014.
12 Donald Macdonald to Frederick Sharp and Elgin Armstrong, 12 January 1971, file 2530, 73-1223, series 5, box 114, DHH.
13 Donald Macdonald to Pierre Trudeau, 16 March 1971, file 8, MG 26 O11, vol. 2, LAC.
14 Pierre Trudeau to Donald Macdonald, 22 March 1971, file 8, MG 26 O11, vol. 2, LAC.
15 M.A. Crowe to Pierre Trudeau, "The Role of Canadian Land Forces in Europe," 22 March 1971, file 8, MG 26 O11, vol. 2, LAC.
16 Gordon Robertson to Pierre Trudeau, "The Role of Canadian Land Forces in Europe," 23 March 1971, file 8, MG 26 O11, vol. 2, LAC. There was no mention of this episode in Robertson's personal papers or his *Memoirs of a Very Civil Servant: Mackenzie King to Pierre Trudeau* (Toronto: University of Toronto Press, 2000).
17 Mary E. McDonald to Gordon Robertson, 7 April 1971, file 8, MG 26 O11, vol. 2, LAC.
18 Donald Macdonald to Pierre Trudeau, "Role of the Canadian Land Forces Stationed in Europe: Assignment to ACE Mobile Force (Land)," 30 April 1971, file 8, MG 26 O11, vol. 2, LAC.
19 Pierre Trudeau to Donald Macdonald, 13 May 1971, file 8, MG 26 O11, vol. 2, LAC.
20 Donald Macdonald, "White Paper on Defence," 22 April 1971, 5–6, Cabinet Document 438-71, RG 2-B-2, vol. 6388, LAC; P.A. McDougall, "White Paper on Defence," 4 June 1971, Cabinet Document 652-71, RG 2-B-2, vol. 6391, LAC.
21 M.A. Crowe to Pierre Trudeau, "Briefing Note for Cabinet Meeting of 8 July 1971 – White Paper on Defence," 2 July 1971, file 8, MG 26 O11, vol. 2, LAC.
22 Cabinet of the Government of Canada, "The White Paper on Defence," Privy Council Office, 22 July 1971, Cabinet Conclusions Database, LAC.
23 Canada, Department of National Defence, *Defence in the 70s* (Ottawa: Information Canada, 1971), 16, 32.
24 See Chapter 5 in Douglas L. Bland, *The Administration of Defence Policy in Canada* (Kingston, ON: Frye, 1987).
25 Douglas L. Bland, *Chiefs of Defence: Government and the Unified Command of the Canadian Armed Forces* (Toronto: Canadian Institute of Strategic Studies, 1995), xiv.
26 Secretary of State of Canada, *Organization of the Government of Canada*, 9th ed. (Ottawa: Queen's Printer, 1978), 342–45.

27 Orlando Figes, *Revolutionary Russia, 1891–1991: A History* (New York: Metropolitan Books, 2014), 264.
28 See Annex J of Director Force Development, "Force Development Objective (FDO), FDO L 1/71, Land Force, 1974 to 1985," 28 June 1972, which includes the final report on Armor / Anti Armor from NATO's "Alliance Defence Problems for the 1970s," 1–3, file DRBS 100–15-L1/71, RG 24, vol. 29747, LAC.
29 Canadian Liaison Officer at NATO, "From CDN [Canadian] LNO [Liaison Officer] for Commanders, following is text of message I discussed with Commander 25 July 72," received 31 July 1972, file 1901–0, part 2, RG 24, vol. 23712, LAC. Two cables communicated the message.
30 Frederick Sharp to Andrew Goodpaster, "Canadian Post 1974 Land Force Structure Europe," August 1972, file 2530, 73–1223, series 5, box 114, DHH.
31 G. Crean, "Following for Prime Minister, from Bonn," 16 July 1975, file 27–8-GFR, part 1, RG 25, vol. 10318, LAC.
32 John Halstead, interview by Roger Hill, 3 and 5 June 1987, *In Alliance*, 429.
33 A.E. Ritchie to Mitchell Sharp, "Memorandum to the Minister: Use of Canadian Defence Facilities for Training of Forces from other Countries," 4 May 1971, file 27–20–3, part 1, RG 25, vol. 10404, LAC.
34 "Canada/Federal Republic of Germany Defence Cooperation," [February 1975?], file 27–8-GFR, part 1, RG 25, vol. 10318, LAC.
35 "Kissinger and Schlesinger," 5 December 1973, National Security Adviser Collection, Gerald R. Ford Presidential Library, Ann Arbor, MI.
36 John Wickham and H. Lobdell Jr., "Memorandum of Conversation: Canadian-US Bilateral in Brussels," 6 December 1973, in *Documents on Western Europe, 1973–1976*, vol. E-15, part 2, of *Foreign Relations of the United States, 1969–1976*, ed. Kathleen B. Rasmussen (Washington, DC: Government Printing Office, 2014), 391–93.
37 Charles J. Gauthier, "Chapter IV: Between White Papers – Major Developments from the Mid 70s to Mid 80s," 8, file 56, 92–228, series 3, DHH.
38 "Summary Record of Discussions, Commanders' Conference Held in Chief of Defence Staff Conference Room," 10–12 January 1972, Annex F, 5, file DRBSG 190–352, part 4, RG 24, vol. 29914, LAC.
39 Director Force Development, "Force Development Objective (FDO), FDO L 1/71, Land Force, 1974 to 1985," 28 June 1972, 64, file DRBS 100–15-L1/71, RG 24, vol. 29747, LAC.
40 Ibid., 105–7.
41 Ibid., 101.
42 W.C. Leonard, "FDO L 1/71 Land Force 1974 to 1985," 7 September 1972, file 3185–1, part 1, RG 24, vol. 23485, LAC.
43 R. Bérubé, "Force Development Objective, FDO L 1/71, Land Forces 1974 to 1985 First Draft," 24 August 1972, 3, 10–20, and Annex B, 6, file 3185–1, part 1, RG 24, vol. 23485, LAC.
44 W.E. Sills, "Comments, Commander CFE Land Force FDO L-1/71," 22 September 1972, file 3185–1, part 1, RG 24, vol. 23485, LAC.
45 Gauthier, "Chapter IV," 19.
46 Jim Fox, telephone interview with author, 12 August 2013, confirmed in email to author, 29 January 2014.
47 "Land Force Policy Review, 1974," 5 October 1973, 79, file 44, 2 Combat Group fonds, 86–383, series 2, DHH.
48 "Minutes of the 95th Meeting of the Defence Management Committee," 18 February 1974, file 3, Defence Management Committee fonds, 79–560, box 2, DHH.

49 Draft of a Memorandum to Cabinet, "Land Force Policy," 6 September 1974, Annex J, 11, file – Canadian Force Europe Miscellaneous, 96–26, box 1, DHH; Gauthier, "Chapter IV," 19.
50 G. Simpson, "Land Force Policy Review," 3 December 1973, file 1901–2, part 3, RG 24, vol. 23571, LAC.
51 S.C. Waters, "Second Draft – Land Forces Policy Review," 12 December 1973, file 1901–2, part 3, RG 24, vol. 23571, LAC.
52 Andrew Godefroy, "Chasing the Silver Bullet: The Evolution of Capability Development in the Canadian Army," *Canadian Military Journal* 8, 1 (2007): 53–66. Also see Chapters 5 and 6 of Peter Kasurak, *A National Force* (Vancouver: UBC Press, 2013).

Chapter 6: The Scorpion and the Centurion

1 "Estimates – 1973–74, Department of National Defence," 22, file 1, 75–457, series 1, box 21, DHH.
2 Christopher F. Foss and Simon Dunstan, *Scorpion Reconnaissance Vehicle 1972–94* (Oxford: Osprey, 2005), 6–10.
3 A.J. Tedlie, "Light Armoured Regiment: Tracked and Wheeled Armoured Vehicles," 19 December 1968, file 891, 73–1223, series 1–2, box 48, DHH; Ross Campbell, "Defence Planning Questionnaire(69)," 24 October 1969, file 27–4-NATO-1–9, RG 25, vol. 10291, LAC.
4 Foss and Dunstan, *Scorpion Reconnaissance Vehicle,* 11–16; J.L. Drewry, "Future Resource Requirements," 30 October 1970, Annex A, file 3136–10, part 1, RG 24, accession 1994–95/725, box 3, LAC.
5 "Briefing of CDAC, Direct Fire Support Vehicle," 1969, file 20, 79–527, box 2, DHH.
6 Bob Caldwell, email to author, 14 April 2014.
7 Doug Green, email to author, 17 January 2014.
8 Foss and Dunstan, *Scorpion Reconnaissance Vehicle,* 10.
9 "Approval of Capital Project," 6 March 1972, 5, file 3136–5-L0980, RG 24, accession 1993–94/257, box 27, LAC.
10 J.R. Chisholm, "Minutes of the 7th Meeting of the Defence Management Committee," 21 February 1972, file 2, 79–560, box 1, DHH.
11 "Approval of Capital Project," 6 March 1972, 1, file 3136–5-L0980, RG 24, accession 1993–94/257, box 27, LAC. The Treasury Board's most important role during the procurement process in the 1970s was the final approval of the military's plan for procurement, after it had been approved by all levels of the military and by Cabinet, if necessary. The Treasury Board looked at the requirement and choice of equipment but focused on costing. If it did not meet the Treasury Board's standards, the military could not proceed with the purchase.
12 J.R. Chisholm, "Minutes of the 22nd Meeting of the Defence Management Committee," 14 August 1972, file 3, 79–560, box 1, DHH.
13 F.R. Sharp (CDS), "CDS Action Directive D24/71, Implementation White Paper, Second Report – Land Forces, Europe," 23 August 1972, file 2530, 73–1223, series 5, box 114, DHH.
14 J.R. Chisholm, "Minutes of the 29th Meeting of the Defence Management Committee," 25 September 1972, file 3, 79–560, box 1, DHH.
15 Gerry Koeller, interview with author, 17 June 2014.
16 Sean M. Maloney, "'A Proportion of Their Cavalry Shall Be Converted': Light Armoured Force Development in Canada's Army, 1952–1976." *Army Doctrine and Training Bulletin* 2, 4 (1999): 98.
17 Charles J. Gauthier, "Chapter IV: Between White Papers – Major Developments from the Mid 70s to Mid 80s," 10, file 56, 92–228, series 3, DHH.

18 Ibid., 11.

19 James Richardson, "Replacement of the Centurion Tank," Cabinet Document 1228–72, quoted in Gauthier, "Chapter IV," 11.

20 Cabinet of the Government of Canada, "Replacement of the Centurion Tank," Privy Council Office, 25 January 1973, Cabinet Conclusions Database, LAC.

21 L. Denis Hudon, "Configuration of the Canadian Land Forces in Europe," 20 March 1973, file 8, MG 26 O11, vol. 2, LAC. Richardson's draft of the Cabinet memo from February 1973 was attached to the letter.

22 Ibid.

23 Ivan Head to Pierre Trudeau, "Configuration of the Canadian Land Forces in Europe," 4 April 1973, file 8, MG 26 O11, vol. 2, LAC.

24 Ivan Head to Pierre Trudeau, "NATO Land Forces," 12 April 1973, file 1, MG 26 O19, vol. 139, LAC. A draft of the letter to J. Richardson was attached.

25 James Richardson, "Configuration of Canadian Land Forces in Europe," 10 May 1973, Cabinet Document 461–73, RG 2-B-2, vol. 6427, LAC.

26 Cabinet of the Government of Canada, "Configuration of Canadian Land Forces in Europe," Privy Council Office, 31 May 1973, Cabinet Conclusions Database, LAC.

27 Brereton Greenhous, *Dragoon* (Belleville, ON: Guild of the Royal Canadian Dragoons, 1983), 473.

28 "Extension of Life of Centurion Tanks until Dec 76," September 1973, 3A, file 3136–5-P2930, RG 24, accession 1993–94/257, box 27, LAC.

29 William J. Porter to the Department of State, "Reported Plan to Refit Centurion Tanks," 14 November 1974, Access to Archival Databases, National Archives and Records Administration (hereafter AAD, NARA).

30 Simon Dunstan, *Centurion Universal Tank 1943–2003* (Oxford: Osprey, 2003), 39.

31 Royal Canadian Dragoons, *The Springbok* (Lahr, Germany, 1974), 34–38, Military History Research Centre, Canadian War Museum, Ottawa (hereafter CWM).

32 "Extension of Life of Centurion Tanks until Dec 76," 8.

33 J.G. Mumford, "Minutes of the 60th Meeting of the Defence Management Committee," 28 May 1973, file 2, 79–560, box 2, DHH.

34 H.H. Winter, "Minutes of PCB Meeting 10/73," 7 November 1973, file 1150–100/P15, part 1, RG 24, accession 1997–98/625, box 1, LAC; J.G. Mumford, "Minutes of the 85th Meeting of the Defence Management Committee," 3 December 1973, file 2, 79–560, box 2, DHH.

35 Mac Campbell, telephone interview with author, 6 December 2013, confirmed in email to author, 18 January 2014.

36 Royal Canadian Dragoons, *The Springbok* (Lahr, Germany, 1975), 46–48, CWM.

37 Wayne D. Ralph, "The Bell AH-1Q TOW Cobra: Operational Experience and Field Trials," *Canadian Defence Quarterly* 4, 2 (1974): 24–26, FFL.

38 Jim Fox; Ramsey Withers, email to author, 17 January 2014.

39 D.L. Craig, "The Anti-Armour Helicopter," *The Springbok* (Lahr, Germany, 1975), 33–36, CWM.

40 Gordon Kitchen, "A Canadian View of the Organization, Role and Employment of Attack Helicopters," 9 November 1976, Annex A, 7, file 3185–1, part 7, RG 24, vol. 23546, LAC.

41 Randall Wakelam, "A Fine Mess: How Our Tactical Helicopter Force Came to Be What It Is," *Canadian Air Force Journal* 1, 3 (2008): 50.

42 Charles Nixon, interview by Roger Hill, 16 and 25 March 1987, *In Alliance*, 306.

43 J.C. Arnell, "The Economics of Defence (Part II: Inflation Strikes Hardest at Personnel Costs)," *Canadian Defence Quarterly* 3, 2 (1973): 25, FFL.

44 Dr. J.C. Arnell, "Funding of New Capital in the Future," 11 April 1972, file 3136–10, part 2, RG 24, accession 1994–95/725, box 3, LAC.
45 C.R. Nixon, deputy minister of national defence from 1975 to 1982, and General Gérard Thériault, CDS from 1983 to 1986, suggested this in their interviews with Doug Bland for Bland's *Chiefs of Defence: Government and the Unified Command of the Canadian Armed Forces* (Toronto: Canadian Institute of Strategic Studies, 1995). Gérard Thériault, interview by Doug Bland, March 1992, and C.R. Nixon, interview by Doug Bland, July 1992, transcripts, CWM.
46 H.H. Winter, "Minutes of PCB Meeting 2/71," 22 February 1971, see Annex F, which includes the memo by Rear Admiral J.A. Charles, file 1150–100/P15, part 1, RG 24, accession 1997–98/625, box 1, LAC.
47 Ibid.
48 Sylvain Cloutier, interview by R. Bothwell and J.L. Granatstein, 20 January 1988, 4, file 145, box 9, F0316, accession 1989–036, CTASC.
49 Arnell, "Funding of New Capital in the Future."
50 Charles Mills Drury and James Richardson, "Financing the Defence Program," 21 March 1973, Cabinet Document 422–73, RG 2-B-2, vol. 6426, LAC. The Cabinet Committee on External Policy and Defence supported the paper. Wilfrid Lavoie, "Financing the Defence Program," 24 May 1973, Cabinet Document 502–73, RG 2-B-2, vol. 6427, LAC.
51 Jean-Jacques Blais, email to author, January 2014.
52 "Notes for Remarks by Rt. Hon. P.E. Trudeau, Prime Minister of Canada, at the NATO Summit Meeting, Brussels, 30 May 1975," MG 26 O13, vol. 47, LAC.
53 Cabinet of the Government of Canada, "Financing the Defence Program," Privy Council Office, 31 May 1973, Cabinet Conclusions Database, LAC.
54 Bland, *Chiefs of Defence*, 19–20, 123.
55 Ivan Head and Pierre Trudeau, *The Canadian Way: Shaping Canada's Foreign Policy, 1968–1984* (Toronto: McClelland and Stewart, 1995), 85.
56 Peter Kasurak, *A National Force* (Vancouver: UBC Press, 2013), 124, 126.
57 Léo Cadieux, interview by Peter Stursberg, 12 September 1978, 14, file 139, box 9, F0316, accession 1989–036, CTASC.
58 Kasurak, *A National Force*, 130.
59 Cabinet of the Government of Canada, "The White Paper on Defence," Privy Council Office, 22 July 1971, Cabinet Conclusions Database, LAC.
60 Gordon Smith, interview by R. Bothwell and J.L. Granatstein, 8 October 1987, 4, file 148, box 10, F0316, accession 1989–036, CTASC.

Chapter 7: Tanks, Trade, and Strategy

1 T.G. Fraser, *The Arab-Israeli Conflict*, 3rd ed. (New York: Palgrave Macmillan, 2008), 98–104.
2 Abraham Rabinovich, *The Yom-Kippur War: The Epic Encounter That Transformed the Middle East* (New York: Schocken Books, 2004), 111–12; George W. Gawrych, *The 1973 Arab-Israeli War: The Albatross of Decisive Victory*, Leavenworth Papers No. 21 (Washington, DC: US Army Center of Military History, 1996), 39.
3 Saul Bronfeld, "Fighting Outnumbered: The Impact of the Yom Kippur War on the U.S. Army," *Journal of Military History* 71, 2 (2007): 466–67. http://dx.doi.org/10.1353/jmh.2007.0096.
4 J. Clarkson, "Spark at Yom Kippur: Many Surprises in an Eighteen Day War," *Canadian Defence Quarterly* 3, 4 (1974): 20–22, FFL.
5 L.W. Bentley and D.C. McKinnon, "The Yom Kippur War as an Example of Modern Land Battle," *Canadian Defence Quarterly* 4, 1 (1974): 18–19, FFL.

6 Rabinovich, *Yom Kippur War,* 509.
7 [?] Johnson to the Department of State, "Canadian Defense Debate," 6 December 1974, AAD, NARA.
8 J.F. Anderson, interview by R. Bothwell and J.L. Granatstein, 7 August 1987, 5, file 141, box 9, F0316, accession 1989–036, CTASC.
9 Jim Fox.
10 M.A. Stevenson to Pierre Elliott Trudeau, 26 November 1974, and Pierre Elliott Trudeau to M.A. Stevenson, 6 January 1975, file 117, MG 26 O7, vol. 52, LAC.
11 Daniel Yergin, *The Prize: The Epic Quest for Oil, Money, and Power* (New York: Free Press, 2008), 596–98.
12 Statistics Canada, "Consumer Price Index (CPI)," series V735319 in CANSIM database.
13 Charles J. Gauthier, "Chapter III: Funding the Defence Program from 1970 to 1975," 105–8, file 55, 92–228, series 3, DHH.
14 Allan MacEachen and James Richardson, "Financing the Defence Program in 1975–76," 13 October 1974, 12–18, Cabinet Document 578–74, RG 2-B-2, vol. 6449, LAC.
15 R.F. Charron, "Record of Cabinet Discussion, Meeting of 28 November 1974, Financing the Defence Program from 1975–76 to 1979–80," 2 December 1974, Cabinet Document 578–74, RG 2-B-2, vol. 6449, LAC.
16 Ivan Head to Pierre Trudeau, "Financing the Defence Program," 12 November 1974, 1, file 9, MG 26 O19, vol. 139, LAC.
17 Ivan Head to Pierre Trudeau, "Comments on The Defence Program Paper," 4 February 1975, 3, file 8, MG 26 O11, vol. 2, LAC.
18 Mitchell Sharp, "Canada-U.S. Relations: Options for the Future," special issue, *International Perspectives* (Autumn 1972): 1, 17, FFL; Mitchell Sharp, *Which Reminds Me ... : A Memoir* (Toronto: University of Toronto Press, 1994), 184.
19 J.L. Granatstein and Robert Bothwell, *Pirouette: Pierre Trudeau and Canadian Foreign Policy* (Toronto: University of Toronto Press, 1990), 164–65.
20 Ivan Head and Pierre Trudeau, *The Canadian Way: Shaping Canada's Foreign Policy, 1968–1984* (Toronto: McClelland and Stewart, 1995), 272–73.
21 "The Defence Program – Tasks," 24 March 1975, file 5, MG 26 O11, vol. 2, LAC.
22 William J. Porter to the Department of State, "Canadian Defense Effort to Be Reduced," 18 October 1974, AAD, NARA.
23 Memorandum of Conversation between Trudeau, Ford, and senior members of the Canadian and American governments and militaries, 4 December 1974, National Security Adviser Collection, Ford Library.
24 William J. Porter to the Department of State, "High-Level US-Canadian Defense Consultation," 13 February 1975, AAD, NARA.
25 "Canada/Federal Republic of Germany Defence Cooperation," [February 1975?], file 27–8-GFR, part 1, RG 25, vol. 10318, LAC.
26 Wolfgang Behrends, interview by R. Bothwell and J.L. Granatstein, 7 December 1987, 1, file 141, box 9, F0316, accession 1989–036, CTASC. In 2011, a ninety-two-year-old Schmidt visited Trudeau's tomb. Paul Chiasson, "Chrétien and Former German Leader Visit Trudeau's Tomb," *Toronto Star,* 1 June 2011, http://www.thestar.com/news/canada/2011/06/01/chrtien_and_former_german_leader_visit_trudeaus_tomb.html.
27 G. Crean, "PMs Visit: Assessment," 7 March 1975, MG 26 O13, vol. 68, LAC.
28 K. Leonberger, "Gespräch des Bundeskanzlers Schmidt mit Ministerpräsident Trudeau," 4 March 1975, in *Akten zur Auswärtigen Politik der Bundesrepublik Deutschland 1975, 1.*

Januar bis 30. Juni, ed. Michael Kieninger, Mechthild Lindemann, and Daniela Taschler (Munich: R. Oldenbourg, 2006), 212–14.

29 Head and Trudeau, *Canadian Way*, 273–74.

30 Menzies recalled that he set up a meeting between Schmidt and Trudeau on Canada's contributions to NATO in 1974, although he might have been referring to the March or May 1975 meetings because there is no reference to a 1974 meeting between the two leaders. There is also the suggestion that Menzies thought that Schmidt would be better able to convince Trudeau of the need for Canadian tanks in Europe, and this was indeed correct. Michael Posner, "Arthur Menzies was an extraordinary diplomat for 40 years," *Globe and Mail*, 21 March 2010, http://www.theglobeandmail.com/news/national/arthur-menzies-was-an-extraordinary-diplomat-for-40-years/article1209695/?page=all.

31 Rupprecht von Keller to the German Foreign Office, "Beteiligung Kanadas an den NATO-Streitkräften in Deutschland," 27 March 1975, in Kieninger, Lindemann, and Taschler, *Akten zur Auswärtigen Politik*, 321–22.

32 William J. Porter to the Department of State, "Annual Policy Assessment: Canada," 11 April 1975, AAD, NARA.

33 Douglas L. Bland, *Chiefs of Defence: Government and the Unified Command of the Canadian Armed Forces* (Toronto: Canadian Institute of Strategic Studies, 1995), 136–38.

34 J.A. Dextraze, interview by R. Bothwell and J.L. Granatstein, 12 April 1988, 2, file 141, box 9, F0316, accession 1989–036, CTASC.

35 Charles Nixon, interview by Roger Hill, 16 and 25 March 1987, *In Alliance*, 306.

36 Charles J. Gauthier, "Chapter IV: Between White Papers – Major Developments from the Mid 70s to Mid 80s," 39, file 56, 92–228, series 3, DHH.

37 James Richardson, "The Defence Program – The Tasks," 6 February 1975, 2, Cabinet Document 78–75, RG 2-B-2, vol. 6460, LAC.

38 Ibid., 15–17.

39 Cabinet of the Government of Canada, "The Defence Program – The Tasks," Privy Council Office, 17 April 1975, Cabinet Conclusions Database, LAC.

40 Wilfrid Lavoie, "Ministerial Meeting of the Defence Planning Committee 22–23 May 1975 – NATO Ministerial Guidance," 13 May 1975, James Richardson, "Ministerial Meeting of the Defence Planning Committee 22–23 May 1975 – NATO Ministerial Guidance," 2 May 1975, Cabinet Document 277–75, RG 2-B-2, vol. 6465, LAC.

41 Franz Krapf to the German Foreign Office, "Vorschau auf die bevorstehende NATO-Konferenz unter Teilnahme von Staats- und Regierungschefs," 23 May 1975, in Kieninger, Lindemann, and Taschler, *Akten zur Auswärtigen Politik*, 594–95.

42 "Notes of the Cabinet Meeting," 4 June 1975, file 1975/06/04 Cabinet Meeting, James E. Connor files, box 4, Gerald R. Ford Presidential Library, Ann Arbor, MI.

43 E. Mcauliffe, US Mission to NATO, to the Department of State, "Canadian Prime Minis Trudeau's Meeting with North Atlantic Council," 24 October 1974, AAD, NARA; Arthur Menzies, interview by Roger Hill and Nancy Pawelek, 5 July 1987, *In Alliance*, 390.

44 Memorandum of Conversation between Trudeau, Ford, and senior members of the Canadian and American governments and militaries, 30 May 1975, National Security Adviser Collection, Ford Library.

45 A.R. Menzies, "MTG between PM Trudeau and Chancellor Schmidt," 30 May 1975, file 27-NATO-12-SPRING-75, part 1, RG 25, vol. 14601, LAC.

46 G. Crean, "Following for Prime Minister, from Bonn," 16 July 1975, file 27–8-GFR, part 1, RG 25, vol. 10318, LAC; Arthur Menzies, interview by Roger Hill and Nancy Pawelek, 5 July 1987, *In Alliance*, 392.
47 "Notes for Remarks by Rt. Hon. P.E. Trudeau, Prime Minister of Canada, at the NATO Summit Meeting, Brussels, 30 May 1975," MG 26 O13, vol. 47, LAC.
48 "Background Notes on the Federal Republic of Germany: Biography of Mr. Hans-Dietrich Genscher, Minister of Foreign Affairs," [September 1975?], file 20–1-2-GFR, part 10, RG 25, vol. 8654, LAC.
49 G. Crean, "Following for Prime Minister, from Bonn," 16 July 1975, file 27–8-GFR, part 1, RG 25, vol. 10318, LAC.
50 E. Streator, US Mission to NATO, to the Department of State, "Canadian Defense Structure Review; Consultations," 18 June 1975, AAD, NARA.
51 R. Menzies, "CDN Defence Review – Consultations with FRG," 25 June 1975, file 27–4-NATO-1–9, part 3, RG 25, vol. 14598, LAC; David Bruce, US Mission to NATO, to the Department of State, "Canadian Defense Structure Review: FRG Follow-Up Paper," 5 July 1976, AAD, NARA.
52 Robert Ingersoll to the US Mission to NATO, "Canadian Defense Structure Review – US Comments," 3 July 1975, AAD, NARA.
53 David Bruce, US Mission to NATO, to the Department of State, "Canadian Defense Structure Review; Consultation June 26," 27 June 1975, AAD, NARA.
54 David Bruce, US Mission to NATO, to the Department of State, "Canadian Defense Structure Review; United States Comments," 27 June 1975, AAD, NARA.
55 Robert Ingersoll to the US Mission to NATO, "Canadian Defense Structure Review," 3 July 1975, AAD, NARA.
56 R. Menzies, "CDN Defence Review – Consultations with USA," 3 July 1975, file 27–4-NATO-1–9, part 3, RG 25, vol. 14598, LAC.
57 G. Crean, "CDN Defence: Consultation with FRG and USA," 6 August 1975, file 27–8-GFR, part 1, RG 25, vol. 10318, LAC.
58 J. Halstead, "PM's Talk with FRG Chancellor," 7 August 1975, file 20–1-2-GFR, part 10, RG 25, vol. 8654, LAC; Carl-Werner Sanne, "Gespräch des Bundeskanzlers Schmidt mit Ministerpräsident Trudeau," 31 July 1975, in Kieninger, Lindemann, and Taschler, *Akten zur Auswärtigen Politik*, 1084–86.
59 G.G. Riddell, "PDM's Lunch with the CDS," 29 August 1975, file 27–1-1–3, part 6, RG 25, vol. 10277, LAC.
60 William J. Porter to the Department of State, "SecDef Schlesinger Visit to Ottawa Sep 15–16," 11 September 1975, AAD, NARA.
61 John Wickham, "Highlights of Discussions between Secretary Schlesinger and Canadian Officials during Visit to Ottawa, 15–16 September," 17 September 1975, in *Documents on Western Europe, 1973–1976*, vol. E-15, part 2, of *Foreign Relations of the United States, 1969–1976*, ed. Kathleen B. Rasmussen (Washington, DC: Government Printing Office, 2014), 417–20.
62 William J. Porter to the Department of State, "SecDef's Visit to Ottawa Sept 15–16," 17 September 1975, AAD, NARA.
63 "Defence of Canada – Part 3: The Space Between," YouTube video, 2013, http://www.youtube.com/watch?v=unXd9Yz87Gs.
64 David Bruce, US Mission to NATO, to the Department of State, "Canadian Forces for NATO: DRC Multilateral Review," 29 October 1975, AAD, NARA.
65 See Joel J. Sokolsky, "Learning to Speak the Same Language: American Military Multilateralism and the Fraternity of the Uniform," paper presented to the conference "Lost in Translation? The Impact of Military Culture on Alliance and Coalition Politics," Centre for International and Defence Policy, Queen's University, 17–18 April 2015.

66 Ivan Head to Pierre Trudeau, "The Canadian Defence Program (Including Equipment Acquisitions)," 10 November 1975, 4, 16–17, file 9, MG 26 O19, vol. 139, LAC. Head attached a lengthy paper to his memo.
67 James Richardson, "The Defence Program – Force Structure," 9 November 1975, 4, 13–14, and 22, Cabinet Document 640–75, RG 2-B-2, vol. 6473, LAC.
68 R.F. Charron, "Defence Structure Review – Analysis of the Strategic Situation and Canadian Foreign Policy Implications," 20 November 1975, file 9, MG 26 O19, vol. 139, LAC.
69 Donald Macdonald to Pierre Trudeau, 12 November 1975, file 9, MG 26 O19, vol. 139, LAC.
70 Ivan Head to Pierre Trudeau, "Defence Purchases," 17 November 1975, file 9, MG 26 O19, vol. 139, LAC.
71 Cabinet of the Government of Canada, "The Defence Program Force Structure," Privy Council Office, 20 November 1975, Cabinet Conclusions Database, LAC.
72 See Granatstein and Bothwell, *Pirouette,* 254–55; Bland, *Chiefs of Defence,* 136–38; and Roy Rempel, *Counterweights: The Failure of Canada's German and European Policy, 1955–1995* (Montreal and Kingston: McGill-Queen's University Press, 1997), 86–87.
73 "Defence of Canada – Part 3: The Space Between."
74 [?] Johnson to the Department of State, "Visit of Secretary Kissinger to Ottawa October 14–15," 3 October 1975, AAD, NARA.
75 See Gerald Ford's letter to Pierre Trudeau on the purchase of the long-range patrol aircraft, 28 May 1976, National Security Adviser Collection, Ford Library.
76 Marilyn Eustace, *Canada's European Force: 1964–1971* (Kingston, ON: Centre for International Relations, Queen's University, 1982), 148.
77 Byers, "Defence and Foreign Policy in the 1970s: The Demise of the Trudeau Doctrine," *International Journal* 33, 2 (1978): 332. http://dx.doi.org/10.1177/002070207803300203.
78 Granatstein and Bothwell, *Pirouette,* 254–55.
79 Head and Trudeau, *Canadian Way,* 76.
80 Rempel, *Counterweights,* 86–87.
81 John Marteinson and Michael R. McNorgan, *The Royal Canadian Armoured Corps: An Illustrated History* (Toronto: Canadian Royal Armoured Corps Association and Canadian War Museum, 2000), 386.
82 Robert Bothwell, *Alliance and Illusion: Canada and the World, 1945–1984* (Vancouver: UBC Press, 2007), 383, 440n40.
83 Ramsey Withers, email to author, 17 January 2014.
84 John Halstead, interview by Roger Hill, 3 and 5 June 1987, *In Alliance,* 427.
85 Thomas S. Axworthy, "G8: The Most Exclusive Club in the World," *Historica Canada,* 2015, http://www.thecanadianencyclopedia.com/en/article/g8-the-most-exclusive-club-in-the-world-feature/.
86 Rempel, *Counterweights,* 103, 30.
87 See M.M. Kostecki, "Canada's Grain Trade with the Soviet Union and China," *Canadian Journal of Agricultural Economics / Revue canadienne d'agroeconomie* 30, 2 (1982): 223–38. http://dx.doi.org/10.1111/j.1744-7976.1982.tb01980.x.
88 Ross Campbell, interview by Roger Hill, David Cox, and Nancy Pawelek, 13 and 16 April 1987, *In Alliance,* 352.
89 Karl Carstens, interview by R. Bothwell and J.L. Granatstein, 22 October 1987, 1, file 149, box 10, F0316, accession 1989–036, CTASC.
90 This was similar to STAFEUR's argument that Canada needed to provide forces that were not only acceptable to allies to get the benefits of the alliance but were also supported by concrete evidence. Michael Shenstone, interview by R. Bothwell and J.L. Granatstein, 2 February 1989, 1, file 148, box 10, F0316, accession 1989–036, CTASC.

91 Tom Axworthy.
92 François Richard, interview by R. Bothwell and J.L. Granatstein, 8 October 1987, 1, file 148, box 10, F0316, accession 1989–036, CTASC.
93 "Record of Conversation – Visit of Chancellor Schmidt, July 1976," [July 1976?], file 20-GFR-9-SCHMIDT, H, part 1, RG 25, vol. 9297, LAC.
94 Tom Axworthy.
95 "Statement by Prime Minister Trudeau at the NATO Summit, Washington D.C., May 30, 1978," MG 26 O13, vol. 48, LAC.

Chapter 8: "From a Beetle to a Porsche"

Portions of this chapter previously appeared in a shortened analysis of the Leopard purchase in the *Canadian Military Journal* 16, 4 (2016): 16–27.

1 Mac Campbell, telephone interview with author, 6 December 2013, confirmed in email to author, 18 January 2014.
2 G.G. Brown, "Comparative Tank Data," 9 June 1975, attached to a memo from Jacques Dextraze to Ivan Head, 17 June 1975, file 8, MG 26 O19, vol. 139, LAC.
3 Jacques Dextraze to Ivan Head, 17 June 1975, "Comparative Tank Data," file 8, MG 26 O19, vol. 139, LAC.
4 G.G. Riddell, "Retrofitting of Tanks for Canadian Mechanized Brigade Group in Europe," 27 August 1975, file 27–1-1–3, part 6, RG 25, vol. 10277, LAC.
5 G.G. Riddell, "PDM's Lunch with the CDS," 29 August 1975, file 27–1-1–3, part 6, RG 25, vol. 10277, LAC.
6 Larry Brownrigg, interview with author, 12 August 2013.
7 Charles J. Gauthier, "Chapter VII: Important Equipment Acquisitions during the 1970–1990 Period," 50, file 56, 92–228, series 3, DHH.
8 J.A. Dextraze, interview by R. Bothwell and J.L. Granatstein, 12 April 1988, 3, file 141, box 9, F0316, accession 1989–036, CTASC.
9 R.J. Baxter, "Minutes of PCB Meeting 6/75," October 21, 1975, RG 24, file 1150–100/P15, part 1, accession 1997–98/625, box 1, LAC; R.J. Baxter, "Minutes of PCB Meeting 26/75," November 27, 1975, file 1150–100/P15, part 1, RG 24, accession 1997–98/625, box 1, LAC.
10 Mac Campbell.
11 G.J. Koeller, "Leopard Project Post-Project Report, April 1981, Executive Summary," April 1981, 3–4, file 8344–006, part 2-PA, Records of the Treasury Board Secretariat, RG 55, accession 2002–00077–8, box 22, LAC; Larry Brownrigg.
12 Mac Campbell.
13 The steering committee was composed of the Director General Land Engineering Procurement and Maintenance, Brigadier-General E. Creber, as chair; Director General of Procurement and Supply, Brigadier-General D. Day; the head of Director Land Requirements, Lieutenant-Colonel C. Conway; the Chief Industrial Products Division at DSS, R. Longhurst; and another official from Industry, Trade, and Commerce. G.G. Riddell from External Affairs, Bureau of Defence and Arms Control, was also kept abreast of events. Koeller, "Leopard Project Post-Project Report," 3–4.
14 For a time, Killick was replaced by M. Matusiak, acting chief of supply. W.E. Grant to T. Charland, "Report on Leopard Tank Offset Negotiations with Krauss-Maffei AG, Munich, July 27–August 6, 1976," 10 August 1976, Records of the Department of Supply and Services, RG 98, vol. 390, file ERO-6500–36, LAC.
15 Larry Brownrigg.
16 Christopher F. Foss, ed., *Jane's Armour and Artillery: 1990–91* (London: Jane's Information Group, 1990), 39, 133.

17 Koeller, "Leopard Project Post-Project Report," 1–2.
18 Larry Brownrigg.
19 Koeller, "Leopard Project Post-Project Report," 12.
20 Ibid.
21 J.G. Mumford, "Minutes of the 196th Meeting of the Defence Management Committee," 5 April 1976, file 2, 79–560, box 5, DHH.
22 James Richardson, "The Tank Replacement Program," 28 April 1976, Cabinet Document 224–76, RG 2-B-2, vol. 6503, LAC.
23 Cabinet of the Government of Canada, "The Tank Replacement Program," Privy Council Office, 20 May 1976, Cabinet Conclusions Database, LAC.
24 Koeller, "Leopard Project Post-Project Report," 10.
25 J. Halstead to National Defence Headquarters, "Official Visit to Bonn by MND [Minister of National Defence]," 17 January 1977, file 27–8-GFR, part 1, RG 25, vol. 10318, LAC.
26 Koeller, "Leopard Project Post-Project Report," 24.
27 Mac Campbell.
28 W.E. Grant to T. Charland, "Report on Leopard Tank Offset Negotiations with Krauss-Maffei AG, Munich, July 27–August 6, 1976," 10 August 1976, RG 98, vol. 390, file ERO-6500–36, LAC; from Bonn to DSS, "Krauss-Maffei Contract," 13 October 1976, RG 98, vol. 390, file ERO-6500–36, LAC.
29 C.R. Nixon to G.F. Osbaldeston, 8 October 1976, file 3779–05–07, RG 19, vol. 6166, LAC.
30 Larry Brownrigg.
31 F.R. Blythman, Annex to "Report of Leopard Tank Discussions – Bonn – Lahr 3 Dec 76–9 Dec 76," 21 December 1976, file 1180–120/L8, part 1, RG 24, accession 1997–98/122, box 242, LAC.
32 Koeller, "Leopard Project Post-Project Report," 11.
33 D.V. Hampson, "Leopard Project – Briefing to PCB, 12 Jan 78," attached to "Minutes of PCB Meeting 1/78," 17 January 1978, file 1150–110P15, part 1, RG 24, accession 1997–98/625, box 3, LAC.
34 Mac Campbell.
35 B.A. Sulzenko to A.J. Barry, "Leopard Tank," 1 October 1976, file 3779–05–07, RG 19, vol. 6166, LAC.
36 G.C. Wesley, "Minutes of a Meeting on the Leopard Club Held in ADM(MAT) Conference Room," 25 October 1976, file 1180–120/L8, part 1, RG 24, accession 1997–98/122, box 242, LAC.
37 Koeller, "Leopard Project Post-Project Report," Annex C.
38 "Centurion/Leopard Ceremonies," *The Springbok* (Lahr, Germany, July 1977), 7, CWM.
39 D.V. Hampson, "Leopard Project – Briefing to PCB, 22 Nov 79," attached to "Minutes of PCB Meeting 36/79," 22 November 1979, file 1150–110P15, part 3, RG 24, accession 1997–98/625, box 3, LAC.
40 Koeller, "Leopard Project Post-Project Report," Annex H.
41 D.V. Hampson, "Leopard Project – Briefing to PCB, 12 Jan 78."
42 Koeller, "Leopard Project Post-Project Report," 16.
43 "Additional Information for the Briefing Officer," 6 January 1982, 16, file 8344–006, part 2-PA, RG 55, accession 2002–00077–8, box 22, LAC.
44 "Agreement between the Federal Minister of Defence of the Federal Republic of Germany and the Minister of National Defence of Canada Regarding the Loan of Leopard Battle Tanks, Recovery and Bridgelayer Tanks, Logistic Support, and the Training of Personnel," signed 14 October 1976, file 48, 2007–9, box 2, DHH.
45 Koeller, "Leopard Project Post-Project Report," 10, 15.

46 Clive Milner, telephone interview with author, 5 August 2013, confirmed in email to author, 20 January 2014.
47 Harry Mohr, interview by J.R. "Digger" MacDougall, October 2004, transcript, CWM; Harry Mohr, "Leopard," *The Springbok* (Lahr, Germany, July 1977), 11–12, CWM.
48 S.B. MacKinnon, "The Troop Leaders Speak Out," *Armour Bulletin,* October 1977, Armoured Department, Combat Arms School (Gagetown, NB), 10–11, FFL.
49 "Agreement between the Federal Minister of Defence of the Federal Republic of Germany and the Minister of National Defence of Canada," 5, 8.
50 Koeller, "Leopard Project Post-Project Report," 19; Terry Seeley, interview by J.R. "Digger" MacDougall, July 2004, transcript, CWM.
51 Clive Milner; Jim Fox.
52 "Agreement between the Federal Minister of Defence of the Federal Republic of Germany and the Minister of National Defence of Canada," 5.
53 Terry Seeley.
54 S.B. MacKinnon, "The Troop Leaders Speak Out," *Armour Bulletin,* October 1977, Armoured Department, Combat Arms School (Gagetown, NB), 10–11, FFL.
55 Clive Milner.
56 Terry Seeley.
57 Clive Milner; Koeller, "Leopard Project Post-Project Report," Annex M, 12; S.B. MacKinnon, "The Troop Leaders Speak Out"; Harry Mohr, interview by J.R. "Digger" MacDougall, October 2004, transcript, CWM.
58 Terry Seeley.
59 Clive Milner.
60 "Canadian Army Trophy 1977," *The Springbok* (Lahr, Germany, July 1977), 10–11, CWM.
61 Clive Milner.
62 Clive Milner, "Message from the Commanding Officer," *The Springbok* (Lahr, Germany, July 1977), 3–4, CWM.
63 Larry Brownrigg.
64 G.J. O'Connor, "Centurion to Leopard C1," *Armour Bulletin*, January 1977, Armoured Department, Combat Arms School (Gagetown, NB), 14, FFL.
65 Bill Coupland, email message to author, 20 January 2014.
66 Koeller, "Leopard Project Post-Project Report," 22.
67 Gerry Koeller.
68 Bill Coupland.
69 "Driving and Maintenance," *Armour Bulletin,* October 1977, Armoured Department, Combat Arms School (Gagetown, NB), FFL.
70 Jim Fox.
71 Gerry Koeller.
72 Mac Campbell.
73 Jim Gervais, telephone interview with author, 23 June 2014.
74 Foss, *Jane's Armour and Artillery: 1990–91,* 33–39; Lieutenant M.J. Pacey, "The SABCA – Tank Fire Control System," *The Springbok* (Lahr, Germany, January 1977), 24, CWM.
75 John Marteinson and Michael R. McNorgan, *The Royal Canadian Armoured Corps: An Illustrated History* (Toronto: Canadian Royal Armoured Corps Association and Canadian War Museum, 2000), 387.
76 Darrell Dean, telephone interview with author, 23 May 2014.
77 Walter J. Spielberger, *From Half-Track to Leopard 2* (Munich: Bernard and Graefe, 1979), 227–28.
78 Terry Seeley.

79 Koeller, "Leopard Project Post-Project Report," Annex M, 12.
80 Ibid., 25.
81 Ibid., 14.
82 K.R. Black, "Brief on the Leopard Report," attached to "Visit Report," 29 June 1976, file 1180–120/L8–2, part 1, RG 24, accession 1997–98/122, box 244, LAC.
83 Federal Office for Military Technology and Procurement, "Minutes of a Meeting Regarding the Establishment of the Technical Working Group of the LEOPARD User Nations," 16 February 1978, file 1180–120/L8–6, part 1, RG 24, accession 1997–98/122, box 247, LAC. Translated from the original German in 1978.
84 D.V. Hampson, "Leopard Project – Briefing to PCB, 22 Nov 79."
85 Bill Coupland.
86 From National Defence to Treasury Board, "Authority to Enter into an Agreement," 10 March 1977, file 1180–120/L8, part 2, RG 24, accession 1997–98/122, box 242, LAC.
87 Gerry Koeller.
88 Koeller, "Leopard Project Post-Project Report," 25.
89 Ibid., 19, 22.
90 Bill Coupland; Clive Milner; Darrell Dean.
91 Gerry Koeller.
92 "Additional Information for the Briefing Officer," 6 January 1982, 3, file 8344–006, part 2-PA, RG 55, accession 2002–00077–8, box 22.
93 W.E. Grant to T. Charland, "Report on Leopard Tank Offset Negotiations with Krauss-Maffei AG."
94 Larry Brownrigg.
95 A.W. Allan to J.M. Desroches, "Leopard Tank Procurement, Draft Provisions for Industrial Offsets," 27 August 1976, file ERO-6500–36, RG 98, vol. 390, LAC.
96 "Canadian-German Relations in the Field of Defence," [November 1976?], file 27–8-GFR, part 1, RG 25, vol. 10318, LAC.
97 D.V. Hampson, "Leopard Project – Briefing to PCB, 12 Jan 78."
98 D.V. Hampson, "Leopard Project – Briefing to PCB, 22 Nov 79," attached to "Minutes of PCB Meeting 36/79," 6 December 1979, file 1150–110P15, part 3, RG 24, accession 1997–98/625, box 3, LAC; Koeller, "Leopard Project Post-Project Report," 18.
99 D.V. Hampson, "Leopard Project – Briefing to PCB, 22 Nov 79," attached to "Minutes of PCB Meeting 36/79," 6 December 1979.
100 Industry, Trade, and Commerce – Defence Programs Branch, "Cross-Canada Industrial Tour By Krauss-Maffei & Sub-Contractors of Germany in Support of Leopard Tank Offset Agreement," 1980, file APB 3350–004–02 V, RG 55, accession 2010–00088–9, box 7, LAC.
101 Koeller, "Leopard Project Post-Project Report," 12; Larry Brownrigg.
102 D.V. Hampson, "Leopard Project – Briefing to PCB, 22 Nov 79."
103 "Treasury Board Submission – Amendment to Approval of the Leopard Project – DSP L1373," 27 September 1978, included in Koeller, "Leopard Project Post-Project Report."
104 Koeller, "Leopard Project Post-Project Report," 17.
105 "Canadian-German Relations in the Field of Defence."
106 "German-Canadian Relations Defence Cooperation," 27 June 1977, file 27–8-GFR, part 1, RG 25, vol. 10318, LAC.
107 KM produced Leopard 1s for Greece and Turkey in the early 1980s. Christopher F. Foss, ed., *Jane's Armour and Artillery: 2010–2011* (London: Jane's Information Group, 2010), 49–52.
108 Al Ditter, "Project Tank: Replacing the Leopard," *Aerospace and Defence Technology* (March/April 1989): 17.

109 See the testimony on 13 May 1976, 29 November 1976, 1 December 1976, 17 May 1977, 2007–11, boxes 6 and 7, DHH.
110 Standing Committee on External Affairs and National Defence, 1 December 1975, file 7, 2007–11, box 6, DHH.
111 Ibid., 17.
112 A.A. Stuck, "Minutes of Meeting PCB 22/81," 6 November 1981, file 1150–110/P15, part 4, RG 24, accession 1997–98/625, box 5, LAC; Koeller, "Leopard Project Post-Project Report," 22.
113 D.V. Hampson, "Leopard Project – Briefing to PCB, 22 Nov 79."
114 Office of the Auditor General of Canada, "1984 Report of the Auditor General of Canada: Chapter 12 – Department of National Defence," Reports to Parliament (Ottawa: Office of the Auditor General of Canada, 1984).

Conclusion

1 See Joseph Jockel and Joel Sokolsky, "Emphasizing the Assets: A Proposal for the Restructuring of Canada's Military Contribution to NATO," *Canadian Defence Quarterly* 9, 2 (1979), FFL; Gérard Thériault, interview by Doug Bland, March 1992, transcript, CWM.
2 For example, see Isabel Campbell, *Unlikely Diplomats: The Canadian Brigade in Germany, 1951–64* (Vancouver: UBC Press, 2013), for a recent challenge to the narrative. See J.L. Granatstein, *Canada's Army: Waging War and Keeping the Peace,* 2nd ed. (Toronto: University of Toronto Press, 2011), for the most prominent example of this arc.
3 See Charles J. Gauthier, "Chapter I: Preface," 12–13, file 53, 92–228, series 3, DHH.
4 See Chapters 5 and 6 of Peter Kasurak, *A National Force* (Vancouver: UBC Press, 2013).
5 Henry Kissinger, *The White House Years* (Boston: Little Brown, 1979), 382–83.
6 William Peters did not directly address the brigade in Europe, but allied pressure for tanks clearly fits his analysis of Canada's relationship with its alliances. See William Peters, *Club Dues: The Relevance of Canadian Expeditionary Forces* (Toronto: Irwin, 2001), 101, 104.
7 Roy Rempel, *Counterweights: The Failure of Canada's German and European Policy, 1955–1995* (Montreal and Kingston: McGill-Queen's University Press, 1997), 87–97.
8 For an overview of the literature, see Alex Roland's excellent pamphlet *The Military Industrial Complex* (Washington, DC: American Historical Association, 2001).
9 See James Burton, *The Pentagon Wars* (Annapolis, MD: Naval Institute Press, 1993), and the film *The Pentagon Wars,* directed by Richard Benjamin (New York: HBO, 1998).
10 Irving Brinton Holley, *Buying Aircraft for the Army Air Forces in World War II* (1962; reprint, Washington, DC: Ross and Perry, 2001), 573.
11 This concept was helpfully suggested by one of the anonymous reviewers for an article based on this research.
12 For example, see J.L. Granatstein and Robert Bothwell, *Pirouette: Pierre Trudeau and Canadian Foreign Policy* (Toronto: University of Toronto Press, 1990), 255.
13 Barney Danson, *Not Bad for a Sergeant: The Memoirs of Barney Danson,* with Curtis Fahey (Toronto: Dundurn Group, 2002), 218–22.
14 Granatstein and Bothwell, *Pirouette,* 254.
15 See Eliot A. Cohen, *Supreme Command: Soldiers, Statesmen, and Leadership in Wartime* (New York: Free Press, 2002), for an analysis of Lincoln, Clemenceau, Churchill, and Ben-Gurion and their leadership during wartime and how they questioned and directed their subordinates.

Bibliography

Archival Sources

Canadian Command and Staff College, Fort Frontenac Library, Kingston
Mobile Command Annual Historical Reports
Special Committee on Defence, 1963
Standing Committee on National Defence, 1966 and 1967

Canadian War Museum, Military History Research Centre, Ottawa
Doug Bland interviews
J.R. MacDougall interviews

Clara Thomas Archives and Special Collections, York University, Toronto
J.L. Granatstein Fonds, F0316

Directorate of History and Heritage, Ottawa
2 Combat Group Fonds (86–383)
Canadian Embassy (Germany) Fonds (2007–09)
Charles J. Gauthier Fonds (92–228)
Defence Management Committee Fonds (79–560)
Department of National Defence Estimates Collection (75–457)
Director General Land Force Development Fonds (96–26)
Director of Combat Development (80–499)
File 112.1.009 (D37)
Jean Victor Allard Fonds (84–126)
Robert Lewis Raymont Fonds (73–1223)
William B.S. Sutherland Fonds (79–527)

Gerald R. Ford Presidential Library, Ann Arbor, MI
James E. Connor Files
National Security Adviser Collection

Library and Archives Canada, Ottawa
Cabinet Conclusions
Department of External Affairs
Department of Finance
Department of National Defence
Department of Supply and Services
H. Basil Robinson Fonds
John Halstead Fonds

Lester B. Pearson Fonds
Maxwell Yalden Fonds
Mitchell Sharp Fonds
Paul Martin Fonds
Pierre Trudeau Fonds
Treasury Board Secretariat

National Archives and Records Administration, College Park, MD
Access to Archival Databases (https://aad.archives.gov/aad/)

NATO Archives
North Atlantic Council Fonds, Defence Planning Committee Series

University of Toronto Archives and Record Management Services, Toronto
Robert Selkirk Bothwell Fonds, Accession B1988–0074

Magazines and Journals

ARMOR
Armour Bulletin
Canadian Army Journal
Canadian Defence Quarterly
International Perspectives
Sentinel
Springbook
Strathconian

Other Sources

Addinall, Robert. "To Transform an Army: The Canadian Interpretation of the RMA and the Transformation of Armoured Vehicle Design, 1992–2008 – The Case of the LAV III." PhD diss., War Studies, Royal Military College, Kingston, ON, 2011.

Allard, Jean V. *The Memoirs of General Jean V. Allard.* With Serge Bernier. Vancouver: UBC Press, 1988.

Axworthy, Thomas S. "G8: The Most Exclusive Club in the World." *Historica Canada.* 2015. http://www.thecanadianencyclopedia.com/en/article/g8-the-most-exclusive-club-in-the-world-feature/.

Bennett, M. Todd, ed. *National Security Policy, 1969–1972.* Vol. 34 of *Foreign Relations of the United States, 1969–1976.* Washington, DC: Government Printing Office, 2011.

Bijker, Wiebe E. *Of Bicycles, Bakelites, and Bulbs: Toward a Theory of Sociotechnical Change.* Cambridge, MA: MIT Press, 1995.

Bijker, Wiebe E., Thomas Hughes, and Trevor J. Pinch, eds. *The Social Construction of Technological Systems: New Directions in the Sociology and History of Technology.* Cambridge, MA: MIT Press, 1987.

Bland, Douglas L. *The Administration of Defence Policy in Canada.* Kingston, ON: Frye, 1987.

–. *Chiefs of Defence: Government and the Unified Command of the Canadian Armed Forces.* Toronto: Canadian Institute of Strategic Studies, 1995.

Bothwell, Robert. *Alliance and Illusion: Canada and the World, 1945–1984.* Vancouver: UBC Press, 2007.

Bronfeld, Saul. "Fighting Outnumbered: The Impact of the Yom Kippur War on the U.S. Army." *Journal of Military History* 71, 2 (2007): 465–98. http://dx.doi.org/10.1353/jmh.2007.0096.

Burton, James. *The Pentagon Wars.* Annapolis, MD: Naval Institute Press, 1993.

Byers, Michael, and Stewart Webb. *That Sinking Feeling: Canada's Submarine Program Springs a Leak*. Ottawa: Canadian Centre for Policy Alternatives and Rideau Institute, 2013.

Byers, R.B. "Defence and Foreign Policy in the 1970s: The Demise of the Trudeau Doctrine." *International Journal* 33, 2 (1978): 312–38. http://dx.doi.org/10.1177/002070207803300203.

Campbell, Isabel. *Unlikely Diplomats: The Canadian Brigade in Germany, 1951–64*. Vancouver: UBC Press, 2013.

Canada, Department of National Defence. *Defence in the 70s*. Ottawa: Information Canada, 1971.

–. *White Paper on Defence*. Ottawa: Queen's Printer, 1964.

Clearwater, John. *Canadian Nuclear Weapons*. Toronto: Dundurn Press, 1998.

–. *"Just Dummies": Cruise Missile Testing in Canada*. Calgary: University of Calgary Press, 2006.

–. *U.S. Nuclear Weapons in Canada*. Toronto: Dundurn Press, 1999.

Cohen, Eliot A. *Supreme Command: Soldiers, Statesmen, and Leadership in Wartime*. New York: Free Press, 2002.

Danson, Barney. *Not Bad for a Sergeant: The Memoirs of Barney Danson*. With Curtis Fahey. Toronto: Dundurn Group, 2002.

"Defence of Canada – Part 3: The Space Between." YouTube video. 2013. https://www.youtube.com/watch?v=unXd9Yz87Gs.

Dingwall, Don. *The Centurion in Canadian Service*. Ottawa: Service, 2005.

Ditter, Al. "Project Tank: Replacing the Leopard." *Aerospace and Defence Technology* (March/April 1989): 17–25.

Donaghy, Greg. *Tolerant Allies: Canada and the United States, 1963–1968*. Montreal and Kingston: McGill-Queen's University Press, 2002.

Duffield, John. *Power Rules: The Evolution of NATO's Conventional Force Posture*. Palo Alto, CA: Stanford University Press, 1995.

Dunstan, Simon. *Centurion Universal Tank 1943–2003*. Oxford: Osprey, 2003.

Eibl, Franz, and Hubert Zimmermann, eds. *Akten zur Auswärtigen Politik der Bundesrepublik Deutschland 1969, 1. Januar bis 30. Juni*. Munich: R. Oldenbourg, 2000.

–, eds. *Akten zur Auswärtigen Politik der Bundesrepublik Deutschland 1969, 1. Juli bis 31. Dezember*. Munich: R. Oldenbourg, 2000.

English, John. *Just Watch Me: The Life of Pierre Elliott Trudeau*. Toronto: Knopf, 2009.

–. "Problems in Middle Life." In *Canada and NATO: Uneasy Past, Uncertain Future*, edited by Margaret MacMillan and David Sorenson, 47–66. Waterloo, ON: University of Waterloo Press, 1990.

Eustace, Marilyn. *Canada's European Force: 1964–1971*. Kingston, ON: Centre for International Relations, Queen's University, 1982.

Fetterly, Ross. "Arming Canada: Defence Procurement for the Twenty-First Century." PhD diss., War Studies, Royal Military College, Kingston, ON, 2011.

Figes, Orlando. *Revolutionary Russia, 1891–1991: A History*. New York: Metropolitan Books, 2014.

Fortmann, Michel, Martin Larose, and Susan M. Murphy. "An Emerging Strategic Counterculture? Pierre Elliott Trudeau, Canadian Intellectuals and the Revision of Liberal Defence Policy Concerning NATO (1968–1969)." *International Journal* 59, 3 (2004): 537–56.

Foss, Christopher F., ed. *Jane's Armour and Artillery: 1990–91*. London, UK: Jane's Information Group, 1990.

–, ed. *Jane's Armour and Artillery: 2010–2011*. London, UK: Jane's Information Group, 2010.

Foss, Christopher F., and Simon Dunstan. *Scorpion Reconnaissance Vehicle 1972–94*. Oxford: Osprey, 1995.

Fraser, T.G. *The Arab-Israeli Conflict*. 3rd ed. New York: Palgrave Macmillan, 2008.

Gavin, Francis. *Nuclear Statecraft: History and Strategy in America's Atomic Age*. Ithaca, NY: Cornell University Press, 2012.

Gawrych, George W. *The 1973 Arab-Israeli War: The Albatross of Decisive Victory*. Leavenworth Papers No. 21. Washington, DC: US Army Center of Military History, 1996.

Gellner, John. *Canada in NATO*. Toronto: Ryerson Press, 1970.

Godefroy, Andrew. "Chasing the Silver Bullet: The Evolution of Capability Development in the Canadian Army." *Canadian Military Journal* 8, 1 (2007): 53–66.

–. *In Peace Prepared*. Vancouver: UBC Press, 2015.

Granatstein, J.L. *Canada's Army: Waging War and Keeping the Peace*. 2nd ed. Toronto: University of Toronto Press, 2011.

–. *A Man of Influence*. Ottawa: Deneau, 1981.

Granatstein, J.L., and Robert Bothwell. "Pierre Trudeau on His Foreign Policy: A Conversation in 1988." *International Journal* 88, 1 (2010–11): 171–81.

–. *Pirouette: Pierre Trudeau and Canadian Foreign Policy*. Toronto: University of Toronto Press, 1990.

Greenhous, Brereton. *Dragoon*. Belleville, ON: Guild of the Royal Canadian Dragoons, 1983.

Hart, Michael. *A Trading Nation: Canadian Trade Policy from Colonialism to Globalization*. Vancouver: UBC Press, 2002.

Head, Ivan, and Pierre Trudeau. *The Canadian Way: Shaping Canada's Foreign Policy, 1968–1984*. Toronto: McClelland and Stewart, 1995.

Hecht, Gabrielle. *The Radiance of France: Nuclear Power and National Identity after World War II*. Cambridge, MA: MIT Press, 1998.

Holley, Iriving Brinton. *Buying Aircraft for the Army Air Forces in World War II*. 1962. Reprint, Washington, DC: Ross and Perry, 2001.

Jenkins, Tom. *Canada First: Leveraging Defence Procurement through Key Industrial Capabilities – Report of the Special Adviser to the Minister of Public Works and Government Services*. February 2013. http://www.tpsgc-pwgsc.gc.ca/app-acq/documents/eam-lmp-eng.pdf.

Kasurak, Peter. *A National Force*. Vancouver: UBC Press, 2013.

Kieninger, Michael, Mechthild Lindemann, and Daniela Taschler, eds. *Akten zur Auswärtigen Politik der Bundesrepublik Deutschland 1975, 1. Januar bis 30. Juni*. Munich: R. Oldenbourg, 2006.

Kissinger, Henry. *The White House Years*. Boston: Little Brown, 1979.

Kostecki, M.M. "Canada's Grain Trade with the Soviet Union and China." *Canadian Journal of Agricultural Economics/Revue canadienne d'agroeconomie* 30, 2 (1982): 223–38. http://dx.doi.org/10.1111/j.1744-7976.1982.tb01980.x.

Lackenbauer, Whitney P., Franklyn Griffiths, and Rob Huebert. *Canada and the Changing Arctic: Sovereignty, Security and Stewardship*. Forewords by Bill Graham and Hugh Segal. Waterloo, ON: Wilfrid Laurier University Press, 2011.

Lackenbauer, Whitney P., and Peter Kikkert. *The Canadian Forces and Arctic Sovereignty*. Waterloo, ON: Wilfrid Laurier University Press, 2010.

Lewis, Adrian R. *The American Culture of War*. New York: Routledge, 2007.

Lindemann, Mechthild, and Matthias Peter, eds. *Akten zur Auswärtigen Politik der Bundesrepublik Deutschland 1968, 1. Januar bis 30. Juni*. Munich: R. Oldenbourg, 1999.

–, eds. *Akten zur Auswärtigen Politik der Bundesrepublik Deutschland 1968, 1. Juli bis 31. Dezember*. Munich: R. Oldenbourg, 1999.

MacKenzie, Donald. *Inventing Accuracy: A Historical Sociology of Nuclear Missile Guidance*. Cambridge, MA: MIT Press, 1990.

Maloney, Sean M. "Fire Brigade or Tocsin? NATO's ACE Mobile Force, Flexible Response and the Cold War." *Journal of Strategic Studies* 27, 4 (2004): 585–613. http://dx.doi.org/10.1080/1362369042000314529.

–. *Learning to Love the Bomb*. Washington, DC: Potomac Books, 2007.

–. "'A Proportion of Their Cavalry Shall Be Converted': Light Armoured Force Development in Canada's Army, 1952–1976." *Army Doctrine and Training Bulletin* 2, 4 (1999): 85–103.

–. "Sean M. Maloney.com - The Royal Canadian Armoured Corps: An Illustrated History." Accessed May 14, 2012. http://www.seanmmaloney.com/canadian-armed-forces-operations/the-royal-canadian-armoured-corps-an-illustrated-history-co-authored-with-john-marteinson-and-michael-mcnorgan-foreword-by-desmond-morton-toronto-robin-brass-200/.

Männistö-Funk, Tiina. "The Crossroads of Technology and Tradition: Vernacular Bicycles in Rural Finland, 1880–1910." *Technology and Culture* 52, 4 (2011): 733–56. http://dx.doi.org/10.1353/tech.2011.0151.

Marteinson, John, and Michael R. McNorgan. *The Royal Canadian Armoured Corps: An Illustrated History*. With Sean M. Maloney. Foreword by Desmond Morton. Toronto: Canadian Royal Armoured Corps Association and Canadian War Museum, 2000.

Martin, Paul. *A Very Public Life*. 2 vols. Toronto: Deneau, 1983–85.

Miller, James E., and Laurie Van Hook, eds. *Western Europe; NATO, 1969–1972*. Vol. 41 of *Foreign Relations of the United States, 1969–1976*. Washington, DC: Government Printing Office, 2012.

Norcliffe, Glen. "G-COT: The Geographical Construction of Technology." *Science, Technology and Human Values* 34, 4 (2009): 449–75. http://dx.doi.org/10.1177/0162243908329182.

Office of the Auditor General of Canada. "1984 Report of the Auditor General of Canada: Chapter 12 – Department of National Defence." Reports to Parliament. Ottawa: Office of the Auditor General of Canada, 1984.

The Pentagon Wars. Directed by Richard Benjamin. New York: HBO, 1998.

Peters, William N. *Club Dues: The Relevance of Canadian Expeditionary Forces*. Toronto: Irwin, 2001.

Pinch, Trevor. "The Social Construction of Technology: A Review." In *Technological Change: Methods and Themes in the History of Technology*, edited by Robert Fox, 17–36. Amsterdam: Harwood Academic Press, 1996.

Pinch, Trevor J., and Wiebe E. Bijker. "The Social Construction of Facts and Artefacts: Or How the Sociology of Science and the Sociology of Technology Might Benefit Each Other." *Social Studies of Science* 14, 3 (1984): 399–441. http://dx.doi.org/10.1177/030631284014003004.

Plamondon, Aaron. *The Politics of Procurement: Military Acquisition in Canada and the Sea King Helicopter*. Vancouver: UBC Press, 2010.

Qaimmaqami, Linda W., and Adam M. Howard, eds. *Middle East Region and Arabian Peninsula, 1969–1972: Jordan, September 1970*. Vol. 24 of *Foreign Relations of the United States, 1969–1976*. Washington, DC: Government Printing Office, 2014.

Rabinovich, Abraham. *The Yom-Kippur War: The Epic Encounter That Transformed the Middle East*. New York: Schocken Books, 2004.

Rasmussen, Kathleen B., ed. *Documents on Western Europe, 1973–1976*. Vol. E-15, Part 2 of *Foreign Relations of the United States, 1969–1976*. Washington, DC: Government Printing Office, 2014.

Rempel, Roy. *Counterweights: The Failure of Canada's German and European Policy, 1955–1995*. Montreal and Kingston: McGill-Queen's University Press, 1997.
Richter, Andrew. *Avoiding Armageddon: Canadian Military Strategy and Nuclear Weapons, 1950–63*. Vancouver: UBC Press, 2002.
Robertson, Gordon. *Memoirs of a Very Civil Servant: Mackenzie King to Pierre Trudeau*. Toronto: University of Toronto Press, 2000. http://dx.doi.org/10.3138/9781442677203.
Roland, Alex. *The Military Industrial Complex*. Washington, DC: American Historical Association, 2001.
Rosen, Paul. "The Social Construction of Mountain Bikes: Technology and Postmodernity in the Cycle Industry." *Social Studies of Science* 23, 3 (1993): 479–513. http://dx.doi.org/10.1177/030631293023003003.
Sampson, Charles S., ed. *Western Europe Region*. Vol. 13 of *Foreign Relations of the United States, 1964–1968*. Washington, DC: Government Printing Office, 1995.
Secretary of State of Canada. *Organization of the Government of Canada*. 9th ed. Ottawa: Queen's Printer, 1978.
Sharp, Mitchell. "Canada-US Relations: Options for the Future." Special issue, *International Perspectives* (Autumn 1972): 1–24.
–. *Which Reminds Me ... : A Memoir*. Toronto: University of Toronto Press, 1994.
Shimooka, Richard. *Towards an International Model for Canadian Defence Procurement*. Ottawa: Conference of Defence Associations Institute, 2013.
Smith, Louis J., and David H. Herschler, eds. *Foundations of Foreign Policy, 1969–1972*. Vol. 1 of *Foreign Relations of the United States, 1969–1976*. Washington, DC: Government Printing Office, 2003.
Sokolsky, Joel J. "Learning to Speak the Same Language: American Military Multilateralism and the Fraternity of the Uniform." Paper presented to the conference "Lost in Translation? The Impact of Military Culture on Alliance and Coalition Politics," Centre for International and Defence Policy, Queen's University, 17–18 April 2015.
Spielberger, Walter J. *From Half-Track to Leopard 2*. Munich: Bernard and Graefe, 1979.
–. *The Leopard 1 and Leopard 2 Weapon Systems*. Stuttgart: Motorbuch Verlag, 2000.
Stone, J.C. *A Separate Defence Procurement Agency: Will It Actually Make a Difference?* Ottawa: Canadian International Council and Canadian Defence and Foreign Affairs Institute, 2012.
"Supreme Allied Commander Europe (SACEUR)." *NATO*. 2016. http://www.nato.int/cps/en/natolive/topics_50110.htm.
Trudeau, Pierre Elliott. "The Relation of Foreign Policy to Defence Policy." 12 April 1969. In *Canadian Foreign Policy 1966–1976: Selected Speeches and Documents*, edited by Arthur E. Blanchette, 342–48. Montreal and Kingston: McGill-Queen's University Press, 1980.
Wakelam, Randall. *Cold War Fighters: Canadian Aircraft Procurement, 1945–54*. Vancouver: UBC Press, 2012.
–. "A Fine Mess: How Our Tactical Helicopter Force Came to Be What It Is." *Canadian Air Force Journal* 1, 3 (2008): 50–51.
Williams, Alan S. *Reinventing Canadian Defence Procurement: A View from the Inside*. Montreal and Kingston: McGill-Queen's University Press, 2006.
Yergin, Daniel. *The Prize: The Epic Quest for Oil, Money, and Power*. New York: Free Press, 2008.
Zaloga, Steven J. *M551 Sheridan: US Airmobile Tanks 1941–2001*. Oxford: Osprey, 2009.
Zimmermann, Hubert. *Money and Security: Troops, Monetary Policy and West Germany's Relations with the United States and Britain, 1950–1971*. Cambridge: Cambridge University Press, 2002. http://dx.doi.org/10.1017/CBO9781139052290.

Index

Note: "(i)" after a page number indicates an illustration; AMF stands for Allied Command Europe Mobile Force; NATO, for North Atlantic Treaty Organization; OPEC, for Organization of the Petroleum Exporting Countries; SACEUR, for Supreme Allied Commander Europe

Studies in Canadian Military History

John Griffith Armstrong, *The Halifax Explosion and the Royal Canadian Navy: Inquiry and Intrigue*

Andrew Richter, *Avoiding Armageddon: Canadian Military Strategy and Nuclear Weapons, 1950–63*

William Johnston, *A War of Patrols: Canadian Army Operations in Korea*

Julian Gwyn, *Frigates and Foremasts: The North American Squadron in Nova Scotia Waters, 1745–1815*

Jeffrey A. Keshen, *Saints, Sinners, and Soldiers: Canada's Second World War*

Desmond Morton, *Fight or Pay: Soldiers' Families in the Great War*

Douglas E. Delaney, *The Soldiers' General: Bert Hoffmeister at War*

Michael Whitby, ed., *Commanding Canadians: The Second World War Diaries of A.F.C. Layard*

Martin Auger, *Prisoners of the Home Front: German POWs and "Enemy Aliens" in Southern Quebec, 1940–46*

Tim Cook, *Clio's Warriors: Canadian Historians and the Writing of the World Wars*

Serge Marc Durflinger, *Fighting from Home: The Second World War in Verdun, Quebec*

Richard O. Mayne, *Betrayed: Scandal, Politics, and Canadian Naval Leadership*

P. Whitney Lackenbauer, *Battle Grounds: The Canadian Military and Aboriginal Lands*

Cynthia Toman, *An Officer and a Lady: Canadian Military Nursing and the Second World War*

Michael Petrou, *Renegades: Canadians in the Spanish Civil War*

Amy J. Shaw, *Crisis of Conscience: Conscientious Objection in Canada during the First World War*

Serge Marc Durflinger, *Veterans with a Vision: Canada's War Blinded in Peace and War*

James G. Fergusson, *Canada and Ballistic Missile Defence, 1954–2009: Déjà Vu All Over Again*

Benjamin Isitt, *From Victoria to Vladivostok: Canada's Siberian Expedition, 1917–19*

James Wood, *Militia Myths: Ideas of the Canadian Citizen Soldier, 1896–1921*

Timothy Balzer, *The Information Front: The Canadian Army and News Management during the Second World War*

Andrew B. Godefroy, *Defence and Discovery: Canada's Military Space Program, 1945–74*

Douglas E. Delaney, *Corps Commanders: Five British and Canadian Generals at War, 1939–45*

Timothy Wilford, *Canada's Road to the Pacific War: Intelligence, Strategy, and the Far East Crisis*

Randall Wakelam, *Cold War Fighters: Canadian Aircraft Procurement, 1945–54*

Andrew Burtch, *Give Me Shelter: The Failure of Canada's Cold War Civil Defence*

Wendy Cuthbertson, *Labour Goes to War: The CIO and the Construction of a New Social Order, 1939–45*

P. Whitney Lackenbauer, *The Canadian Rangers: A Living History*

Teresa Iacobelli, *Death or Deliverance: Canadian Courts Martial in the Great War*

Graham Broad, *A Small Price to Pay: Consumer Culture on the Canadian Home Front, 1939–45*

Peter Kasurak, *A National Force: The Evolution of Canada's Army, 1950–2000*

Isabel Campbell, *Unlikely Diplomats: The Canadian Brigade in Germany, 1951–64*

Richard M. Reid, *African Canadians in Union Blue: Volunteering for the Cause in the Civil War*

Andrew B. Godefroy, *In Peace Prepared: Innovation and Adaptation in Canada's Cold War Army*

Nic Clarke, *Unwanted Warriors: The Rejected Volunteers of the Canadian Expeditionary Force*

David Zimmerman, *Maritime Command Pacific: The Royal Canadian Navy's West Coast Fleet in the Early Cold War*

Cynthia Toman, *Sister Soldiers of the Great War: The Nurses of the Canadian Army Medical Corps*

Daniel Byers, *Zombie Army: The Canadian Army and Conscription in the Second World War*

J.L. Granatstein, *The Weight of Command: Voices of Canada's Second World War Generals and Those Who Knew Them*

Colin McCullough, *Creating Canada's Peacekeeping Past*

Douglas E. Delaney and Serge Marc Durflinger, eds., *Capturing Hill 70: Canada's Forgotten Battle of the First World War*

Brandon R. Dimmel, *Engaging the Line: How the Great War Shaped the Canada–US Border*

Geoffrey Hayes, *Crerar's Lieutenants: Inventing the Canadian Junior Army Officer, 1939–45*

Meghan Fitzpatrick, *Invisible Scars: Mental Trauma and the Korean War*
Patrick M. Dennis, *Reluctant Warriors: Canadian Conscripts and the Great War*

Studies in Canadian Military History
Published by UBC Press in association with the Canadian War Museum